STUDIES IN GLOBAL CHRISTIANITY

# Revisioning Christian Unity

# The Global Christian Forum

STUDIES IN GLOBAL CHRISTIANITY

## Series Preface

The latter part of the twentieth century witnessed a global level change in Christian dynamics. One significant development was the rise of the churches in the global south, not only in their number but also in their engagement with their socio-cultural contexts. Studies in Global Christianity is a Regnum series dedicated to studies on various issues that the global church, especially churches in Africa, Asia, Latin America and Eastern Europe struggle with. The series plans to publish studies so that the global church will learn not only from the past and present, but also from provocative and prophetic voices for the present and the future. The editors and the publisher particularly pray that the series as a public space will encourage the southern churches to make an important contribution to the shaping of a healthy future for global Christianity. The editors, therefore, invite theological seminaries and universities both in the West and in the "South" to submit relevant scholarly dissertations for possible publication in the series. In turn, it is hoped that the series provides a forum for South-to-South as well as South-to-North dialogues.

## Series Editors



A full listing of titles in this series
appears at the end of this book

STUDIES IN GLOBAL CHRISTIANITY

# Revisioning Christian Unity

## Journeying with Jesus Christ, the Reconciler

## at

## The Global Christian Forum, Limuru, November 2007

Edited by Huibert van Beek

First published 2009 by Regnum Books International

Regnum is an imprint of the Oxford Centre for Mission Studies
P.O. Box 70, Oxford, OX2 6HB, UK
15 14 13 12 11 10 09 7 6 5 4 3 2 1



British Library Cataloguing in Publication Data
A catalogue record for this book is available from the British Library

ISBN 978-1-506477-38-1

Typeset by BB Ltd

Distributed by 1517 Media in the US and Canada

# Contents

# Foreword

*The Rev. Wesley Granberg-Michaelson is General Secretary of the Reformed Church in America and a member of the Committee on the Global Christian Forum.*

The world is experiencing what the scholar Lamin Sanneh calls a "post-Western Christian awakening." Patterns of Christian vitality and witness are shifting in breath-taking ways that are reshaping the globe's religious landscape, and Christianity today seems divided in new ways. On the one hand are those churches, largely in the North, and rooted in the heritage of the East and the West, which have a deep sense of the historic Christian Tradition, and an ecumenical commitment to what the Nicene Creed names as "the one holy catholic and apostolic Church." But these churches find themselves struggling to maintain a resonant and vital witness amidst their modern, or post-modern cultures.

On the other hand are those churches, located largely in the South (but moving through migration into the global North) which exhibit a vital, even explosive spiritual power, and are propelling a Christian resurgence within their societies and regions of the world. Yet, in their creative contextualization, links to the historic Christian Tradition can seem tenuous, and the sense of belonging to the wider, global church, in all its expressions, is minimized in their focused and frequently sectarian enthusiasm.

While the United States sees those who call themselves "non-religious" as the fastest growing religiously classified group in its population, now at 15%, and most of Europe becomes increasingly settled in its secularized cultural identity, a Christian, post-colonial presence has grown remarkably in Africa, Latin America, and many places in Asia.

The Christian population in Africa, only a few million at the beginning of the 20th century, now includes over 360 million people, and is projected to grow to 633 million by 2025. By that same time, 640 million Christians would be in Latin America, and 460 million in Asia. The contemporary face of Christianity in today's world is a woman from a Kenyan village or a Brazilian favela.

This shift in Christianity's global foundations is not only geographical, but also confessional. Modern Pentecostalism, for example, recently celebrated its birth 100 years ago at Azusa Street. Today its adherents are estimated to include about 580 million Christians, or one of four Christians in the world, constituting one of the most dramatic stories of modern Christian history. Further, this number equals or exceeds the total membership of all the churches which belong to the World Council of Churches. If present growth continues, by the middle of the 21st century the world will be home to one billion Pentecostal Christians.

The rapid growth of the church in the global South has changed the contours of modern Evangelicalism as well. A few decades ago, 70% of the world's Evangelical community lived in the global North. Today it is the opposite—70% are in the global South, where context shapes a witness that is becoming more holistic, integrating personal evangelism and social justice.

The Catholic Church as well is experiencing the pervasive changes brought by these shifts in the tectonic plates of global Christianity. In the first quarter of this century, Catholicism is projected to lose 20 million members in Europe, but to gain 140 million members in Latin America, 100 million in Africa, and 50 million in Asia. Similar dynamics are having an impact on the Orthodox Church.

Part of our contemporary dilemma is that the member churches of the WCC primarily reflect the presence of historic Protestantism, Anglicanism and the Orthodox. While WCC member churches from the global South share much of the vitality of other growing churches in their regions, the WCC's ethos is still predominantly shaped by the historic Protestantism inherited from the North, with serious accommodations in the last decade to the sensitivities and gifts of the Orthodox. Pentecostal, Evangelical, and new culturally indigenous expressions of Christianity such as the African Instituted Churches are mostly absent. So the movements of fresh vitality and growth that are shaping the future of global Christianity are largely isolated from the structures of the present ecumenical movement, to the impoverishment of both. A new "space" had to be created to draw those representing the diversity of world Christianity together, and a new style had to be developed to build bonds of trust. The Global Christian Forum has been created for this purpose, in response to this context of Christianity's shifting global expressions.

It explains why many of the 230 Christian leaders who gathered at Limuru, Kenya in November, 2007 described this event as a watershed in modern Christian history. Those days in Limuru, and the nine years of preparation and regional encounters that led to that point, provided a fresh vision for how the global church could build a unity of fellowship and witness that reflected the new realities of world Christianity.

Participants at Limuru stressed that this promising journey was built on 60 years of ecumenical history. However, it represented an initiative toward a more broadly inclusive movement of Christian unity. The approach leading to the gathering at Limuru seemed simple, almost elemental. But it has touched a nerve among so many participants who have been yearning for a fuller expression of Christian *koinonia* today. The final message from the Limuru gathering was met with a spontaneous doxology from the participants. The shared feeling was that something new was being born in their midst, and that this was a work of God's Spirit.

Three words can best describe the space and style that has emerged in the process of the Global Christian Forum: testimonial, relational, and missional. From its first exploratory meetings, those who gathered decided to share with each other their stories of their journey of faith in Christ. This simple exercise established a starting point of trust rather than division.

From this beginning, relational bonds were established and nurtured among participants. Understanding across barriers that long have divided the Christian family began to emerge as participants formed relationships in a climate hospitable to acceptance and growth.

Recognizing that fellowship in Christ, and the quest for Christian unity, is never for its own sake, but for the world, hopes for the Global Christian Forum are often framed in a missional way. These new and promising experiences of encounter and trust across chasms of division in the Christian family are meant to serve the church's witness and mission in the world.

As these religious tectonic plates continue to shift, dramatically altering the forms and fissures that are shaping world Christianity, the initiative offered by the Global Christian Forum becomes ever more crucial. Building bridges across this contemporary chasm in world Christianity is the most urgent ecumenical challenge facing the church today. New forms and paradigms are necessary, requiring honest analysis, creative exploration, and humble discernment. The story of the Global Christian Forum, and what transpired during one week in Limuru, Kenya, is a modest, fragile, and yet deeply promising contribution toward building those bridges of fellowship. This movement is embracing the diversity of Christian expressions today and nurturing a spirit and breadth of unity that has not been seen in modern history.

# Preface

This book is in the first place a record of the Global Christian Forum gathering that took place on 6 – 9 November 2007 at the Jumuia Conference and Country Home in Limuru, near Nairobi, Kenya. The gathering turned out to be an extraordinary and historic event, not just in its own right but as a decisive moment in a process that began in 1998 and since then continues to gain momentum. To preserve the memory and provide access to the full collection of documents for contemporary and furture church workers, theologians, students and researchers is, therefore, the main purpose of this volume.

The book opens with an introduction highlighting the significance of the Global Christian Forum in the present context of the church worldwide and against the background of its modern history. The introduction goes on to explain how the Limuru gathering was organized, why the flow of the event was conceived the way it was and what was achieved.

Part I offers a comprehensive overview of the origin and the history of the Global Christian Forum since its inception in the late 1990s and of the process leading up to the 2007 global gathering. It also sets out the scope of the Forum embracing all the main Christian traditions and its specific methodology as it has evolved from the early meetings and as it continues to be at the heart of the Forum's journey with Jesus Christ, the Reconciler.

The Limuru gathering, like all Forum meetings, was designed in a way to maximize the participation and input of the participants. For this reason Part II of the book, which gathers the documents of the meeting, begins with a chapter echoing the voices of the assembled through their discussions in groups, their faith stories, affirmations, expectations and regional testimonies. This is followed by chapter four presenting the papers that were read in the plenary sessions and which provided part of the substance for the discussions. In chapter five the reader will find the outcome of the event as it was put on record through the action of the participants in two brief but dense texts, a Message addressed to the widest possible audience and a set of proposals brought to the attention of those in charge in order to carry on the process. Part II concludes with a collection of conference documents including the list of participants.

The Limuru global Forum was the result of almost ten years of work. The gathering asked that this course of action up to and including the event be evaluated. Eventually three evaluations were carried out simultaneously in 2008, by three different institutes. The reports constitute the content of Part III. Although *stricto sensu* they do not pertain to the meeting itself the evaluations have on purpose been included because they present a thorough assessment of the past and propose important directions for the future. The latter are already being taken into account by the Committee on the Global Christian Forum as it proceeds with the implementation of a Three – Year Plan that will culminate in a new global gathering in late 2011.

Huibert van Beek

# Dedication

This book is dedicated to all brothers and sisters in Christ throughout the world who, coming from many different Christian traditions and from various cultures and regions, yearn and labour for greater Christian unity and more common witness of the churches in the world.

# Acknowledgements

The Committee on the Global Christian Forum wants to express its deep appreciation for the commitment and work of the Local Organising Committee under the leadership of its moderator the Rev. Dr. Julius Karanja[1], for the administrative assistance granted by the National Council of Churches of Kenya through the office of its Deputy General Secretary Mr. Oliver Kisaka, and for the dedication of the volunteers staff team[2] led by Mr. Douglas Chial of the World Council of Churches.

The Committee would like to put on record its gratitude towards the Churches and Organisations that together provided the financial resources which made it possible to hold the Global Christian Forum gathering at Limuru, Kenya. These are, in alphabetical order:

Areopagos (Norway)
Association of Protestant Churches and Missions (EMW, Germany)
Christian Aid UK/Ireland
Church of Norway
Church of Sweden
Council for World Mission
Episcopal Church USA
Evangelical Lutheran Church in America
Evangelical Lutheran Church of Finland
FAP – Fondation pour l'Aide au Protestantisme réformé
Finnish Evangelical Lutheran Mission
International Church of the Foursquare Gospel
Kerk in Actie (Netherlands)
Mennonite Central Committee
Methodist Church Great Britain
Mission Covenant Church of Sweden
Pontifical Council for Promoting Christian Unity
Presbyterian Church (USA)
Protestant Church in the Netherlands
Reformed Church in America
Stichting Rotterdam
United Church of Canada
United Methodist Church – GBGM
United Methodist Church – GCCUIM
World Vision International

---

[1] For the names of the committee members see the List of Participants, page 136

[2] For the names of the team members see the List of Participants, page 136

The Global Christian Forum gathering at Limuru would not have been possible without the journey that preceded it. The Committee is deeply grateful for the trust and confidence of the Churches and Organisations that through their commitment and financial support sustained the process and enabled the Committee to realise the vision. It would like to mention in particular those who have contributed annually to the administrative budget:

> The World Council of Churches, as well as the Anglican Communion, Baptist World Alliance, Disciples Ecumenical Consultative Council, General Conference of the Seventh-Day Adventists, Lutheran World Federation, Mennonite World Conference, Pontifical Council for Promoting Christian Unity, the Salvation Army International Headquarters, World Alliance of Reformed Churches, World Evangelical Alliance and the World Methodist Council;

those who funded the various regional consultations and other meetings:

> Church of Norway, Church of Sweden, Council for World Mission, EMW Germany, Franciscan Friars, Methodist Church of Great Britain, Presbyterian Church (USA), Protestant Church in the Netherlands, Reformed Church in America, Salvation Army, United Church of Canada, United Methodist Church, World Vision International;

and those who made contributions in kind

> the Evangelical Fellowship of India and the Syrian Orthodox Church of Antioch.

The Committee would also like to acknowledge with gratitude the Churches and Organisations that have become contributors in the period following the Global Christian Forum gathering at Limuru:

> Assemblies of God Malaysia, Baptist Union of Great Britain, Church of Greece, International Old-Catholic Bishops' Conference, International Pentecostal Holiness Church, Kerk in Actie (Netherlands), Russian Orthodox Church, Union of Evangelical Free Churches (Baptists, Germany), United Pentecostal and Gospel Churches (Assemblies of God, Netherlands).

# Introduction

*Huibert van Beek is the Secretary of the Global Christian Forum*

In September of the year 2000, a group of leaders of Evangelical and Pentecostal churches and organisations responded to an invitation for a conversation with the Continuation Committee of what was to become the Global Christian Forum, at Fuller Theological Seminary in Pasadena, USA. In the room was an awareness that the timing of their meeting – at the turn of a century and the dawn of a new millennium– had a bearing on their deliberations. As the leaders responded to the ideas that were laid out on the table, one of them said: *it is about time that we get over the divisions that have kept us apart for a century....*

## One century, three movements

The twentieth century has brought profound changes in the Christian Church worldwide. On the one hand the modern Ecumenical movement – usually dated back to the 1910 World Mission Conference in Edinburgh, Scotland – has resulted in entirely new relationships between many traditions and confessions. The creation of the World Council of Churches in 1948, the founding of united churches such as in South India in 1947, the decision of the Catholic Church to join the movement following the Second Vatican Council of 1962 – 1965, the striking from memory of the mutual excommunication of 1054 between Rome and Constantinople in 1965, the Joint Declaration on the Doctrine of Justification signed by the Lutheran World Federation and the Catholic Church in 1999: these are but a few illustrations of what became possible in a time-span of less than a hundred years.

At the same time, the Evangelical movement has equally affirmed itself, in particular since the middle of the 20th century, as a significant and growing movement with its own identity that cuts across all the churches and also has its own distinctive denominations. Its history is even older because the first Evangelical Alliance was formed in 1846. Two of the landmarks of the Evangelical movement are the (re)-establisment of the World Evangelical Fellowship (now Alliance) in 1951 and the Lausanne movement which developed from the International Congress on World Evangelization in 1974. The Lausanne Covenant is one of the foundational theological and missiological documents of the last century that has had a profound impact on the movement and beyond.

Thirdly, the beginning of the 20th century was marked by the irruption of the Pentecostal movement – e.g. at the Azusa Street revival in Los Angeles in

1906 – which spread like fire and impacted churches across confessional and geographical boundaries. The expansion and growth of Pentecostalism in the last century is unprecedented in the history of Christianity. It has added a new Christian tradition along with Orthodoxy, Catholicism, the Reformation churches and Evangelicalism. From the 1950s onwards, it has also deeply touched the established churches from within through the Charismatic movement. The Charismatic Renewal in the Catholic Church alone numbers over 100 million adherents. Besides the classical Pentecostal denominations of the early period, the Pentecostal – Charismatic movement of the latter part of the 20th century has brought about wholly new forms of churches such as mega-churches and non-denominational churches.

The Ecumenical, Evangelical and Pentecostal movements are contemporary with one another. Moreover, they have common roots in the same source, the Pietistic and Evangelical revivals of the 18th and especially the 19th century in Europe and North America. They each claim to be a fruit of the Spirit, and rightly so. Pentecostalism is by its very nature Spirit – driven. Ecumenism has at its heart the thirst for unity which is *that we are all made to drink of one Spirit* (1 Cor. 12 : 13). For Evangelicalism the Spirit is equally central to its self-understanding. The three movements, each in their own way, have been sources of extraordinary renewal in the life of the churches. And yet : the Ecumenical movement on the one hand, and the Evangelical – Pentecostal – Charismatic movements on the other, have taken their courses separately and away from each other, largely ignoring each other and sometimes opposing and rejecting one another. The Ecumenical movement has fallen short of embracing the Evangelicals and Pentecostals. The Evangelical and Pentecostal movements have turned their back on the established churches. That is an amazing, and humbling reality of our recent history as churches and as Christians.

There have been attempts in the last century to bridge the gap. Well known are the efforts of David du Plessis, a visionary Pentecostal pioneer from South Africa who from the 1950s to the 1980s laboured hard to bring Pentecostals into dialogue with the World Council of Churches and the Catholic Church. The World Council of Churches and the World Evangelical Fellowship (Alliance) have sought to be in conversation on several occasions. In the last quarter of the past century the Commission on World Mission and Evangelism (WCC) and the Lausanne Committee on World Evangelization have been able to achieve some degree of mutual consultation. But none of these efforts, or any others, led to any comprehensive movement toward rapprochement.

The pioneers of the Ecumenical movement were inspired by the vision of the Una Sancta and 'winning the world for Christ in the 20th century' (John R. Mott), their missionary calling which the Evangelical leaders of the time shared with them. The Pentecostals of the first hour believed in the imminence of Christ's second coming which was the driving force of their Evangelistic zeal. At the end of the century neither the former nor the latter vision have come true. The church is not united and the world has not been won for Christ. What has come about is that Christianity is one of several world religions and that the church has become truly global. Not only is it global, its centre of gravity is shifting from the 'old' Christian North to the global South. The church is also more diverse than it ever has been. It has taken on many different faces. The Pentecostal and Evangelical churches and movements now constitute about a quarter of world Christianity, the Catholic Church about one half, and the Orthodox, Anglican, Protestant and some independent churches which form the fellowship of the World Council of Churches form the other quarter.

## A new space

It is at this intersection of events and in this entirely new configuration that the Global Christian Forum has emerged. Its aim is to create a space where *all* the main Christian traditions, Orthodox, Catholic, Anglican / Protestant, Evangelical and Pentecostal / Charismatic can come together in mutual confidence and respect. There are many 'bilateral dialogues' going on, between churches and church families within the Ecumenical movement, e.g. Catholic – Anglican, Lutheran – Orthodox, Reformed – Methodist and many more. There are also some bilateral conversations across the fence that separate the Ecumenical part of the Christian family and the Evangelical and Pentecostal part. The Catholic Church and Pentecostals have been in dialogue for over thirty years and recently new impulses were given to discussions between the Catholic Church and the World Evangelical Alliance. Dialogue and consultations have also been initiated between the World Council of Churches and Pentecostals and similar initiatives have brought together the Reformed and the Lutheran families with Pentecostals. But a place where all sit at the table has been wanting until now and the response that the Forum has received has shown that the need for it is being felt increasingly on all sides. It has also become clear that for this to happen something new had to come about.

Whether the Global Christian Forum is the appropriate answer in the long run remains an open question. It is still tentative, provisional and fragile. But there is no doubt that overcoming the new divisions which the 20th century has brought and creating a space where the whole Christian family can gather for the sake of unity and common witness is a response to a major challenge of our time. In addressing it the Forum has endeavoured to break new ground, establish new relationships, propose new configurations of encountering one another and develop new methodologies of entering in discussion with one another.

## The Limuru gathering

From the beginning of the Forum process there was the intention to convene a representative gathering at world level. For several reasons this took much longer than was initially foreseen[1]. The meeting that took place on 6 – 9 November 2007 at Jumuia Conference Centre in Limuru, Kenya thus became the culmination of almost ten years of work. It was attended by 226 leaders and representatives of an extraordinary broad spectrum of Christian churches, movements and global organisations, and from all parts of the world. This made it probably the most diverse Christian gathering ever to discuss unity and common witness.

The fact that the World Evangelical Alliance and the Conference of Secretaries of Christian World Communions had decided to hold their 2007 annual meetings in conjunction with the gathering underlined the uniqueness of the event and contributed to its representation. Care had been taken to ensure that half of the participants were from Evangelical, Holiness, Pentecostal and Independent constituencies. The relative over-representation of these parts of the Christian church has been a principle of all the Forum meetings. It is done in recognition of their extraordinary growth over the past century and in order to strengthen their presence as they meet with the 'older' churches and make their voice(s) heard. The majority of them was from the global South[2].

Under the theme *Our Journey with Jesus Christ, the Reconciler*, the four-day programme[3] of the gathering was designed on the basis of the experience of previous Forum meetings. It began with an introduction to the history, purpose and process of the Global Christian Forum and the sharing of faith journeys on the first day, followed by two days focussing on the discernment of what God is doing in the churches and organizations, and a final day of conclusions and action. Each day began and ended with a time of prayer led by different traditions represented in the meeting. Bible studies in small groups took place on the mornings of the second, third and last day. The opening session on the first day was organized by the local hosting committee and was marked by moments of lively Kenyan worship. The gathering ended with a closing celebration prepared and led by a group of participants.

Three plenary speakers addressed the gathering. Samuel Kobia, general secretary of the World Council of Churches spoke 'words of encouragement' inviting the participants to take the risk of working together. He stressed the unprecedented breadth of the event and shared his own faith journey. Pentecostal theologians Wonsuk Ma (Korea) and Cheryl Johns (USA) presented papers on questions of unity and mission which have been the issues

[1] The origin, history and process of the Global Christian Forum are described more in detail in Chapter 1.

[2] See the Participants' List in Chapter 5.

[3] See Chapter 5

at the centre of the Global Christian Forum process from the beginning[4]. Both speakers were stimulating and provocative. Wonsuk Ma pointed to the contradictions between what he typified the life-before-death emphasis and the life-after-death emphasis which have separated the 'mainline' and 'Evangelical' approaches to mission. Taking his personal faith story as an illustration, he affirmed that the two approaches are actually complementary and one is never complete without the other. Cheryl Johns stressed that the old 'mainstream' Ecumenical paradigm is dying and that nothing less than a re-birth of Ecumenism is needed to embrace the challenges of the new faces, the different worldviews and the new voices of non-Western Christianity. Those wishing to create a new space for Christian unity, she said, need to undergo a process of conversion and all of us from the North, the South, the East and the West need to die to old assumptions regarding each other. These presentations sparked off animated discussions in the groups.

The programme ensured an interaction between plenary sessions and meetings in groups. Each participant was assigned to one of eight groups and to a smaller Bible study group. Each group reflected in its composition the broad range of traditions and the diversity of regions that was characteristic of the gathering. This enabled the participants to experience in the more intimate setting of the groups the uniqueness of the Forum. The groups met each day and were free to choose the issues they wished to focus on. Brief reports were shared in plenary each day.

An absolute highlight of the gathering was the sharing of the individual faith journeys on the opening day. Because of the size of the meeting this was done in the groups. Although it meant that all stories could not be shared with everybody, as had been possible in earlier gatherings, the exercise of listening to one another's journey with the Christian faith and encounter with Christ was a tremendous experience of opening up the minds and spirits of Christians belonging to so many different traditions. There is no doubt that one of the strengths of the Forum is this way of beginning a meeting rather than with formal speeches and academic papers.

As this was a gathering that was expected to speak a word about the Forum itself, a process was built into the programme to make that possible. A small drafting group was set up on the first day to work on a Message or Letter to be issued as a result of the event. Secondly, a group of leaders of the main church families or movements and from global organizations present in the meeting[5] met twice to discuss a set of proposals for the future of the Forum submitted by the Continuation Committee. The participants were fully informed of these actions.The draft message as well as the proposals were shared in plenary for

---

[4] See Chapter 3

[5] The Orthodox Churches (Eastern and Oriental), the Pontifical Council for Promoting Christian Unity, the Evangelical and Pentecostal movements, the World Council of Churches and the Conference of Secretaries of Christian World Communions.

comments and the groups were invited to discuss the two documents. Their remarks were fully taken into account. The transparency of the process and the quality of the work done by the drafting group and the leaders group enabled the gathering to approve by consensus the Message and the Proposals for the Future of the Forum on the last day[6].

The gathering was characterized by a remarkable spirit of openness and eagerness to listen to one another and break down barriers. As the momentum built up there was a growing awareness among the participants of being part of an extraordinary, even a historic event. The participatory and flexible style of the meeting helped to create numerous opportunities for conversation and mutual discovery. For many of the representatives of the churches and organisations involved in the Ecumenical movement it was a unique occasion to interact with such a powerful group of Evangelicals and Pentecostals, and vice-versa.

One of the most important moments was the plenary on the morning of the third day when leaders and representatives of the Catholic Church, the Evangelical and Pentecostal movements, the Orthodox Churches, the Conference of Secretaries of Christian World Communions and the World Council of Churches expressed in unequivocal terms the importance of the Global Christian Forum and their resolve to be part of this new space. Some of them did so affirming also the importance of other, existing instruments for Christian unity others pointed to the need to hold on to the priority of mission along with the search for unity.

Another essential result was that the Pentecostal World Fellowship could be listed with the Churches, Church families and Organizations that signed the Message, although it was not officially represented at the gathering. The decision taken by its leaders who were present to subscribe to the Message was a major step forward.

There were also shortcomings. Not enough time had been scheduled in the programme for discussion in plenary with the two key-note speakers. The time reserved for the Bible studies in the small groups was also too short. In spite of the efforts to achieve a balanced representation and of the emphasis on the role of the churches in the global South in shaping the new faces of Christianity, the South was not sufficiently visible in the leadership of the gathering (including the GCF Committee itself). The representation of women and young adults and other groups, i.e. people with disabilities, indigenous groups etc. was not at all satisfactory.

The meeting did not go into any in-depth discussion of potentially divisive issues. It was not intended and not equipped to do so. Some felt that if such issues were put on the agenda major divergencies could be expected to emerge rapidly along the well-known fault lines, taking the process back to square one. Limuru 2007 may have indicated that the Forum approach, based on the sharing

---

6 See Chapter 4

of faith journeys as the preamble for discussion, offers a new way of dealing with divisions. The reference to repentance, which is present in the Message and was expressed in a moving way in the closing celebration points in the same direction.

In the planning of the Limuru gathering the expected outcome was formulated as follows :

- to encourage the continuation of the Forum process, especially locally and nationally
- to decide that global Forum gatherings be held from time to time
- to set up a new GCF Committee
- to ensure the continuation of the Forum process administratively.

All in all, the gathering achieved far more than could be expected. The Message contains a very strong affirmation of the Forum and an invitation to all brothers and sisters in Christ throughout the world to join the process. The Proposals for the Future of the Forum provide a clear direction and a comprehensive set of guidelines for carrying the process forward. Our task now is to take these next steps on the journey toward unity to which Christ calls all who follow him.

To God be the glory.

*The participants of the Limuru Global Forum gathering, in front of the conference building*

# PART I: THUS FAR…

# CHAPTER 1

## THE GLOBAL CHRISTIAN FORUM – A NARRATIVE HISTORY

**Rev. Sarah Rowland Jones**

*The Rev. Sarah Rowland Jones is an Anglican priest from the UK currently working as the Research and Ecumenical Advisor to the Archbishop of Cape Town, Anglican Church of Southern Africa. She is a member of the Committee on the Global Christian Forum. This article was written in mid-2007. It reflects the origin, history and purpose of the Forum and the hopes and expectations in the lead-up to the Limuru global event.*

### Introduction

The Global Christian Forum evolved from a process that first began to take shape in the 1990s. It arose from reflections on the nature of the World Council of Churches, and the recognition that the range of contemporary Christianity was far wider than the Council was ever conceivably going to be able to cover. There was thus a need to find other ways for making contacts and realising potential relationships between brothers and sisters in Christ who had little if any encounter, or current likelihood of encounter, with one another. Cautious conversations led to careful consultations with a widening circle of participants, and a greater confidence in pursuing the possibilities of this vision to facilitate ever increasing interactions.

Building on these tentative beginnings, and taking a markedly different approach to the customary ways of conducting ecumenical encounters, the initiative has gradually developed a flexible and open-ended process to help Christians recognise their faith in the Lord Jesus Christ in other Christians who are from very different traditions, cultures, and backgrounds. Through a series of regional meetings on five different continents, it has opened up new possibilities for future encounters and deeper exchanges, and even brought unanticipated commitments to common witness, and to co-operation and collaboration, in areas of shared concern.

November 2007 will see the culmination of these gatherings in the form of a rather larger 'Global Event'. Christian leaders meeting in Nairobi[1] will have similar opportunities for fresh encounters among themselves, and, in the light

[1] At the time of writing of this article it was not yet confirmed that the global event would take place at Jumuiah Conference and Country Home in Limuru, near Nairobi.

of these, will be invited to harvest together the fruit of the last eight years. It will be for them to reflect on how best to take forward all that has been gained, and so to respond together more fully to the prayer of Jesus Christ that we might all be one.

What follows is the story of how, by the grace of God, the Forum grew from small beginnings into a movement with the potential to make a significant impact on global Christianity in the first decade of the twenty-first century.

## The Seeds of an Idea

'Nothing does more to activate Christian divisions than talk about Christian Unity' wrote the Irish historian and diplomat Connor Cruise O'Brien in *The Times* newspaper in 1989. Though cynical, there was some truth in the suggestion that towards the end of the twentieth century, a century that had seen unprecedented developments in the breadth and depth of contacts between churches and other Christian bodies, there was nonetheless some loss of momentum and direction.

This was evident within the World Council of Churches itself – a body that was launched through an inaugural General Assembly in Amsterdam in 1948. By the end of the century it enjoyed the membership of churches and other bodies in over a hundred countries, which together accounted for five to six hundred million of the world's Christians. Yet these were drawn heavily from the historic churches of the Reformation and the Orthodox families of churches, and constituted about a quarter of the world's Christians. The Catholic Church, with around a billion faithful, remained outside the WCC, though, particularly after Vatican II, it has enjoyed a close relationship, with full membership in the commission on Faith and Order and a Joint Working Group.

At the same time, the overwhelming majority of Evangelical and Pentecostal churches were not only not members of the WCC, but most also had little or no contact with the historical ecumenical movement. Indeed, for a number of these it was a matter of conviction, sometimes rooted in their own historical foundations, that such contacts should not be pursued, or that certain of those also bearing the name of Christians should be held at a distance.

In the mid-1990s, all this was evident to the then General Secretary of the WCC, Rev. Dr. Konrad Raiser. At that point he was engaged in reflecting on the 'Common Understanding and Vision of the World Council of Churches'. Recognising that ecumenism as most fully understood went far beyond the WCC, he suggested that there was call for a new initiative. This initiative should aim to foster relationships between those Christians who, up to that time, were not in touch with one another.

The idea was that there might be some 'forum', some neutral space, in which it might be possible to foster and conduct a broader pattern of relationships than that reflected within the WCC. It was hoped that this might bring together not just those already participating in the 'ecumenical movement', but also extend to Evangelical, Pentecostal and Independent churches, as well as ecumenical and quasi church organisations.

**Beginning the Consultation Process**

The first step was a survey to test the forum idea, mainly with globally diffused churches and groupings of churches. In August 1998 a consultation was held at the Chateau de Bossey (the World Council of Churches' Ecumenical Institute in the Swiss countryside). Twenty-eight participants, largely but not wholly from within the 'ecumenical movement', met over four days, and produced a comprehensive document, 'Proposals Regarding a Forum of Christian Churches and Ecumenical Organisations' (the full text is given in document 1, page 23).

This document noted there had been a proliferation of ecumenical contacts – indeed, almost to the point of becoming unsustainable. Though to be welcomed, there was also an attendant risk of proliferation becoming fragmentation between all the different dialogues and movements and encounters. Thus the meeting asserted 'A more effective, more sustaining, more inclusive network of relationships is needed to bring differences of understanding among the partners into a mutually committed dialogue so that all may find their way to a clearer discernment and a more faithful obedience.'

But this was not merely an aspiration driven by organisational efficiency. The meeting also believed there was a need and a calling for a forum that could promote 'more significant, more inclusive relationships' among participants, in this way helping them, by 'transcending the limitations of existing frameworks, to think new thoughts, dream new dreams, and glimpse new visions.'

From the first there was an insistence that in order to achieve this vision the forum would rely on participation, and be very clear that it was not an organisation operating through formal membership. Similarly, it would rely on a minimum number of rules and structures.

Given this general endorsement of the need to pursue the idea further, a small 'Continuation Committee' was established among participants from the following: the Moscow Patriarchate, the World YWCA, the South African Council of Churches, the Syrian Orthodox Patriarchate, the Pontifical Council for Promoting Christian Unity, the Anglican Communion and Dr. Cecil M Robeck, of the Assemblies of God, who took part in a personal capacity. Dr. Robeck had been a significant and pioneering figure in building bridges between Pentecostal and other Christians since the night when he received a clear call from God to become engaged in ecumenical contacts, at a time when these were explicitly against the by-laws of his church. Huibert van Beek, at that time a WCC staff member, was asked to serve as secretary to the committee. The task of the Continuation Committee was to refine the details of the proposal, and prepare for a global 'forum' gathering within a few years.

The 'Proposals' document was presented to the Eighth Assembly of the World Council of Churches, held in Harare in December 1998, and discussed in both the Policy Reference Committee I and in a plenary session, alongside the WCC.'s own ongoing work on a 'Common Understanding and Vision'. The Assembly encouraged the Central Committee to continue promoting the process of consultation envisaged by the Bossey meeting.

At its first meeting, in August 1999, the Continuation Committee decided that more groundwork was needed before proceeding to the unique global consultation that had been envisaged at Bossey. Certainly, it would be necessary to hold one or more preparatory meetings to develop the concept into a more mature form. Indeed, even before proceeding to this stage, there was a prior need to explore more fully the extent of potential interest in the forum idea among Evangelical and Pentecostal constituencies, which had not been adequately represented at the 1998 consultation.

To this end, the Committee invited a number of Evangelical and Pentecostal leaders from around the world for a discussion at Fuller Theological Seminary, Pasadena, USA, where Dr. Robeck teaches. Some thirty people gathered from 9 to 11 September 2000, and, after presentations on the history of inter-church relations and on regional and other challenges, they discussed frankly their hopes and aspirations. An atmosphere of mutual partnership, trust, and consensus prevailed, and a warm sense of fellowship emerged as many participants experienced a new breadth and depth of Christian encounter. There was a strongly shared sense that the time was ripe for pursuing a rapprochement of the 'ecumenical' and 'evangelical' parties of world Christianity, and in the course of discussions, the forum proposal took on a more substantive shape, and acquired the name which it now enjoys, the 'Global Christian Forum.'

As the communiqué of the meeting (document 2, page 26) makes clear, the potential success of the Forum has depended to a considerable degree on its independence from any and all existing bodies and movements. Though the initiative first came from the WCC. and has since received considerable and sustained support from the WCC., Konrad Raiser recognised from the first that it must exist independently of the WCC. It could not be a disguised attempt by the WCC and its members to reach out to other Christians and draw them into existing configurations. Rather, it had to have a life of its own, in order to be able to do this 'new thing' for which there appeared to be a growing vision among Christians of a great diversity of perspectives and traditions. Thus the responsibility of the Forum should lie, and be seen clearly to lie, with an autonomous Continuation Committee, accountable to the various churches and organisations participating in the process.

Not only did the meeting provide the Forum with a clear name, it also began the important work of drawing up a 'purpose statement' enunciating more fully the scope of the Forum's aspirations. These initial proposals, set out in the communiqué, have significantly shaped the subsequent development of the process. The life of the Forum is seen as grounded in John 17:12, Jesus' prayer that '... that all of them may be one ... so that the world may believe,' and in 2 Corinthians 5:18-21, our common faith in a reconciling God. From this basis, as well as pursuing better ways of handling Christian differences creatively and peaceably and working to strengthen the wholeness of the church, the Forum should also include a focus on the mission of the church as a means of fostering common witness. The gathering requested that the Continuation Committee pursue further work on these tentative principles.

The Committee accomplished this through its subsequent meeting, held in London the following December. They recognised that considerable progress had been made in Pasadena, but that more work remained to be done in testing and refining the Forum, not least among a wider circle of Christians that, as the communiqué indicated, more fully reflected the global perspective and inclusivity.

Thus planning began for a further, rather larger consultation. This sought to bring together representatives from the most diverse Christian traditions including: the African Instituted, Anglicans, Baptists, Catholics, Disciples, Evangelicals, Friends (Quakers), the Holiness Church, Independents, Lutherans, Mennonites, Methodists, Moravians, Old-Catholics, the Orthodox Church (Eastern and Oriental), Pentecostals, the Reformed Church, the Salvation Army, Seventh-day Adventists, the United and Uniting Churches, together with those from ecumenical bodies (such as national and regional councils of churches) and quasi church organisations (including World Vision, YWCA, YMCA and IFES, and various other Evangelical and Pentecostal alliances, federations and groupings). Such a commitment has been followed in all subsequent meetings, each of which is thus to some degree a microcosm of the global Christian family. Generally around half of those invited come from explicitly Evangelical, Pentecostal and Independent constituencies (though of course evangelical and charismatic Christians are also present within many of the historic churches). This balance reflects the major objective of pursuing and extending the exploration of the Forum proposal with these constituencies.

This larger meeting was held in June 2002, once again at Fuller Theological Seminary, and became the first of a series of encounters that spread around the world in preparation for the fully Global Forum event scheduled for November 2007.

### Broadening the Conversation – Back to Pasadena

Around sixty mid-ranking church and organisational leaders gathered in Pasadena from 15 to 20 June 2002. The meeting began with an introduction to the history of the Forum to date, described in their presentations by members of the Continuation Committee as 'The Conversation so Far'. Also on the first day, Dr. Howard Loewen, Dean of Fuller Theological Seminary, gave the keynote address on the theme *'Strengthening the Fellowship We Share – Maintain the Unity of the Spirit in the Bond of Peace'*, in which he focussed on the centrality of the issue of scripture and tradition for the future of dialogue and co-operation between the Orthodox, Catholic, Protestant and Anglican traditions on the one hand, and the Evangelicals and Pentecostals on the other.

However, by far the greater part of the first two days was taken up by 'sharing', a process that has become perhaps the most powerful tool of the Forum in building relationships between Christians from very different traditions. Participants are invited to take a few minutes to introduce themselves by saying something about their tradition, and something of their personal experience of faith. This might range from an account of how they became Christians or how Christianity became central to their lives, to some particular pivotal event in which their faith was central, to a narrative of how they came to a position of Christian leadership. This process had been followed at earlier meetings, but now acquired a more intentional and fundamental role in the building of new relationships.

The first contributions were made by participants who were familiar with the process, from a breadth of backgrounds, who spoke in a variety of styles expressed in different uses of language. This low-key introduction reduced any expectation that everyone was required to give the sort of 'personal testimony' that characterizes Pentecostalism. Even so, it was evident that while some were familiar with speaking freely about their faith in this way, for others it was a rather new experience. However, it proved such a powerful means of introducing participants that later in the meeting several of those who had spoken very briefly on the first day asked to have the microphone back in order to share their stories at greater length!

'If there is any encouragement in Christ, any consolation from love, any sharing in the Spirit, any compassion and sympathy, make my joy complete: be of the same mind, having the same love, being in full accord and of one mind' wrote Paul to the Church at Philippi (Phil 2:1,2). As people spoke it became increasingly evident that the variety of language employed could not disguise authentic sharing in the same Spirit. Here were people of traditions which at first might seem almost incompatible, and who yet were undeniably also 'in Christ'. Thus there was deep and challenging listening between everyone from those from churches that had existed since the first or second century, to others whose general expectation was that anyone with the gifts of leadership would start their own church. Encouragement and joy really did overflow at this 'discovery' of brothers and sisters in the faith, which allowed people better to 'hear' the uniqueness of each tradition on its own terms, and this warmth generated for the rest of the meeting.

The compassion that flowed from this encounter with fellow-members of the body of Christ provided the context for deeper reflection on the two major issues of evangelisation and inter-church relations. A number of chosen participants from the diversity of traditions were given time in groups to prepare themselves before giving a panel presentation on each topic, followed by discussion. Within the new atmosphere, it became possible to discuss honestly some divisive issues, especially proselytism (as proved also to be the case in most subsequent meetings).

It is worth recording that proselytism is not only a problem between 'mainline' churches and Evangelicals or Pentecostals, but also between churches of the same tradition. It often reflects a lack of trust that 'the other' has the same commitment to Jesus Christ, and feeds on ignorance of respective histories with little effort at mutual understanding. Discussion at Pasadena suggested that the problem might better be handled in discussions directly between the concerned parties, rather than in the arena of the ecumenical organisations such as the W.C.C. As an illustration of this, Pentecostal and Catholic participants spoke about the Report from the fourth phase of the *Catholic–Pentecostal dialogue on Evangelism, Proselytism and Common Witness*, copies of which were circulated.[2]

The meeting then went on to discuss the possibility of producing a brief report or communiqué; the refining of the draft purpose statement contained in the communiqué of two years' earlier; and the role and composition of the Continuation Committee in taking forward the process. Some participants expressed concern about being publicly identified with the meeting, in that they had accepted the invitation to attend as uncommitted observers. Nonetheless, there was widespread support for taking forward and extending what had been so far achieved. On this basis, a communiqué, 'Towards a Global Christian Forum' was unanimously agreed, with general rather than specific reference to the supporting Christian bodies, and the draft purpose statement was finalised (texts of these are given in Documents 3 and 4, pages 27 and 28).

It was also agreed that the membership of the Continuation Committee would be expanded by four additional members to represent Evangelicals, Pentecostals, women and young people.

Two important considerations can be drawn from this consultation, which are reflected in the agreed texts.

Firstly, there was a clear – and joyful – affirmation of the vision of a Forum, which could bring around one table Christians from all the major traditions, for prayer, dialogue and mutual engagement. The only requirement for being present was an affirmation of orthodox Trinitarian and Christological beliefs, namely to 'confess the triune God and Jesus Christ as perfect in His divinity and humanity' yet even here there was acceptance that those like the Friends (Quakers), who do not make such a commitment, would certainly be welcomed.

Secondly, there was an understanding of the Forum as an unfolding process rather than a single 'event' to be reached at some point in the near future.

To this end, it was recommended that the Continuation Committee would consider proceeding by means of a number of regional meetings, through which the Forum process could be given wider exposure and its possibilities explored

---

[2] Available on line at http://www.prounione.urbe.it/dia-int/pe-rc/doc/e_pe-rc_pent04.html

and tested further. There should also be a continuing commitment to invite those not yet present at the table to join the dialogue and so enlarge the circle of those involved.

The draft purpose statement would be used as a basis for discussion in these meetings, but would not be submitted for further changes at this stage of the process. Rather, comments and suggestions would be noted, with the intention being to produce an improved formulation possibly at the time of the global Forum event in 2007.

## Regional Meetings around the Globe

The Continuation Committee now had, in the draft purpose statement, a clear mandate to take forward the 'creation of an open space wherein representatives from a broad range of Christian churches and inter-church organisations … can gather to foster mutual respect, to explore and address together common challenges.' They now put together an Action Plan, to run through to 2007, to pursue this comprehensive effort to create a space where Christians and churches from all sides can meet in a multilateral setting, and so promote dialogue and possible co-operation on unity and common witness among all the main traditions in the today's global Christian Church.

Following the advice of the June 2002 consultation, it was decided to hold consultations in four other major regions of the world (Asia, Africa, Europe and Latin America – the second Pasadena meeting being considered as having covered North America, from which a high proportion of participants came) and then to convene a fully global 'Forum event' in 2007, as a culmination of the process. The theme for each gathering would be 'Jesus Christ in [*name of region*] – our journey with him.' It was agreed that there should generally be keynote speakers, one from within those historically engaged with ecumenism, and one from the Evangelical / Pentecostal sides, and that certain individuals would be invited to participate in panel discussions on aspects of faith within the region.

### *Asia*

The first of these regional consultations took place in May 2004 in Hong Kong, with participants drawn from Asia and the Pacific. It was organised in co-operation with the Christian Conference of Asia (CCA), the Federation of Asian Bishops' Conferences (FABC), and the Evangelical Fellowship of Asia (EFA)[3]. The meeting brought together 47 Asian participants, 27 coming from Evangelical and Pentecostal churches. Another 14 people came from the Continuation Committee and participants in the Pasadena consultation in 2002, who would be able to share their experiences of the process.

[3] Now called Asian Evangelical Alliance.

The programme followed a similar structure to that in Pasadena, with the bulk of the first two days being allocated to 'sharing' as people introduced themselves. Two keynote speakers gave papers on the theme of '*Jesus Christ in Asia – our Journey with Him'*. Dr. Wonsuk Ma, with his wife Julie C. Ma, spoke on *Our Journey with Him as Pentecostal Believers*. The second paper was given by Dr. Feliciano V. Carino, who had attended the 1998 Bossey meeting in his capacity as the then General Secretary of the Christian Conference of Asia. Two panels initiated discussions on inter-church relations, and on challenges faced by Christians within Asia.

The meeting was characterised by a huge diversity. There were Orthodox and Mar Thoma participants from Churches established in the earliest centuries of Christianity, through to the newest movements of faith. Some came from countries where the majority affirmed Christian allegiance, while others were in small, often persecuted, minorities. Some knew great affluence, others extreme poverty. The vast populations of China and India contrasted with the few millions in Cambodia and Laos.

Yet the shared experience of faith created a unity among the participants that transcended all these differences. The objectives of making the Forum known in Asia, and facilitating a conversation between groups in the region that had never met before were more than achieved. Pentecostal and Roman Catholic participants from one particular country were able, through this face-to-face encounter to tackle long-running and previously insoluble issues. It was remarkable how few participants, even from the churches of the Reformation, had previously had any contact with the Catholic church, or vice versa, and the opening up here of new possibilities for dialogue and for co-operation on areas of mutual interest was a significant achievement of the gathering.

The meeting enthusiastically issued a statement (document 5, page 29) which not only affirmed 'the need to work together and continue the initiative at the regional, national and local level' but which went on to 'urge the Evangelical Fellowship of Asia, the Christian Conference of Asia and the Federation of Asian Bishops' Conferences to assist in forwarding this initiative.' An informal commitment was made in principle to form a Continuation Committee for Asia from representatives of these three bodies, to work together- an unprecedented co-operation.

### *Africa*

The regional consultation for Africa was held in August 2005, in Lusaka (Zambia). The All Africa Conference of Churches (AACC) as the regional ecumenical body, the Association of Evangelicals in Africa (AEA), and the Organisation of African Instituted Churches were involved, as well as several other continent-wide organisations. Catholics and the Orthodox were also represented. Of the 59 participants from Africa, 32 were from Evangelical, Pentecostal and African Instituted churches. As before, 12 participants with prior experience of the process came from outside the continent. The meeting operated in English, with a translation for French speakers. The Portuguese speakers present were fortunately able to operate in English.

The meeting again began with a focus on sharing. Keynote addresses on '*Jesus Christ in Africa – Our Journey with Him*' were given by Dr. Hlope Brigalia Bam, the head of the South African electoral commission, an Anglican who had served as General Secretary of the South African Council of Churches and who also worked with the World Council of Churches and Rev. Dr. Kwabena Asamoah-Gyadu, Assistant Professor at Trinity Theological Seminary, Ghana, and West Africa Sub-Regional Co-ordinator of the African Theological Fellowship, who approached the theme from an Evangelical and Pentecostal background.

Dr. Bam made a passionate plea for the involvement of Christians and the churches in the public arena, on the moral, social and political issues confronting Africa. Talking about her own journey with Christ she explained how she had learned that faith is not private. Dr. Asamoah-Gyadu noted that the reform and growth of Christianity in Africa was developing particularly through the life of the Pentecostal, Evangelical, and African Indigenous churches, and that the challenge of Africa's journey with Jesus was to apply the Evangelical/Pentecostal experience of the faith to all areas of life on the continent.

The two presentations together underlined the need for the church to be involved in moral and socio-political issues, while also giving clear attention to personal evangelism and spiritual renewal. In much of Africa, the prevalence of such challenges to all the churches as poverty, HIV-AIDS, corruption and good governance, and the spread of Islam, meant that there was much less of the tension experienced in other parts of the world between issues of evangelism over and against social action. Similarly, differences of liberal versus conservative, ecumenical versus evangelical, and discordant historic legacies, seemed far less pronounced, despite the wide diversity of churches and organisations that were present, and despite the fact that many had never met with one another before.

For this reason the programme focused more on common concerns than in previous Forum meetings. Yet it was again the mutual discovery of Christians who usually do not sit together in meetings that profoundly marked the event. There was particular interest in both the Coptic Church, present on the continent since the first century, and in the African Instituted Churches. The representatives of the latter were able to explain, in ways others clearly found reassuring, their insistence on the core orthodox doctrines as necessary for membership of the Organisation of African Instituted Churches. They were also now addressing various issues where African culture appeared to be in conflict with traditional Christian teaching, even allowing for a process of inculturation.

The gathering appointed an African continuation committee (recognising that they had fallen short of their own aspirations to ensure gender and linguistic balance and youth representation), and adopted a statement (document 6, page 30).

*Europe*

The Europe Consultation on the Global Christian Forum took place on 19 – 22 June 2006, in Warburg, Germany, attended by 51 participants from the various Christian traditions in Europe, including diaspora and migrant communities. The main regional organisations were represented (Ecumenical as well as Evangelical and Pentecostal), and members of the Continuation Committee also took part.

This consultation was a day shorter than elsewhere. Introductions through the sharing of personal stories and denominational uniqueness were followed by reports on recent local or regional ecumenical developments: the merging of the Council of Free Churches and the Christian Council in Norway; the growing relationship between the Pentecostal Federation and the Federation of Protestant Churches in Italy; similar developments in France, including the establishment of the National Council of Evangelical Churches, which links the Evangelicals and Pentecostals that are part of the Protestant Federation and the Federation of Evangelical Churches and the Assemblies of God.

Five key areas were identified for deeper group discussions, of which the most acute were proselytism, mission and evangelism. As in Asia, there was an unprecedented opportunity for exposure between people who had not previously met. Sharp words were exchanged – but also bridges built, and suggestions made for moving forwards.

A second area was that of common witness in the public sphere, addressing the need to avoid undermining one another publicly, and wherever possible provide a common voice. There was recognition that it was often feasible to stand together even when there is not total agreement of positions, to affirm one another as having more in common unity than in division, and to affirm legitimate diversity. This was seen as particularly important in ensuring that faith perspectives are given a place in public and political discourse, which increasingly emphasises the secular. Thus a third concern was the need for 'new apologetics' and 'new hermeneutics' to enunciate and communicate faith appropriately for today (including in non-verbal ways), instead of relying on language and paradigms several centuries old. The fourth group considered the tensions that arise between large and officially recognised and small or unrecognised denominations, while the fifth group addressed immigrant Christian communities and their faith traditions, such as the African Approach churches in Europe, and the challenges of Islam.

In advance of the meeting, some members of the Continuation Committee had feared that this might be the most difficult of the regional meetings, given that Europe had been the crucible of so many of Christianity's divisions. However, holding the meeting in a Syrian Orthodox monastery immediately distanced the gathering from the dynamics of the Reformation. It became a safe context in which it became possible to voice criticisms and share painful experiences. Substantive common concern was shared, over losses to secularism, high levels of ignorance about the essence of Christianity (not only in the formerly Warsaw Pact countries), and the need to re-evangelise Europe; and a conviction these would best be tackled through working together.

As with previous regional meetings, such broad encounters were unprecedented, and gave rise to great enthusiasm for the Forum process as a means of adding a missing dimension to current ecumenical practices. Alongside this was a concern not to institutionalise and add to the already overburdened European ecumenical calendar. Many participants said they hoped to use the faith-sharing element in local, national and sub-regional bodies, and to find ways of broadening participation in, or in parallel with, existing forums. It was recognised that it would be inappropriate to try to subsume the steering of the Forum process in Europe within any existing body (such as the Conference of European Churches), since all these lacked the breadth of Warburg, and so would replicate the limitations GCF aims to overcome.

Though initially it had felt that a statement would not be necessary, in the end a subgroup worked through and beyond the end of the meeting to produce a communiqué (document 7, page 32).

### *Latin America and the Caribbean*

The final regional gathering, for Latin America and the Caribbean, was held in Santiago, Chile, from 26 to 29 June 2007, working closely with the Consejo Latinoamericano de Iglesias (the Latin American Council of Churches), with additional support in facilitation from Rev. Carlos Ham, a Cuban working with the World Council of Churches. 68 participants gathered, all from or working in the region apart from the six who were from the Continuation Committee. The Catholic delegation was larger than in previous meetings, which reflected not only their significant role within the region but also the warmth with which the process had been received by CELAM (the Catholic Bishops' Conference of Latin America). The meeting was conducted in Spanish, with 'whispering translation' for the handful of people who required it.

Though for a variety of reasons there was not as extensive a Pentecostal and neo-Pentecostal participation as hoped, the breadth of the gathering was nonetheless unprecedented on the continent, which has seen deep tensions in many places between Catholics on the one hand and Pentecostals and Evanglicals on the other. Some participants recounted first hand experiences of threats and even violence. Yet a remarkable spirit of joy and openness rapidly emerged, which allowed for such frank sharing of experiences.

This was in many ways the least diverse regional meeting, perhaps reflecting the dominance of two languages, Spanish and Portuguese across all of Central and Southern America, and also the fact that nearly everywhere the churches had been confronted with a common experience of political strife, dictatorship, or even civil war. One participant also commented on the overwhelming influence of Catholic culture as a unifying factor, 'even as Pentecostals, we are Catholic Pentecostals!'

There were three panel presentations by participants, on the Latin American context (including political, social, economic, and ecclesiastical perspectives); on the 'Faces" of the Church (Anglican, Catholic, Evangelical, Orthodox, Pentecostal, Protestant); and on examples of inter-church co-operation. By chance, the Latin American Bible Societies were meeting simultaneously in a nearby hotel, and joined the consultation for part of a morning, presenting everyone with a Spanish Bible.

On one evening, the meeting joined a special service held at the Police Academy, which honoured the role played by the churches in Chile, working together, in returning the country to democracy. The participants were also received at the offices of the President by the current Chaplain, a Methodist and the first non-Catholic to be appointed to this role, and at a later session the meeting prayed for the incoming Pentecostal Chaplain. These events underlined the potential for a joint Christian witness when Christians of very differing backgrounds are able to work together, and were a great encouragement to others present. (It is worth noting that the Forum process claims no particular ownership over contacts that extend beyond those of 'traditional ecumenism' but is always glad to find these, and ready to offer whatever support is appropriate.) On the final evening, a 'prayer vigil' for Christian unity was held at a Santiago Pentecostal Church, at which one of the Roman Catholic participants spoke very movingly about God's grace in bringing his children together.

Discussions in groups on the nature of the Forum process and its potential to enliven Christian life within the region led to the agreement of a 'Message to the Churches' (document 8, page 34). This agreement also underlines the interdependence of all areas of mission and ministry, and the holistic nature of the gospel which addresses not only spiritual but also all other human needs.

## Continuing Developments within Regions

As the Continuation Committee pursued its programme of regional meetings, the momentum generated in earlier gatherings took on a life of its own.

### *Asia*

Thus, a follow-up to the Asian regional meeting was held in Bangkok, Thailand, on 21-23 September 2006, with representatives from the three Asian regional bodies. This was the first time that the Christian Conference of Asia (CCA, ecumenical), the Federation of Asian Bishops' Conferences (FABC, Catholic) and the Evangelical Fellowship of Asia (EFA) had met together.

Prior to this, the CCA and the FABC had had a history of meeting and working together since 1996 and had formed the Asian Movement for Christian Unity (AMCU). After two days of sharing and listening to each other, the participants decided to recommend, firstly, that the CCA and the FABC invite the EFA to join this bi-partite process so as to make it tri-partite, and, secondly, that the CCA and the FABC invite the EFA to send about 20 participants to the next AMCU assembly in June 2007 in Kuala Lumpur, Malaysia. The participants also recommended that the first day of this assembly be a kind of 'Forum style event' of trust building, and mutual introductions through the sharing of faith stories.

*Africa*

The Africa Continuation Committee, appointed at the Africa Consultation, held its first meeting from 14 to 16 November 2006 in Nairobi. The committee discussed ways of spreading the information on the Global Christian Forum as widely as possible to churches and church-related organisations in Africa. It decided to encourage the participants at the 2005 consultation to organize national Forum meetings and to focus particularly on Kenya, Ghana and Zimbabwe as pilot countries for such an initiative. The committee had discussions with the General Secretaries of the Association of Evangelicals in Africa, the All Africa Conference of Churches and the Organisation of African Instituted Churches (all three based in Nairobi). Bishop Dandala, the General Secretary of the AACC called on the committee to help in ensuring the presence of all the Christian traditions within Africa at the next assembly of the AACC in December 2008 in Maputo, Mozambique.

*Europe*

In September 2007, the Third European Ecumenical Assembly took place in Sibiu, Romania, at which there was a hearing on the Forum process.

**WCC Ninth Assembly**

While the process of regional meetings and their subsequent developments evolved, the World Council of Churches held its Ninth Assembly in Porto Alegre, Brazil, from 14 to 23 February 2006. Reference was made to the Forum within the report of the Policy Reference Committee, and the recommendations it proposed were endorsed by the plenary assembly (document 9, page 36).

This makes clear the WCC's continuing support for the Forum, including its participation in the Global Event, while recognising it as an independent process. The Forum was also mentioned frequently in other discussions, particularly those on the future of ecumenism, recognising that the WCC would have to reflect further on its relationship with the Forum after the Nairobi meeting, and in the light of its evolving internal debate on ecumenism in the twenty-first century, on the dynamic balance between the deepening convergence among its existing members and the broadening of the scope of its membership.

A generally high level of awareness, and appreciation, of the Forum among participants at the Assembly, was taken as a great encouragement by the Continuation Committee, who recognised that their efforts at communication had been under-resourced. The Evangelical Fellowship of India oversaw the printing of a brochure in 2005, which was updated with a further printing by the Syrian Orthodox Church in 2007. A website was finally launched in 2006 (www.globalchristianforum.org), and a regular electronic newsletter has since been circulated. Some 500 copies of the brochure were distributed at Porto Alegre, while others have been widely disseminated through participants at regional meetings, and through various targeted mail shots and other means.

## Looking Towards Nairobi – The Global Event

The series of regional meetings will culminate with a global gathering to take place from 6 to 9 November 2007 in Nairobi, Kenya. This will bring together some 250 representatives, including high level leaders, of all the main Christian traditions in the world and their global bodies (that is, confessional umbrella organisations, ecumenical councils, and Evangelical and Pentecostal federations and alliances, as well as various inter-church bodies). The global gathering will thus finally bring to fruition the vision of the original Forum proposal. It will provide opportunities to 'harvest' the results of the process to date, to explore the possibilities of such an unprecedented broad gathering at the global level, and to give directions for the future.

In order to give shape to the Global Event, an international planning group composed of the members of the Continuation Committee together with several additional representatives of churches and organisations involved in the Forum process met from 9 to 11 November 2006 in Utrecht, the Netherlands.

Participants will gather under the theme of 'Our Journey with Jesus Christ, the Reconciler'. As the usual form of introductions will not be feasible in a plenary of some 250 members, after the introduction to the Forum participants will meet in groups of 30 to share their faith stories. These same groups will form the nucleus for Bible study and prayer throughout the rest of the gathering.

Keynote speakers will address 'Discerning what God is doing in our Churches and Organisations', 'New Developments and Trends in World Christianity', and 'Discerning Our Place in God's Mission in the World', each of which is designed to prompt fruitful debate within the groups. There will also be panel presentations on the vision of the Global Christian Forum, and expectations of how it might be taken forward, from leaders of some of the main Christian traditions and global organisations. Towards the end of the meeting, the groups will be asked to consider the future of the Forum, guided by two questions. The first of these asks how we discern the Spirit leading us to overcome divisions and enter into new and broader relationships; and the second, how the Forum process might be taken forward globally, regionally, nationally and locally.

Thus the Forum is committed to fulfilling that part of the original vision which places the evolution and future shape of the process within the hands of those who come to the table. There is no prior commitment among the Continuation Committee, the World Council of Churches, or any other body, to any specific institutional or other framework. It is through the dialogues of the participants that the benefits of the process to date will find ways of bearing further fruit into the future.

## Reflections on the Global Christian Forum

While the precise future of the Global Christian Forum lies in the hands of those who will gather in Nairobi, various conclusions can be drawn from all that has happened since the idea of a neutral space with an open invitation was first mooted almost ten years ago.

Perhaps the most important, and overriding, point to arise in all the meetings so far, as well as in many other discussions among church leaders, is that this is an idea whose time has come. 'Now is the time' that we should be working to go beyond the dynamics of inter-church relations that characterised the twentieth century. On all sides the Forum seems to have tapped into a latent, and deeply held, conviction that 'now is the time' to heal the divisions between the so-called 'ecumenical' churches and the Evangelicals and Pentecostals.

Of course, the Forum is not the only place where such expectations have emerged, and it has been encouraging to find ample evidence of many similar initiatives, often at national or local level, to bring together those who were previously separated. Examples include Christian Churches Together in the USA and the National United Christian Forum in India, to name but two. These workings of the Spirit are a sign of encouragement to us all.

The independent nature of the Forum has also been fundamental to all that has been achieved. Only such a free-standing and broadly constituted network would have the capacity to invite an extensive range of participants with such an assurance of neutrality, and so act as a catalyst for the unprecedented encounters and the deepening engagements that have transpired.

The Forum came to life at a time of many changes in the Christian world. The centre of gravity has been shifting strongly towards the global South, where the old historic divisions are often differently experienced, and, especially where a new generation of Evangelical and Pentecostal leaders is emerging. Many of these leaders are active on issues such as poverty, socio-economic and racial justice, gender and human rights that have traditionally been seen as the preserve of the ecumenical movement. Similarly, Pentecostal and Evangelical scholars, in both the North and the South, are affirming themselves increasingly as interlocutors of the theologians of 'mainline' Christianity.

The Continuation Committee was confronted with the reality of this re-orientation when the Africa consultation criticised the lack of representation of the global South among its members. Steps were subsequently taken to improve the regional, gender and confessional representation.

Over the years, it has been evident that participation has broadened and deepened as the process has continued. The size and seniority of the Catholic delegation at Santiago might be taken as one example of this. Another is the decision by the World Evangelical Alliance, several of whose members came to Pasadena in 2002 as 'uncommitted observers', to hold its 2007 annual leadership meeting in Nairobi immediately before the Global Event so that as many participants as possible will be able to attend both gatherings.

In the course of the process, the importance of bringing in new people has become increasingly clear. The term 'new' is intended to refer to those from Christian traditions that have not been in dialogue with each other before. However, it is always stressed that they come to the table as equal partners in the conversation, and the Forum should by no means be seen as intended to 'lure' Evangelicals, Pentecostals and others, into existing ecumenical configurations. The Forum aims at creating a *new* space for encounters, a space where trust can grow.

From such trust the Forum has contributed to creating new relationships. A crucial element in all the meetings has been the exercise of sharing the faith journeys and the stories of the faith communities by the individual participants. This, above all else, has proven to be a powerful means of discovering the experiences of living faith and the convictions that are held in common by Christians coming from very different traditions. Inviting different traditions to take turns to lead prayers at the beginning and ending of each day has also been very valuable. Such a practice was chosen over an attempt to provide some 'lowest common denominator' format, in that it would offer from a different perspective the chance to observe and be drawn into the authentic expressions of worship of each tradition. For many, being present at prayers led by the Orthodox families of churches was a new and moving experience. A particularly unforgettable example of what the Forum process is capable of was the 'African Pentecostal' worship led by London-based Archbishop Fidelia Onyuku-Opukiri, assisted by her deacon, in the chapel of the Syrian Orthodox monastery at Warburg.

It has been possible so far to avoid giving any direction to the Forum process that would inevitably have led to the creation of a new organisation or institution. Similarly it has been possible to steer clear of the concept of 'membership', or proposals to form a new fellowship of churches over against existing ones. The Forum continues to be based on *participation*, with no other structure than a committee and a small secretariat, and this independence and flexibility have been critical in enabling it to play such an effective role as a catalyst.

Another significant outcome of the Forum that arises from having almost no institutional format, is the tiny cost of all that has been achieved so far. One church leader described it as 'the best value-for-money ecumenism anywhere in the world'. The most expensive meeting was that held in Africa for which the cost of attendance was subsidised for a high proportion of participants. Even so, this only cost $ 55'000 whereas the cost of the Europe meeting for the Forum was a mere $ 12,500. With finances being raised on an *ad hoc* basis, the main contributors have been the Council for World Mission, the Church of Norway, the Protestant Church in the Netherlands, the Reformed Church in America, the Salvation Army (International Headquarters), the United Methodist Church, World Vision International and the World Council of Churches. Since October 2004 the WCC has also given financial support to the Forum's secretariat expenses. As mentioned above, the financing of the first information leaflet was entirely covered by the Evangelical Fellowship of India, and the second printing being by the Syrian Orthodox Church.

Support for the Forum, though not always publicly apparent, is very broad. Alongside the WCC, the Christian World Communions have from the start taken a close interest in the Forum. The CWCs themselves represent a wide range of Christian traditions, engaging some of those who are not part of the World Council. There has been regular reporting to the Conference of Secretaries of CWCs, through members of the Conference who are also on the Continuation Committee, and on several occasions the Conference has expressed its support for the Forum. In some of the regional consultations the CWCs were asked to help with the nomination of participants from their church families in the region. Some have provided financial support for their representatives, and from 2006 the CWCs have made a contribution towards the cost of the Forum secretariat.

Among others we can mention the Catholic Church, which has participated from the beginning in the Forum process through the Pontifical Council for Promoting Christian Unity which is represented on the Continuation Committee. The World Evangelical Alliance has been informally involved in the Forum since 2000, and has been officially represented on the Continuation Committee since 2005. There have been representatives of World Vision in Forum consultations since 2000. World Vision's significant financial support for these meetings has been used in particular to subsidize the participation from Evangelical and Pentecostal constituencies. The World YWCA has taken part in the Forum process since 1998 and is represented on the Continuation Committee.

## Challenges to the Forum

Though much has been achieved, the Forum has had to face a number of challenges and difficulties that were not originally envisaged. Some of these arise from the process became much longer, with many more intermediate steps, than was initially thought. In the 1998 proposal it was expected that a high-level, global Forum meeting of 150–250 participants could be held within two years. As the process developed, it became clear that more time was required.

Though there has been a great broadening and deepening of involvement, some major Evangelical and Pentecostal organisations and churches, including neo-Pentecostals have been slow to participate. At times invitations have been issued to individuals rather than through their church groupings, and their presence at meetings has required an informal understanding with their constituency.

Though questions of mission and ministry, and on the nature of the church, have been tackled with enthusiasm at regional meetings, it must be recognised that these have nonetheless remained at a fairly general and preliminary level. In order to go deeper into these issues, it will be necessary to develop a common agenda. It is likely that as more controversial issues are on the table, it will become more difficult to stay together.

Despite improved communication, the Global Christian Forum remains little known within the churches, outside the ranks of those engaged with ecumenism and inter-church relations. The inability to commit more resources is the downside of the Forum's light operating structure. Similarly, though the Forum is highly cost-effective, its lack of a firm financial basis means that activities are subject to *ad hoc* fundraising, which can be time-consuming, and underlines a dependence on a relatively small number of financial supporters.

## Looking to the Future

While the Global Christian Forum lies in the hands of the Nairobi Event, there has been a strong sense within regional consultations that some way should be found of ensuring the process continues, with, at the very least, further Forum-type encounters, at regional, sub-regional and local levels. This might include, but not be limited to, utilising the principles and processes within existing ecumenical frameworks, as a way of breathing new life into them. The question of whether another fully global gathering should be planned for some time in the first half of the next decade is rather more open to debate.

Any commitment to continue the Forum will raise the question of whether a more stable footing is required than the current ultra-light framework, though it should also be recognised that there has been little enthusiasm for any solution that would entail significant costs or cumbersome administrative structures. These considerations need to be set alongside the current commitment to proceed by participation and eschew any question of 'membership', which thus precludes fund-raising through the fees of affiliating bodies. In a similar vein, while suggestions have been made of a closer relationship with the WCC and the CWCs, it should be guaranteed that any move in this direction would not impede the more fundamental goal of maintaining the Forum's relations with those Evangelical and Pentecostal constituencies that remain outside these bodies. The Forum's unique strengths lie primarily in its ability to invite participants to enter an entirely neutral space and join in the dialogue with no other preconditions than the affirmation of orthodox Trinitarian and Christological beliefs.

For this reason, while the Forum must take account of other developments in relationships between Churches and Christian bodies, there is a strong case for remaining independent. This is true not least while the debate within the World Council on 'Ecumenism in the 21st century' continues to unfold, and certainly until it has reached a rather more mature state. The same might be said of suggestions that the next WCC assembly, in 2013, be open to all churches.

Ownership of the Forum process lies with those who come to the table, responding to the invitation to a dialogue that is encapsulated in the Purpose Statement with its aspirations for increasing inclusiveness. It will be for those who gather in Nairobi to tease out these questions, seeking a fresh vision from our Father in heaven of His purpose for His people. May God, by God's Spirit, continue to call us into greater and fuller experiences of the unity that is ours in Christ, his Son, our Lord, who 'by his blood has ransomed for God saints from every tribe and language and people and nation, and made them to be a kingdom and priests serving our God.'

*Part of the GCF Continuation Committee. Far right: Rev. Rowland Jones, author of the article*

## 1. PROPOSALS REGARDING A FORUM OF CHRISTIAN CHURCHES AND ECUMENICAL ORGANISATIONS

1. A consultation took place at the Chateau de Bossey, near Geneva, 26-29 August 1998 to consider the possible creation of a broad-based Forum of Christian churches and ecumenical organisations. Twenty-eight participants represented the WCC, Christian World Communions, Regional Ecumenical Organisations, National Councils of Churches, international ecumenical organisations and churches not at present associated with major ecumenical structures.
2. The gathering noted dramatic changes in the world situation, as well as major developments in relationships between churches and between ecumenical organisations. Efforts to advance Christian unity now take many forms, have many players and focus on many centres. However, this diversity raises urgent questions about how to strengthen the wholeness of the movement against tendencies towards fragmentation and competitiveness, not least in view of shrinking resources. A more effective, more sustaining, more inclusive network of relationships is needed to bring differences of understanding among the partners into a mutually committed dialogue so that all may find their way to a clearer discernment and a more faithful obedience.
3. The following proposal for a Forum of Christian churches and ecumenical organisations emerged in the course of the consultation. It is offered in the hope that churches and ecumenical structures may discern in it a way forward for the years immediately ahead.

*Goals and Objectives*

4. The proposed Forum is *possible* because of the unity that is already given in Christ. It is *called for* because of our common faith in a reconciling God whose church knows that it is summoned to become God's reconciled and reconciling people.
5. The Forum is intended to help build more significant, more inclusive relationships. It will not speak for the participating bodies, but it will provide a way for them, transcending the limitations of existing frameworks, to think new thoughts, dream new dreams, and glimpse new visions.
6. Seeking to be open to the charisma the Spirit gives to Christ's people, the Forum's style will be open, expectant and relying on a minimum of rules and structures. One condition for participation therefore, is a willingness to accept other participants as bona fide partners in a dialogue, the aim of which is to strengthen the obedience of all to Christ.
7. The occasional gatherings of the Forum will provide opportunities for worship, exploration of matters of common Christian concern and development of enhanced mutual understanding. They are not

conceived as decision making, programme initiating or document-producing events. However, they might lead to new forms of co-operation.

*Participation*

8. This is a Forum, not an organisation, therefore the question to be considered is participation, not membership.
9. Participation will be based on confessing the Lord Jesus Christ as God and Saviour according to the Scriptures and seeking to fulfil together the common calling to the glory of the one God, Father, Son and Holy Spirit. It should be characterised by the desire to mutually engage in the search for obedience to Christ.
10. Participants will mainly be representative of church bodies and ecumenical organisations of international significance. Some participants will also be individuals who are representative of and accountable to identifiable constituencies with a commitment to our common calling.
11. Roman Catholics, Orthodox, Evangelicals, Pentecostals, and other families represented in the Conference of Christian World Communions, as well as Regional Ecumenical Organisations, International Ecumenical Organisations and the World Council of Churches, are among those envisaged as participants in the Forum.
12. Criteria of participation include willingness to listen, to talk and respond together with others in the Christian family to God's calling. Participants must have mutual respect and respect for the self-understanding of the others.

*Size, Process and Contents of Forum meeting*

13. The Forum is a concept that will be manifest in many ways, including international meetings. Once the idea has taken root, it could meet in various configurations and locations.
14. The initial meeting should be made up of 150 -250 participants, depending on the response to he invitations issued. The process will be designed to allow maximum participation. This will begin by soliciting issues and challenges from the participating bodies prior to the meeting.
15. There will be a balance of plenary and small group time, with space for celebration and spontaneity. Worship will be an integral part of the forum. The meeting should reflect awareness of the historical forces that bring participants together and should provide opportunities for in-depth discussion.
16. The distinctiveness will be in the style of the meeting that will promote open dialogue of sharing without a focus on documentation and recommendations. No votes will be taken.

17. Provision might be made for a group of "listeners" to help discern and articulate the insights gained by the gathering.

*Funding, Timing*

18. Participants would be expected to cover their costs. In order to ensure fullest participation, the Organising Committee will seek funds to cover certain overhead expenses and make available a modest amount for subsidies.
19. The initial Forum meeting may take place as early as the year 2001.

*Organising Mechanisms*

20. A small Continuation Committee drawn from the consultation of August 1998 will continue as a bridge between the process thus far and its future. It could also become the nucleus of the Organising Committee for the first Forum meeting.
21. The Continuation Committee is to consider responses to this proposal and to work out the modalities of a first meeting of the Organising Committee by October 1999. This Continuation Committee will need to meet before mid-1999.
22. A small group of eminent persons who have a broad basis of credibility among Christians and churches might be constituted by the Continuation Committee to serve as an inviting body. This group may or may not need to meet. Invitations to participate would then go with the signatures and under the patronage of these persons.
23. The Organising Committee should be called by the Continuation Committee in consultation with the leaders of the interested bodies who by the responses to the initial proposal sent after this meeting would have expressed interest in the Forum.
24. It will include representatives of ecumenical partners of international significance who currently have various levels of collaborating as well as new partners representing the wider community such as Pentecostal Churches, World Evangelical Fellowship, the Organisation of African Instituted Churches who may express interest. A strong representation of the Roman Catholic Church was also stressed.
25. The tasks of the Organising Committee will include:
    - i) Receiving and evaluating responses which contribute to building the agenda
    - ii) Building an inclusive agenda
    - iii) Taking care of logistics and budget of the Forum
    - iv) Raising some funds for the overhead costs as well as for granting small subsidies for those who might need it.
    - v) Preparing for a procedure to evaluate the first meeting of the Forum.

## 2. COMMUNIQUÉ – GLOBAL CHRISTIAN FORUM

Thirty representatives from throughout the world gathered from 9-11 September 2000 at Fuller Theological Seminary, Pasadena, California, to explore the idea of a Global Christian Forum that would include a wide spectrum of churches and organisations. Those present came from Orthodox, Roman Catholic, Anglican, Reformation Protestant, Pentecostal and Evangelical churches as well as Christian networks and quasi church organisations.

Although the idea of such a Forum originally arose in conversations within the World Council of Churches, the development of a proposal is now under the leadership of an independent continuation committee. The discussions at the meeting explored ways to go beyond the present ecumenical structures so that churches from a wider range of traditions may have a common space to discuss issues of mutual concern.

Papers were presented on the history of inter-church relations from Evangelical, Orthodox, Pentecostal, Anglican, Protestant and Roman Catholic perspectives. The realities of regional challenges were presented by representatives from Africa, Asia, Caribbean, Europe, Middle East and North America. Hopes and expectations of churches organised on the world-level, as well as traditional state churches and independent or free churches were openly and frankly discussed.

The representatives agreed on the possible contours of a future Forum that would include the following purposes:

> In the spirit of John 17:21 "that all of them may be one…so that the world may believe that you have sent me" and because of our common faith in a reconciling God (2 Cor. 5: 18 – 21), the forum is intended:

- To deepen our commitment to God's mission in the world;
- To enhance our understanding of contemporary expressions of Christian mission (Matt.28: 19, 20, Matt. 22: 37 – 39, John 20:21 and Acts 1:8);
- To pursue principles and practices that would enable us to handle our Christian differences and distinctive characteristics creatively and peaceably;
- To engage in theological reflection in areas of common concern;
- To strengthen the wholeness of the church by encouraging communication and co-operation; and
- To foster relationships that may lead to common witness.

Further work on the proposal will be carried out by the continuation committee over the next few months.

The meeting was marked by an atmosphere of mutual partnership, trust and consensus building and was underpinned by warm and deep fellowship.

Pasadena, California
11 September 2000

## 3. TOWARDS A GLOBAL CHRISTIAN FORUM

A consultation towards a Global Christian Forum took place at Fuller Theological Seminary in Pasadena, California from June 15-20, 2002. Among the 55 participants were representatives from various Orthodox (Eastern and Oriental), Catholic, Anglican, Reformation Protestant, Pentecostal, Evangelical, and African Instituted churches as well as inter-church organisations.

The idea of a Forum, first suggested in the mid-1990s, grew out of a concern that has been growing in different parts of the Church to bring more voices into the search for the reconciliation and co-operation of Christians and their churches. An initial meeting to test the concept was held at the Bossey Ecumenical Institute in Switzerland, 26-29 August 1998. Another meeting to seek the advice and participation of representatives of the Evangelical and Pentecostal churches took place at Fuller Seminary, 9-11 September 2000.

The Forum is understood as a process of bringing Christians from around the world to a common table in an informal atmosphere; it is not to be another organisation. Its stated purpose is to create an open space in which representatives from a broad range of Christian churches and inter-church organisations, which confess the triune God and Jesus Christ as perfect in His divinity and humanity, can gather to foster mutual respect, to explore and address together common challenges.

For this consultation at Fuller Theological Seminary two themes were central: unity and mission. The participants spent two days introducing themselves, sharing their own spiritual journeys as well as the experience of their churches and organisations. The next two days were spent discussing the concerns and challenges they face.

Among the concerns that surfaced and were frankly discussed were the following: the problems of different approaches to the Scriptures; the place of tradition, often unacknowledged, in the different churches; the need to understand each other's use of Christian vocabulary; the movement of the Spirit in today's world; proselytism and religious freedom; and the new co-operation between churches who are in dialogue with each other or are together suffering persecution. Panels and plenary discussions addressed two issues: one session looked at evangelization from a variety of perspectives; another focused on breakthroughs to inter-church relationships, as well as barriers to reconciliation.

The participants were pleased by the open process of the consultation and grateful for the opportunity to meet Christians from different church traditions and parts of the world. Moved by the honest sharing of concerns, the participants seek to continue this process of bringing diverse Christians together so that they may discover each other as brothers and sisters in the Lord. They hope to expand the participation in the Forum process by planning future meetings both regionally and internationally.

## 4. GLOBAL CHRISTIAN FORUM: PROVISIONAL PURPOSE STATEMENT

To create an open space wherein representatives from a broad range of Christian churches and inter-church organisations, which confess the triune God and Jesus Christ as perfect in His divinity and humanity, can gather to foster mutual respect, to explore and address together common challenges.

In the spirit of John 17:21 "that all of them may be one … so that the world may believe that you have sent me" and because of our faith in a reconciling God (2 Cor.5: 18-21) a forum could pursue the following:

- Deepen our commitment to God's Word and mission in the world;
- Enhance our understanding of contemporary expressions of Christian mission;
- Pursue principles and practices that enable us to deal freely, responsibly and peaceably with our Christian differences and distinctive qualities;
- Engage in theological reflection in areas of mutual concern;
- Strengthen the wholeness of the church by encouraging communication and co-operation; and
- Foster relationships that may lead to common witness.

Pasadena, June 20, 2002

## 5. GLOBAL CHRISTIAN FORUM - ASIA CONSULTATION

*'Jesus Christ in Asia – Our Journey with Him'*

Around sixty Christians from a broad range of traditions and organisations – including Anglican, Catholic, Evangelical, Mar Thoma, Orthodox, Pentecostal, Protestant, Salvation Army, the Christian Conference of Asia, Evangelical Fellowship of Asia, Federation of Asian Bishops' Conferences and World Vision – came together in Hong Kong for the purpose of reflecting on our journey together with Jesus Christ in Asia.

This coming together was the initiative of the Global Christian Forum process. It provided space for us as Asian Christians from different traditions to meet with each other and to listen to each one's "faith journey", our particular struggles and challenges in different situations in Asia, with all its plurality. We experienced a fresh sense of unity under the lordship of Jesus Christ, and a shared passion for participating in his mission in the world.

Arising out of this sharing we developed a new awareness of one another's existence and spirituality, and with it the importance of each other in being church in Asia. We affirm that we need to build bridges that would facilitate co-operation in order to have a united voice in confronting the various issues facing Asia. We acknowledge that this in no way means that we would lose our individual identity or distinctiveness. We acknowledge the need to respect and uphold this diversity, among those who confess that God is Father, Son and Holy Spirit and Jesus Christ as perfect in his divinity and humanity. In this spirit, we need to establish trust, openness, honesty, love and humility as we work with one another.

We affirm the need for an emphasis on holiness of life and prayer for the fostering of unity amongst us, and a deepening and strengthening of our participation in God's mission in his world. We commit ourselves to explore together models for working, studying and addressing issues that are of common concern, notably poverty, oppression and religious intolerance.

We further affirm the need to work together and continue this initiative at the regional, national and local level. We urge the Evangelical Fellowship of Asia, the Christian Conference of Asia and the Federation of Asian Bishops' Conferences to assist in forwarding this initiative.

4 May 2004, Hong Kong

## 6. GLOBAL CHRISTIAN FORUM – AFRICA CONSULTATION

*'Jesus Christ in Africa – Our Journey with Him'*

We, being around seventy Christians from a broad range of traditions and organisations – including African Instituted, Anglican, Baptist, Catholic, Evangelical, Orthodox (Eastern and Oriental), Pentecostal, Protestant, Reformed, Salvation Army, Seventh Day Adventist, African Theological Fellowship, All Africa Conference of Churches, Association of Evangelicals in Africa, various National Councils of Churches, International Fellowship of Evangelical Students, United Bible Societies, the World Student Christian Federation and World Vision, and also the Global Continuation Committee – came together in Lusaka, Zambia, from 9 to 13 August 2005 for the purpose of reflecting together on our journey with Jesus Christ in Africa.

This unprecedented gathering was the initiative of the Global Christian Forum process. Its unique breadth included Anglophone, Francophone and Lusophone participants. It provided space for us as African Christians from different traditions to meet with one another and to listen to each one's 'faith journey,' our particular struggles and challenges in different situations in Africa. We experienced a fresh sense of unity under the Lordship of Jesus Christ, and a shared passion for participating in His mission in the world.

Arising out of this sharing we developed a new awareness and understanding of one another's existence and spirituality, and with it the importance of each other in being church in Africa. We affirm that we need to build bridges that would facilitate co-operation in order to have a united voice in confronting the various issues facing Africa. This in no way means that we would lose our individual identity or distinctiveness. We acknowledge the need to respect and uphold this diversity, among those who confess that God is Father, Son and Holy Spirit, and Jesus Christ as perfect in his divinity and humanity. In this spirit, we need to establish and deepen trust, openness, honesty, love, and humility as we work with one another.

We affirm the need for an emphasis on holiness of life, prayer and the centrality of Scripture for the fostering of unity among us, and a deepening and strengthening of our participation in God's mission in his world. We commit ourselves to explore together models for working, studying and addressing issues which are of common interest, and to maintaining and broadening networks of communication that arise from our fellowship with one another.

We discussed issues of mutual concern, among them the inclusion of marginalized groups; HIV/AIDS; history, contextualisation, inculturation and the promoting of the publication and dissemination of the work of African theologians; Islam; and the Church in the world, including corruption, election monitoring, promoting good governance, advocacy and civic education. We also addressed the terminology surrounding relationships between churches and Christian bodies, and the difficulties that may arise from such vocabulary as 'ecumenical,' 'Evangelical,' 'charismatic,' and 'Pentecostal.'

We are encouraged by the existing levels of co-operation, particularly at the grass roots, in both worship and social action. We affirm the need to develop these further. We acknowledge that in many areas, the greater the degree of unity, the more effective our witness and the more influential our voice.

We further affirm the need to work together, and continue this initiative at the continental, regional, national and local level. We urge the Continuation Committee for Africa to proceed with the work that it has been mandated to undertake, and so to explore ways of taking forward the Global Christian Forum process in Africa. We appreciate the effort of the Global Continuation Committee in launching this initiative.

We offer thanks to the Lord for all He has done for us through the Global Christian Forum process. To God be the Glory!

Lusaka, 13 August 2005

*A discussion group at the Lusaka consultation*

## 7. GLOBAL CHRISTIAN FORUM - EUROPE CONSULTATION

*Statement*

Some fifty representatives from a wide range of Christian churches, denominations and organisations in Europe [Anglican, Baptist, Catholic, Evangelical, Friends (Quakers), Lutheran, Mennonite, Methodist, Old-Catholic, Orthodox (Eastern and Oriental), Pentecostal, Reformed, Salvation Army] gathered for a consultation from 19 to 22 June 2006, at the invitation of the Continuation Committee of the Global Christian Forum. The meeting was hosted by the Syrian Orthodox Church and took place at their monastery St. Jacob of Sarug in Warburg, Germany.

We thank God for this opportunity to meet, and to talk in an atmosphere of trust and openness abut the concerns we have in common as Christians coming from so many different traditions, some of whom had never come together before. The spirit of our meeting stood in contrast with the alienation and hostility that sometimes characterize our relationships. We prayed and praised God in the different ways of our traditions. We shared our individual faith journeys and heard about the presence and witness of our churches and faith communities in Europe today. We listened to examples in some countries in Europe where churches belonging to the ecumenical movement and Evangelical and Pentecostal churches are finding ways to overcome the difficulties and bridge the gaps between them. In our discussions we identified several issues which are sometimes obstacles for better relationships, but can also be opportunities for more co-operation in the future:

- common witness in the public sphere ;
- new ways of expressing the Christian faith in a secularized Europe ;
- proselytism, mission and evangelism ;
- migration and majority / minority situations ;
- inter-religious relations, especially Christian – Muslim dialogue.

Speaking frankly of the different perceptions of each other and of the problems between us we realized that lack of contact has given rise to misunderstandings, and we became keenly aware of the importance of meeting face to face. It became clear also that dialogue is necessary not only between us, but that there is equally a need for dialogue and introspection within each of our churches and Christian faith traditions. One of the ideas that emerged is that of elaborating a 'code of conduct' to guide us in our relationships to one another.

We will report on the rich experience of this meeting to the churches and organisations that we represented, and in our local situations at home. It is our conviction that the process of the Global Christian Forum should continue in Europe, especially at local, national and sub-regional levels. We believe that the migrant and diaspora churches in Europe should be fully part of it. As participants in this meeting we will do our share to make this happen. We are asking the different regional church organisations in Europe, e.g. the Council of European Bishops' Conferences, the Conference of European Churches, the European Evangelical Alliance, the Pentecostal European Fellowship, the European Baptist Federation and others to support and promote this process, and in particular to facilitate the coming together of the 'mainline churches involved in the classical ecumenical movement' and the 'Evangelical / Pentecostal' faith traditions in our countries and sub-regions.

Warburg, 22 June 2006

*A Pentecostal and a Catholic participant in conversation at Warburg*

## 8. GLOBAL CHRISTIAN FORUM - LATIN AMERICA CONSULTATION

*MESSAGE TO THE CHURCHES*

*'Father…that they be one in us, so the world may believe that you sent me'*
*(John 17:21)*

We have gathered together in Santiago, Chile, from June 26-29, 2007, Latin American and Caribbean sisters and brothers from the diverse Christian traditions, invited by the Global Christian Forum, under the theme: *Jesus Christ in Latin America, our pilgrimage with Him.*

This Latin American and Caribbean consultation is the last of a series of regional meetings that have been held in Asia, Africa and Europe. This process will culminate with a global meeting of the *Forum* that will take place in Nairobi, Kenya.

The *Forum* is an open space in which representatives from a broad range of Christian churches and inter-church organisations that confess the Triune God and Jesus Christ as perfect in His divinity and humanity, can gather to foster mutual respect, to explore and address together common challenges.

Inspired by the prayer of Jesus, the *Forum* proposes to stimulate co-operation and communication among the churches, broaden mutual understanding and comprehension, and deepen commitment to the Word of God so that the world may believe in Jesus Christ.

During these days we have recognized one another in our pilgrimage with Jesus. The testimonies of encounter with Jesus and of personal calling from each one of the participants allowed us to see each other as our brothers and sisters, beyond differences and traditions, overcoming distrust and hostilities in an environment of humility and frankness. We have rejoiced together in the praise and exaltation of the good name of our God in daily devotionals and times of worship.

The new challenges presented by the world today have affected the life and mission of the Latin American and Caribbean church. In this way, the *Forum* has been an open space which has allowed us to also be challenged by different concerns: the growing number of internally displaced and immigrant populations, the millions of street children, gangs, urban and socio-political violence, violence against women and children, the advance of AIDS and other pandemics, discrimination and offences against human dignity and the environment. In the midst of all this is the temptation of walking without the foundation of faith or of distorting faith. However, the signs of hope are evident in our communities through the varied expressions of faith, particularly among the youth.

We have seen that the attempts for advancing toward the unity for which the Lord prayed, have been many and varied. From the past century, the spaces, movements, instruments and attempts for dialogue and moving closer together have multiplied at the global, regional and national levels, as well as among denominational families and diverse ecclesiastical traditions. All of this has contributed and contributes today to the visible unity of the church, the credibility of witness to faith in Jesus Christ, and to the expansion of the Reign of God. However, we recognize that there is still much to do so that we can see the prayer of Jesus fully accomplished. In Latin America and the Caribbean today, the church presents many faces, old and new. We have tried to identify them in our meeting in Santiago, rejoicing in the richness of their diversity, and have attempted to understand what God asks of us in light of this new reality.

We see in the *Forum* the possibility of a renewed and broadened place in which to meet one another, appreciate our differences, unite our efforts and commit ourselves in mission. Our arms are open so that together we may build in diversity, support one another in hope, and be witnesses to Jesus Christ along the way. Thus, we desire to extend the widest possible invitation to our brothers and sisters of all churches so that with courage they may join this pilgrimage of faith, recognizing one another on a new common foundation in which trust and mutual love may grow and make us capable of proclaiming Jesus Christ with renewed strength so that the world may believe in Him and have life, to the glory of the one God, Father, Son and Holy Spirit.

Anglican Churches
Catholic Church
Evangelical Churches
Orthodox Churches
Pentecostal Churches
Protestant Churches

Santiago, 29 June 2007

(Translation of the original Spanish text, available at www.globalchristianforum.org)

## 9. WORLD COUNCIL OF CHURCHES – NINTH ASSEMBLY, PORTO ALEGRE, BRAZIL, 14-23 FEBRUARY 2006

### *EXTRACT OF THE APPROVED REPORT OF THE POLICY REFERENCE COMMITTEE ON THE GLOBAL CHRISTIAN FORUM*

34. The Harare Assembly affirmed the proposal that the WCC facilitate the process identified in the Common Understanding and Vision document as the " Forum proposal". This process has included a series of meetings preparatory to gathering a broader representation of Christian churches than currently are members in the WCC for consultation on issues common to all Christian churches and inter-church organisations. Several regional consultations have taken place, with participation from a wide range of Evangelical and Pentecostal churches not represented in the WCC, the Roman Catholic Church and from representatives of WCC member churches, gathering together at a global level representatives of all four main streams of Christianity. Demonstrating the timeliness of this initiative, given the changing global Christian landscape and to enhance a common Christian witness and solidarity in a fractured world, the Global Christian Forum process offers a fluid model of initiatives that can be facilitated by the WCC to welcome broader participation in the ecumenical journey.

35. The PRC noted the tension that will continue to be present as the WCC proceeds on the one hand to deepen its relationships among the member churches and explore the areas of theological convergence and divergence, while on the other hand encountering with ecclesiastical challenges presented by engaging with the broader Christian community. The committee reaffirms the centrality of the fellowship of member churches, the Common Understanding and Vision of the WCC, and the particular accomplishments of the Special Commission in deepening the relationships among the member churches, and notes the urgent need for the WCC to continue to facilitate gathering the broader Christian community in consultation and dialogue.

36. The PRC **recommends** that the Ninth Assembly:

1. receive the report on the Global Christian Forum (Programme Book, pages 164 – 168) including the direction for future work and to express its appreciation to the organizers of the consultations and the forum event;
2. instruct the WCC to participate in the global forum event scheduled to take place in late 2007, and following that event to conduct a formal and comprehensive evaluation of the concept and the process.

# Part II:

# The Limuru Global Gathering

# CHAPTER 2

## FROM THE PARTICIPANTS

*It is appropriate to begin the account of the Limuru gathering with a collection of papers reflecting the voices of the participants. The richness of the daily group discussions, which were reported back in plenary each day resonates in the summary that is offered here. A few examples of the faith journies that were shared in the groups give a taste of this practice of beginning a meeting which is an essential part of the Global Christian Forum. The affirmations and expectations, and the voices from the regions and some of the churches illustrate the input of the participants into the process of the gathering.*

## SUMMARY OF GROUP DISCUSSIONS

**Rev. Theo Gill**

### Introduction

From the earliest planning for the Global Christian Forum in Limuru, it was clear that it would be impossible to share participants' faith journeys in plenary sessions of more than 200 people. The alternative was to facilitate this sharing in smaller discussion groups. The experience from regional Forum meetings was that, with around sixty people in the room, this part of the exercise took almost a full day. In the planning for Limuru it was decided to form eight groups of thirty out of the expected 240 participants, so that each group could complete the sharing exercise in about half a day, specifically on the afternoon of the first day. Once this principle was established, it seemed logical that the same groups of thirty should function as discussion groups throughout the meeting.

In order to enhance the potential of the groups, each was carefully composed to ensure that it represented a cross-section of the whole meeting. In each group the percentages of the various traditions present in the meeting were respected (i.e. Anglican, Catholic, Evangelical, Orthodox, Protestant and Pentecostal) as well as the percentages reflecting gender and region. Additionally, in each group about half of the participants were from churches and organisations involved in the conciliar ecumenical movement and the other half from the Evangelical and Pentecostal churches. To avoid groupings based solely on language, simultaneous interpretation was provided in four of the groups of thirty.

Each discussion group of thirty had a moderator and a reporter who had been asked to play the particular role, and briefed in advance, and who met together over meals (in so far as this could be achieved). In all, the eight groups met in four sessions apiece, for a total of 32 encounters. Their discussions, findings and suggestions were recorded and shared in plenary by reporters, but there was no attempt during the Forum to merge the group reports into one document. That purpose is served by the summary presented below.

The eight discussion groups, designated as Groups A through H, met in periods of reflection that allowed each individual to comment on the principal themes of the Global Christian Forum and on presentations made in plenary sessions. The opening sessions of the groups were devoted to self-introductions and a personal account of each participant's life story and faith journey.

**Life stories and personal pilgrimages**

The dynamic of this phase of the encounter was well summarised by the reporter from Group D:

Each member, according to the Global Christian Forum arrangements, had the opportunity to share with us his or her Christian life story. Our stories were different. A majority of people had been born into and brought up in Christian homes, but whether born into Christian families or not, at some point each person had come to make a definite personal decision of commitment to the lordship of Jesus Christ. Thus, in spite of the diversity in our lives' journeys, at the centre of it all was the difference that Jesus Christ had made in our lives. My conclusion, listening to how each life story had developed, was that Jesus Christ does not make us 'denominational': he makes us 'Christian'. Through the various journeys in Christ that we shared, this invariably meant:

1. A deeper faith
2. A better person
3. A commitment to prayer
4. A commitment to the reading and study of the scriptures
5. A call to serve Christ culminating in ordination or some special capacity as a lay leader.

One member concluded his life story by noting that 'our dreams, our plans and our hopes are nothing compared to the fulfillment we receive in serving Christ.' For another, coming to know Christ as Lord established a relationship more profound than any other offered in the world. Members of the group agreed that these sentiments applied to each of their life stories... [and] pointed us to directions in which the Lord might be calling us to pray and support each other. We were not at this forum simply to listen to life stories, but having done so, to take the further step of participating in each other's ministries through prayer and other forms of support.

The groups hailed the approach of recounting one's own story so that every participant came to know one another as a fellow believer. Everyone came to see themselves as Christians who did not fit easily into predetermined categories such as 'Evangelical', 'Pentecostal', 'Catholic' or 'ecumenical'. The reporter for Group A took up this topic:

We recognise that while we talk we must be careful with labels that are invested with prejudice, by which we pre-judge others. It is a problem of perception. We must begin to relate as brothers and sisters. One member noted that the organisations on our name-tags are man-made. We should begin from the basis of our own names, as we did today, for we are all on a journey of faith and travelling in the same direction.

We need to learn to put labels aside or to bracket them, and allow them to be filled with new content emerging from our relationship and growing understanding of one another. We are grappling with histories and legacies, and we must understand the dynamics of each life in finding one another. The last thing we want to do to each other is to close ourselves in boxes.

The possibility presented by this kind of group is not to deny or put aside who we are, but to understand one another as people and create new definitions. Often the definitions we bring with us are calculated to divide. Here we are given the opportunity to discover new meanings and create definitions that provide us with more stable ground for building relationships…

We have a shared passion, and this is the context for our discussion. We must journey together to find each other, to allow self-definition.

## Families of faith

Early in the proceedings, the faith journeys of believers came to be associated with communities of faith, the one body of Christ and the interaction of Christians and their churches with other churches, and with society as a whole. One group reported:

1. As the participants in Group F shared their individual stories there was a great sense of commonality. Most were born into Christian homes where the family, especially the mothers, played an invaluable and integral role in shaping and nurturing. Few were first-generation Christians.
2. However, as we continued our faith journey and as we grew in faith, we had our own personal encounters with Christ, thus developing a new phase in our spirituality. We all agreed that this became a reality only by the grace of God, irrespective of our differences.
3. Further, through our personal exposure to the wider Christian body/family, we were challenged to think and live beyond the boundaries of our individual churches or faith communities. Our faith continued to be shaped and nurtured by personal experiences, justice

and social issues, ecumenical relationships, interfaith relations and dialogue, healthcare, education, politics and issues of survival. Whereas for some many of these challenges were seen as crises of faith within the churches; for others they represented a new dimension of faith.

4. We agreed that we share a common language, which is a real sign of the working of the Spirit of God in our midst.
5. Finally, we agreed to disagree. We agreed to share this observation made by one of our members: in the culture of some of our churches, people who were born in the church are seen as the membership, and 'evangelism' consists mostly in retaining their children and children's children. In other traditions, particularly the 'newer churches', the growth of the church depends on conversion, on persons who are first-generation Christians. (This will be considered in further group discussions.)

Group H provided more details on 'cradle Christianity' and conversion, subjects touched on in all the group reports. In the words of their reporter:

1. We see the influence of parents on our faith, although not in all cases. About half our members are the products of 'mixed marriages' representing two traditions.
2. Many have experiences in different denominations, which have led to an ecumenical spirit.
3. God deals with each of us, in different languages, but always intervenes and creates opportunities for us.
4. We are able to fulfil God's purposes for us but in different ways.
5. Many of us have found mentors who challenged us to believe, or called us into ministry. Some were called into churches, some to go beyond them in mission.
6. Our international experiences have often driven our ecumenical moves.
7. The formative age between 8 and18 was noted by nearly all of us. Our life courses were often set in those years of our lives.

Following the initial group sessions, the Global Christian Forum presented lectures by prominent missiologists and other church leaders. In its report of the discussion on Dr. Wonsuk Ma's presentation, Group B inserted a note of appreciation of 'Wonsuk sharing his own story, which in many ways resonated with our stories, and which invited us to tell our own stories.' The group report continued:

We affirm the principle of sharing our life stories as a sharing of a part of the greater family story. What one person in our group said about the official, theological bilateral dialogues we affirm here, too: 'Conversation is the discovery of a level of communion, or a level of "church" with one another.' Now we are beginning to see the things we have in common, whereas in the past we focused only on the things that drove us apart. The point of ecumenism is to discover what makes us brothers and sisters in Christ, neither for the sake of dialogue, nor for the sake of church politics.

Group B also learned, or discovered again, as if for the first time, that while we are all on a journey, we are at different places in the journey and it becomes an imperative to 'hear' where others are on that journey. This involves honest listening.

**Describing others**

A recurring complaint in the group discussions concerned attempts by speakers from one region or tradition to describe the circumstances of others. Two missiological presentations were offered by the Pentecostal scholars Wonsuk Ma and Cheryl Bridges Johns. Dr. Bridges Johns was intentionally confrontational, pointedly asking participants whether evidence of numerical decline in certain Christian traditions means that those churches and related organisations are dying. Afterwards one reporter recorded some points of the critical response from members of Group C:

Several group members voiced their concern that the past efforts of the historical churches were minimized. Some felt that to say that the historical churches are dying is offensive to those who belong to them…

One said that the paper is counterproductive and is a counter-dialogue. The speaker feels that my tradition is already dead… Another member opined there is a danger of denying what is old. The fire is still burning – historical churches are still here… The Spirit does not have a short-term memory…

Someone from a church of the South (Brazil) said that he wanted to hear a real Pentecostal from the South [not academics who teach in the UK and USA].

This last comment was echoed the report from Group E:

> Many of the Spanish-speaking members of our group were from Latin America. They felt that the paper [on north-south dimensions of Christianity] did not acknowledge the suffering that still continues today because of the church. Many stories were told of social and political 'legacies' that were not Christian but paternalistic. These practices are still robbing people of dignity, and making it difficult to escape a 'welfare mentality' towards churches in the West. It was felt that the South has been and is still 'crying tears'.

Group A cautioned:

> We must always ask the question of who is defining whom? When are we defining (i.e. are we describing the past, or the present)? Where are we doing the defining (e.g. in the North or the South)?

In several discussions there was at this point a renewed endorsement of the principle that participants are to define themselves, their own traditions and regional contexts rather than encouraging the labelling of others in the name of dialogue.

**Proposals regarding the future of the Global Christian Forum**

In the closing sessions of the eight groups, preparatory work was undertaken for the proposals that might emerge from Limuru. The reports of these sessions became grist for the mill in producing the forum's open letter to Christians throughout the world.

A sampling of comments follows to give an insight into the results of the group process.

From Group A:

> One of the great advantages of this process has been allowing people to speak for themselves and to explain their own traditions and beliefs, rather than lodging charges against other traditions. This also encourages participants to own up to their mistakes and to the mistakes of their own cultures or confessions, where an accusatory conversation would force a more defensive tone. Recognising our own imperfections helps us to admit the need for interdependence and reliance on one another. When we are open to a shift in a paradigm and to non-traditional contributions to leadership – for example, from South to North, young to old, poor to wealthy, rural to urban, Pentecostal movement to historic churches – we become more complete.
>
> Still, we must be aware of continuing suspicion and hostility at the grassroots – charges that are still made, accusations still voiced. In many places, there is no interaction of the sort that we have experienced in this Forum. How can we overcome division and foster dialogue at the local level?

From Group B:

> In the closing session, one Pentecostal member asked whether the Forum should seek to become an alternative to the World Council of Churches. 'The reason that I ask is because I believe my Pentecostal colleagues will only consider joining a Forum like this. I would like to see a Forum that operated on a more regional basis, perhaps continent by continent.'
>
> Another participant responded that the Forum is not in a position to replace other ecumenical structures. But it was agreed that the tone of celebration at the Forum was wonderful. Other participants wished to seek ways of underlining the continuity of story-telling despite the story-tellers' differences in background. The Forum has provided a space for people who would not ordinarily meet together.
>
> As diverse Christians come to know one another, it will become possible to address some of the tricky questions that have not been raised this week.

From Group C:

The discussion in the group did not arrive at specific conclusions regarding certain issues, but reached a general consensus on the following:

1. The letter produced at the close of the meeting is useful for the continuing dialogue.
2. Everyone in the group was very positive about their experience of the Global Christian Forum – what it has done so far, and what it will accomplish in the future.
3. The past accomplishments of the World Council of Churches should not be undervalued. As one member said, 'We must recognize that the WCC's social involvement in the past was a service of love.'
4. There are varying understandings of Pentecostalism. It must be remembered that a Pentecostal from the global South may have a very different perspective from a Pentecostal in the global North.
5. Finally, the group felt that we had 'passed the test' as previous sessions have enabled us to be open with one another even in discussing difficult issues.

## From Group D:

Many of the observations we have made in our group sessions are being incorporated into the 'letter to Christians' and 'proposals for the future of the Forum', and so they will not be reiterated in our group report. In addition to our other recommendations, the members of Group D also wish to suggest that:

1. Participants should make conscious efforts to pray for Christian communions other than their own.
2. Decision-making at Global Christian Forum meetings should be by consensus. It was agreed that we cannot resolve every issue of difference among us, but at the very least a consensus would help us to pursue the very lofty aims we have set ourselves.
3. The Global Christian Forum should never lose sight of the great contribution that the historical ecumenical movement has made to global Christianity.

## From Group E:

In one session, we considered the questions, 'what are we not doing, and what do we need to do, to promote unity?' Here are some of the responses:

- We are told to love, yet we hate; we are told to tell the truth, yet we lie.
- Stop monument- and empire-building if it is not for the sake of others and for sharing.
- Resist elitism, triumphalism, tribalism…
- Bottle up your pride. If you need help, do not neglect to turn to other churches in your area.

## From Group F:

A Way Forward

a. We admit that there is a need for contrition and repentance. Both mainline and non-mainline churches have made errors and have been critical of each other. With caution and care we must be reconciled by going through a process of repentance.

b. We need to bring or translate what is happening here at the Global Christian Forum to the grassroots and local congregations. We need to engage in a process of conscientious contextualisation.

From Group G:

Unity is 'Glocal'. What is happening at this global level needs to be filtered down to the local grassroots level. Where unity is emerging at local levels this also needs to be filtered up through to the global context. Space must be created for both these activities to occur.

From Group H:

We appreciate the minimal structure the Global Christian Forum has had to date but we observe that any living thing creates a structure. If we feel we have a task to accomplish then we arrange the means to succeed.

We discussed local, regional and global expressions of the Forum. There is general support for the open model of discourse that the Global Christian Forum embodies. Among our comments:

1. Some thought it necessary to repeat a meeting of the Global Christian Forum in order to help and to motivate the work at local levels.
2. Many affirmed that the real effect would take place locally and regionally.
3. Some strongly affirmed that they believed the Global Christian Forum was a work of the Holy Spirit, moving us closer to one another, but there was not a full consensus on that feeling.
4. Some noted that Pentecostals and Evangelicals resist invitations from the ecumenical councils to sit at their tables, precisely because it *is* 'their' table. The Global Christian Forum is a new table so that all may share equally.

The discussion groups and Bible studies contributed ideas that were formulated into the documents that emerged from the Global Christian Forum and particularly the letter to Christians everywhere. Apart from their collaboration in agreements adopted at the close of the meeting, each group exemplified an adventure in inter-Christian dialogue and the sharing of insights. These smaller groups became microcosms of the Forum as a whole as may be seen in quotations cited throughout this chapter, yet nowhere is it better stated than in this list of suggestions from Group F:

...we believe that the strands of classical ecumenism that dealt with the divisions in the East and West are alive and still in motion, and they continue to be a dynamic process. However, in the 21st century, we face another new situation: Some Christian traditions, which have not been actively involved with mainline churches, are coming into closer contact. This is a new dimension of ecumenism that we should celebrate. In expressing our expectations and visions for the future of this Forum, we propose three points:

1. We humbly believe that the participants in the Global Christian Forum need to make a commitment to become messengers of the Spirit and to translate this experience to the regional, national and local levels. It is at these levels that we already observe a spontaneous ecumenism is taking place.
2. We recognise that we can engage together in specific mission concerns such as the issues on Christian values and religious freedom. We need to be patient and sensitive in dealing with these issues together. We need to engage in further dialogue.
3. Thus it is our hope and expectation that this Forum (because it has captured the imagination of all churches and made us more aware of the need to come together) will take steps to identify collaborative ways and methods to address these issues through a meaningful process, in order that the image of Christ and of his Church may become a visible reality in the world.

*A discussion group at the Limuru gathering*

## From The Participants
## Faith Stories

# H.E. Archbishop Vincent M. Concessao

*H.E. Vincent M. Concessao is the Archbishop of the Roman Catholic Archdiocese of New Delhi, India*

Born and brought up in a large devout Catholic family – we were eight children and I was the fifth – religious practices like prayer, the sacraments etc. were part of life just taken for granted. I grew up in that culture. There was no questioning. To add to the religious atmosphere in the family I had an uncle who was a priest and an aunt who was a nun. For my grandmother, priests were great heroes, known for their works of charity. That appealed to me and from childhood I wanted to be a priest. That aspiration was also part of the prayer that I was taught. In the course of time, my eldest sister became a nun and I became a priest.

The seminary training was on the whole a smooth process. I was given responsibilities and opportunities to grow. Occasionally there would be a sudden realization, like for instance, about the missionary nature of the Church and the inculturation it calls for, the social implications of being faithful to the Gospel and the commitment to the poor it implies and so on. But opportunities to let these insights turn into practice were limited and so they gradually faded away. Of course, I enjoyed my ministry and grew in my appreciation of the faith and the potential of the laity. I carried on but nothing extraordinary happened except the experience of a retreat I made – the best that I have made so far.

It was just a three-day programme. I went for it more out of curiosity than for deepening my spirituality. The parishioners spoke of it highly and I wanted to know what it was all about. The participants ranged from peons and drivers to doctors and professors. Two priests gave some theological input but most of the speakers were lay people who shared their faith experience. After each talk we met in groups to discuss the topics and prayed and celebrated the daily Eucharist. But what happened in these three days was something just amazing. We must have been about fifty people. We came so close to one another with such an intense experience of joy and freedom and generosity that I was ready for anything that God wanted, even if that meant death. And this experience lasted for about a fortnight. I really felt that it was what heaven would be like. It was certainly an unforgettable way of experiencing Christianity and realizing that it was a pure gift of God.

Another conviction that caught hold of me was that I am a Christian because God chose me and called me and that the purpose of my call is precisely to share in the mission of Jesus himself. He came to reveal the Father. Now it is my turn to reveal Jesus. As the Church we are the body of Christ and now we need to make the Risen Lord visible, audible, tangible in what we say and do and the way we live and to be an object of experience like Jesus when on earth two thousand years ago. Nevertheless only faith, a pure gift of God can make him accessible. And with this gift comes the responsibility to evangelize and that is what gives the Church its deepest identity – its mission.

I also learnt that it is my faith that makes all the difference in my perception, attitudes and behaviour and that in all situations it can enable me to praise and thank God, and therefore, no matter how heavy the cross the Lord wants me to bear and the struggle that comes my way, deep down within me there can be joy because of the kind of life my faith enables me to live and the hope that ensures final victory and eternal bliss. Authentic love then becomes possible.

I always gratefully remember what a spiritual Father told us in an exhortation: You are worth what your love is worth. If your love is worth much you are worth much. If your love is worth little, you are worth little.

## Mr. Bruce Clemenger

*Mr. Bruce Clemenger is General Secretary of the Evangelical Fellowship of Canada*

I was raised in a Christian home where the expression of Christianity was out of the Protestant Holiness tradition. As a child I attended a Christian and Missionary Alliance Church and for several years my pastor was A. W. Tozer. I was too young to understand his sermons though when I hear recordings of his sermons his voice is familiar like that of a grandparent. He always had candies in his pocket that he would freely give to children after the morning service. At a young age I noticed that my older sister had a different relationship to God than me.

Like her I wanted to ask Jesus to come into my heart.

My father served on many church and ministry organization boards and my parents knew many missionaries, so there was a constant flow of missionaries and church leaders from a variety of evangelical traditions coming to my home. Through university and other contexts I found that I enjoyed interacting fruitfully with people of varied and different Christian traditions, locating areas of agreement and disagreement, exploring possibilities for constructive dialogue.

In university I began to question the adequacy and relevance of my faith. While never coming to the point of non-belief, I turned in particular to the writings of A. W. Tozer and Francis Schaeffer to ground my faith and explore its implications for all of life. How we live out our faith in Jesus as saviour and Lord in contemporary society became my life question. After university, I attended the Institute for Christian Studies which brought a reformed and particularly Kyperian framework to my thinking and concentrated my focus on political philosophy and the relationship between faith, politics and public life. After a time with Samaritan's Purse, I had the privilege of exploring my life question in the context of my work with the national alliance of Evangelicals in Canada i.e.the Evangelical Fellowship of Canada.

## Rev. Dr. Kate Coleman

*Rev. Dr. Kate Coleman is a minister of the Baptist Union of Great Britain, in charge of the Regeneration Centre in Birmingham, UK*

When I was 18 years old I had what I can only describe as the most surprising encounter of my whole life. I met God. It was surprising, not because I had no spiritual awareness, for I certainly believed in the supernatural in the New Age philosophy and I had already experienced the power of spirituality. I believed so many things that I was not entirely sure what I actually believed in. But at least I was clear about what I did not believe in. I did not believe in the God that Christians spoke about. In fact in my search for spiritual truth and reality, this 'God' was not even in the running. I had dismissed Him as irrelevant. As far as I could see He lacked integrity, credibility and frankly He was downright unfashionable! By this time my limited experience had also taught me to dismiss all Christians as hypocrites.

So you can imagine my surprise, when in no uncertain terms God made me aware of His presence at the end of a Christian rock concert of all places! What can I say? Except that I felt God's presence and heard God 'speak' to me very clearly. This was as real to me then as it was three years later when I had completed my studies at university and was desperately trying to find out what it was that I was going to do with the rest of my life. I had asked God for direction but I was still trying to convince God that some of my ideas for the future were pretty good. However it became increasingly clear that God had something else He wanted me to do and that I should take a simple step of obedience by going 'up a high mountain alone' to hear from Him (cf. Mk 9:2 – Peter, James and John and the Mount of Transfiguration). So that is exactly what I did. I asked myself the obvious question 'where in Britain are there mountains?' and I settled on Scotland (the only place with a 'real' mountain).

I then went away for 3 weeks to the Isle of Skye just to listen to God. Well, God spoke to me and what God said to me there became the second greatest surprise of my life. You see during those 3 weeks God called me to be a shepherd, He called me to Church leadership. I say that it was a surprise because I had been carefully schooled during the first few years of my Christian experience that women and Church leadership did not mix. The problem was that at the time I actually believed in this teaching for myself! I was hearing a call to leadership but it did not fit into my doctrinal understanding of the Church. After a bit of a wrestling match, I told God that if it was really a word from Him he would have to see to it, since I could not even begin to imagine it. Well less than two years later God did just that. Nearly twenty years of leadership later I was the first black woman to serve as the president of the United Kingdom Baptist Union (2006/7). Now here I am, not only still a pastor, but also I have the privilege of sharing my journey with you.

## Mrs. Victoria Kamondji

*Mrs. Victoria Kamondji is Vice-President of the French Protestant Federation and a leader of churches of African expression in France*

Born into a Christian family, to an Anglican father and a Catholic mother, the church or church attendance was one of the fundamental Christian principles valued by my family. In the town where I grew up in Sierra Leone there were only two missions – Catholic and Methodist. Considering Catholic schools more disciplined, my father sent all his children to the Catholic primary school. On certain week days I would attend Mass in the Catholic Church and on Sundays, a service in the small Methodist Church where I had been baptised by an Anglican priest.

At secondary school level up to O' Levels, I found myself in a Catholic boarding school in the capital, Freetown, where I attended Mass almost every morning and even participated in certain church activities. Back home on holidays, I returned to the Methodist church. This oscillation between the Catholic and the Methodist church was interrupted for two years when in the sixth form I chose an Anglican school. As a day student I could then attend my father's Anglican Church in Freetown.

My years in University in Freetown were decisive. All my life I had been moving back and forth from one faith to the other - Catholic, Methodist, and Anglican without effectively belonging anywhere. I felt a certain spiritual emptiness. It was then that I decided to be confirmed in the Methodist Church on the campus. The services were livelier and I believed this expression of faith would bring spiritual meaning to my life. For some time I took an active part in the Methodist youth movement in the capital.

A year after my Bachelor of Arts Degree I pursued my Masters and Doctoral studies in Lille in France, a town where the Methodist Church did not exist at all. For almost six months, I would accompany my fellow students at the hostel to a nearby Catholic Church. Going back to a Catholic Church did not bother me at all. I had no problems either going back to the Anglican Church later when I learnt that there was one in the town centre. I did not stay there long though because meanwhile I had discovered that the service in a Reformed Church situated just next to the Anglican Church was the closest I could come to the Methodist faith. I quickly joined this community helping out from time to time with Sunday school classes. I was still in search of what I used to describe as something that would give more meaning to my life.

In spite of my involvement in the church's activities I continued to feel the emptiness within. I came to the realisation that church attendance and involvement in its activities were not sufficient to bring fulfilment to the soul. This was when invited by a fellow student to an Evangelical Church, I discovered what had been missing in my life all along. For the first time I had a personal encounter with Jesus. I was born again anew. For the first time in my life I felt an indescribable peace and entered into a more profound relationship with the Lord. God, Jesus, the Holy Spirit and even the words in the Bible became more real. I felt really fulfilled. I was enlightened all of a sudden and my desire ever since has been to serve the Lord.

## H.G. Bishop Serapion

*H.G. Bishop Serapion is the Bishop of the Diocese of Los Angeles, USA, of the Coptic Orthodox Church*

My name is Bishop Serapion. Serapion is a Saint's name, which was given to me when I was ordained a monk in 1979 at St. Bishoy Monastery in the desert of Wadi EL Natrun in Egypt. In the rite of ordination of a monk the Prayer of the Departed indicates that the monk dies and rises to a new life (the monastic life) with a new name and the name of the monastery as his last name. Therefore my new name became Serapion Anba Bishoy. When I was ordained a bishop in 1985 my name changed to be Bishop (first name) Serapion (last name). I was born in1951 into a Christian family. My large family has been Christian since the coming of Christianity to Egypt in the first century. My parents delivered to me the Christian faith. I was a born again Christian when I received the Sacrament of Baptism in the Coptic Orthodox Church and my first encounter with my Lord and saviour Jesus Christ was when I received Him in the Sacrament of Eucharist. My Christian family and the Sunday school of my Church brought me up in the Christian faith and shaped my Christian spiritual life.

During my high school time I started to feel the call to consecrate my life completely to my Lord in the monastic life. My father of confession and Bishop Hedra of Aswan, my hometown, guided me in my spiritual journey towards consecration in the monastic life. After I finished my medical studies and worked as a medical doctor for three years I entered St.Bishoy Monastery in 1979 and became a monk. In 1983 I was sent by H.H. Pope Snenouda to serve the Coptic Communities in Switzerland. In Switzerland I had my first ecumenical experience as I lived in Kloster Einsiedeln, a Benedictine Catholic monastery in Einsiedeln. I was impressed by the spiritual life of the monks and their love and kindness towards me and also noticed the many common things we share as Coptic and Benedictine monks. In 1985 I returned to Egypt and was ordained Bishop for Ecumenical and Social Service and started a new deep experience in the ecumenical life through my heavy involvement in the World Council of Churches, the Middle East Council of Churches, the All Africa Conference of Churches and many theological dialogues. In 1995 I became the Bishop of the Coptic Orthodox Diocese of Los Angeles which covers Southern California and Hawaii. I very much appreciate the idea and the work of the Global Christian Forum and Christian Churches Together in the USA.

## Rev. Michael Tawia-Rensford

*Rev. Michael Tawia-Rensford is Assistant General Secretary of the Ghana Pentecostal Council*

For me to live is Christ and to die is to gain. For all what I am today, and what I shall surely be, whether on earth or in the world to come, has come and will come through God's unlimited grace that He showed to me while I was still very young.

I grew up in the West African country called Ghana. In the Western Prefecture where my home is the majority are basically illiterate. Though my father had some informal education, his relationship with many European expatriates as a cook gradually educated him and enabled him to read and write some basic English. However, my mother had no formal education but together they brought up nine children, four girls and five boys. Our parents made sure we had a better education. All their children had the opportunity to attend the local government schools at Asankrangwa and beyond. I did not know whether it was a divine plan or not, but by the time I was in primary six, I had had the opportunity to study in all the three major and seemingly the best mission schools in the town i.e. Roman Catholic, Methodist and Presbyterian. This gave me a better opportunity to learn more of Christianity and drew me much more closely to the ways of the Bible and I dreamt many times of wanting to go to heaven as described in the Holy Scriptures. My mother had time for the church choir and sung joyfully on Sundays whenever the choir ministered.

However, something unusual happened to me around the age of ten. My father had moved earlier to another commercial town, which hosted one of the largest sawmill companies in Africa at the time – The African Timber and Plywood Ltd (AT&P) at Samreboi. He had taken a very good managerial position where he earned a sizable monthly allowance. Daddy had much hopes and visions for his children and prided himself having all his kids in school and going to the church he loved most, and seeing his wife singing in the choir all the time. Then, suddenly, their marriage dissolved, and ended with a sense of finality. As a boy my world was also coming to an end as I had to walk distances to visit my daddy and most of the time met no one at home. It also meant struggling with mother to work after school at the local open market to sell food items and do some sewing to make ends meet. It was during this time that I turned to search seriously but quietly for the truth of the existence of God whom I had heard and read much about in the Bible. I sometimes went to the forest praying with tears running down my cheeks while watching over my shoulders whether someone was coming around. I was startled by many of the dreams I had during my intense prayers and fasting. The hardest time came when I had passed a national examination that provided entry for secondary schools, and gained a scholarship for one of the leading Presbyterian secondary schools for boys in the country. Unfortunately, I was to decline the offer since mother could not buy the common items to prepare me for school. My life at this stage caused my curiosity to search for more of God. The day came when a young boy of a similar age invited me to a the Sunday school of a Pentecostal church, which until this time had always been a laughing stock to most young people in my community. We sung and danced anytime we passed by every Sunday after church. A Pentecostal Church which until this time was only for those who could not afford to go to the dance bar and have the opportunity to have a record player and a TV set at home.

Little did I know that my first visit was to last for over thirty-six years on my journey with the Lord Jesus. My initial sufferings for making this decision were too many to be captured in this short testimony. I ended up being driven away from home for over eleven years. My father never understood why I had made the decision to change churches. It took me many years of prayer to come home and sit with my family and be reconciled with them. Yes, I changed from one church to the other and never wanted to be back and be part of the old church in my life. But along the journey with my Lord, I discovered that I may have changed the church, but not the Christ, who alone is the owner of the Church. Yes, I had some experiences in my newly found faith in Christ that were part and parcel of the experiences that usually accompany the kind of faith one chooses to follow and since they are Biblical in doctrine, we decide to accept them. The experiences over the years through many missionary institutions and inter-denominational missions have enriched my belief in ecumenical participation for a common platform for Christian evangelism. I believe each and every Christian, no matter which denominational group one belongs to, as long as we claim to be Christians and profess to be true followers of Christ, and ruled by God's word, has a common journey with diverse encounters as we head towards the heavenly destination. Let us do everything possible, therefore, to make it to our heavenly home, where our Lord and master awaits us. Like Jesus, let us come together to be united and share our journeys with each other and with those outside the camp.

## From The Participants
## Affirmations and Expectations

On the morning of the third day of the event an important panel presentation took place. Leaders and representatives of the main church groupings and organisations, Catholic, Orthodox, Evangelical, Pentecostal, Holiness, the Christian World Communions and the World Council of Churches had been asked to share their views and hopes for the Forum. It was the time to hear from them if the journey should be continued, and if the church families and global bodies on whose behalf they spoke wanted to be part of it.

### Voices from the panel

Dr. Geoff Tunnicliffe, the International Director of the World Evangelical Alliance said that the decision to hold the annual meetings of the International Council and the International Leadership Team of the World Evangelical Alliance just prior to the global Forum event and in the same venue was in itself an indication of WEA's interest in the Global Christian Forum. Using the image of a bridge and a river that had changed its course – making the bridge stand idle – he pointed to the need for new bridges because the different streams of Christianity were changing their flow all the time. We as WEA he said, rejoice at being at this table and embrace the purpose statement of the Forum. This is a place where we can address common issues such as religious liberty, poverty etc. that concern us all.

Speaking from the Orthodox perspective the Very Rev. Leonid Kishkovsky of the Orthodox Church in America highlighted four points. There is a need for reconciliation among ourselves so that we learn to see one another as Christians. Martyrdom and especially the memory of Christian martyrs of the 20th century could be a unifying force for our different traditions. We should also have the courage to discuss in an open way issues that cause conflict and friction among us, such as our understanding of mission, evangelism and common witness. And spirituality can bind us together. For example, in Orthodox churches the iconostasis carries a message of the Christian way of life ; the royal doors are between the icon of the Virgin Mary with the infant Jesus (on the left) and the icon of Christ (on the right) – signs of the incarnation and the Last Judgment. The eucharist, celebrated on the altar table beyond the royal doors, gives to us fellowship with the Risen One and empowers our Christian journey through the joy of the resurrection.

Rev. Robina Winbush of the Presbyterian Church (USA) spoke on behalf of the World Council of Churches. She said we were here because the Spirit was answering Christ's prayer for unity. The WCC is deeply committed to the vision of unity beyond its own fellowship. It values the already existing bonds with the Catholic Church and with Evangelicals and Pentecostals. The Global

Christian Forum is widely representative and is significant for the WCC and beyond. That is why we came here, she said, with our general secretary, the moderator of our Central Committee and one of our presidents. We notice a limited representation as yet of women, youth, indigenous peoples etc. We acknowledge the Forum as *a* table while there is the pain that we cannot come together to *the* table. We should move to a deeper understandingng of what God is doing in each of us.

On behalf of the Pentecostal participants Rev. Peter Sleebos, General Superintendent of the Assemblies of God in the Netherlands, expressed thanks to the Global Christian Forum for the invitation to the journey of unity . We feel safe here, he said, and challenged to move from our ground to common ground. Some of us Pentecostals are not comfortable with the term ecumenism. Words like 'forum' or 'space' speak more to us. There is a lot we can learn from each other. We need to learn from the passion for unity of the 'mainline' churches. We need your forgiveness for our arrogance. There may be accusations, for example of proselytism, but we believe that there can also be a more exploratory way of dialogue, on what it means to be a Christian, on making disciples, on justice. How can we be a missional church together ?

Bishop Brian Farrell, Secretary of the Pontifical Council for Promoting Christian Unity said the response of the Catholic Church to the Forum was an unequivocal yes. The Catholic Church is fully committed to Christian unity and wants to be part of every effort to restore it. The Second Vatican Council stated that division is a scandal which damages the preaching of the gospel. Our commitment is well served by the Forum. We are a church of tradition, of the community down the centuries, of oneness in sacraments and ministry. The Global Christian Forum is doing something no other instrument can do : breaking down barriers and walls of hostility. It is vital that it continues, especially at regional and national level. At the same time we believe that other instruments in the search for unity are equally essential e.g. the theological dialogues, joint declarations etc.

Commissioner Linda Bond, in charge of external relations of the Salvation Army International Headquarters spoke as a holiness Christian. She said the Salvation Army is a fruit of the Holiness movement. We do what the church should do : making Jesus known to people. If we were together in mission we would experience our unity. Dialogue on unity is important but it should always be in the context of mission. Our mission together is also to serve suffering humanity. The Forum is a sacred place of conversation, of equipping and of calling, a place where we know God has called us to be. The mission of Jesus Christ should be up front in the Forum. We have common aims so we can learn from each other.

As Moderator of the Conference of Secretaries of Christian World Communions, Rev. Dr. Robert Welsh said that the Forum had been on their agenda for many years. The Conference is a widely representative gathering of leadership and representatives of Communions and Catholic, Orthodox,

Protestant, Evangelical and Pentecostal churches that meets annually for fellowship and relationships. We have supported the Forum from its beginning, not as a result of our actions but as an emerging reality reflecting what we are about ourselves. We want to continue to facilitate it. For this reason we decided to hold our 2007 annual meeting immediately after this event to review the results of this gathering and what it means for us and for the future. In this way, Limuru is not an ending, but rather a new beginning.

## Voices from the floor

Bishop Victoria Mathews of the Anglican Church of Canada remarked that the Anglican Communion is a church of bridges, an ecumenical movement in itself. The Forum adds a new dimension, complementing – not replacing – existing mechanisms. It is of great benefit for the Anglicans, she said, and our hope is that it will go on and continue influencing church leaders, especially at local level.

Rev. Fr. Vsevolod Chaplin of the Russian Orthodox Church hailed the broad representation of the Forum, bringing together Orthodox Christians, Roman Catholics, Evangelicals, Pentecostals and so many others. We should support this, he said. Like the Pentecostals, the word ecumenism was not very popular among our people, he added. It is not concrete and can be interpreted in different ways, even as term for religious syncretism. It is better to speak of inter-Christian dialogue if we cannot yet call ourselves the Body of Christ.

Rev. Israel Batista, General Secretary of the Latin American Council of Churches echoed a voice from the South. Let us allow the rivers of the Spirit to flow, he pleaded, and not be too quick in building bridges. Let us allow the churches of the South to formulate their own agenda. Their sprituality is still too western and so is the Forum. Yet we are grateful to the churches that have funded this event for their action reflects a beautiful symbolism.

Rev. Dr. Ishmael Noko, General Secretary of the Lutheran World Federation said Lutherans were present in large numbers, which demonstrated the support of the Lutheran church family for the Forum. We are in dialogue with many traditions, he pointed out, and the Forum is a gathering of these conversations. He called for more national and regional forums to take place.

# From The Participants
# Regional Voices

The Limuru global gathering was preceded by several regional Forum consultations, notably in Africa, Asia, Europe and Latin America. With hindsight it can be said that the gathering in Limuru would hardly have been possible, and certainly would not have had the same results, without these regional consultations. During one of the plenary sessions testimonies from the regions were given, some focussing on these meetings and their follow-up, others highlighting developments that reflect the purpose and the spirit of the Global Christian Forum but were not initiated by it.

## Asia

### Rev. Dr. Richard Howell

*The Rev. Dr. Richard Howell is General Secretary of the Evangelical Fellowship of India and since August 2008 also the General Secretary of the Asian Evangelical Alliance. He is a member of the Committee on the Global Christian Forum.*

Asia is the continent where the first regional consultation on the Global Christian Forum was held in Hong Kong in May 2004. It brought together some sixty participants, of whom close to fifty were from Asia, representing all the Christian traditions in the region : Anglican, Catholic, Evangelical, Orthodox, Pentecostal and Protestant. At the end of the meeting the participants asked three regional bodies, the Federation of Asian Bishops' Conferences (FABC, Catholic), the Christian Conference of Asia (CCA, ecumenical) and the Evangelical Fellowship of Asia (EFA) to jointly take responsibility for a follow-up. They did so two years later, at a meeting which took place in September 2006 in Bangkok. It was the first time that these three Asian church bodies had met together. The meeting recommended that the EFA be invited to join the Asian Movement for Christian Unity which had been started ten years earlier by the FABC and the CCA.

So it came to pass that unity was visibly manifested when representatives of the Catholic Church in Asia, of the member churches of the Christian Conference of Asia and of the Evangelical Fellowship of Asia met together at the IVth Seminar of the Asian Movement for Christian Unity, in June 2007 in Kuala Lumpur. They were able to issue a joint statement. As a pentecostal we should be shouting hallelujah because something very special happened. I read from the statement:

> The three bodies can concretely promote Christian unity by getting to know one another better through mutual discussions and invitations to assemblies and plenary sessions, by engaging in joint projects such as the Asia Conference of Theological Students (ACTS) and the Congress of Asian Theologians (CATS), and by undertaking joint actions such as summer camps for Christian unity for young people. Mutual co-operation and activities at national and local levels are also to be strongly encouraged.

We thank God for this visible coming together of three traditions, recognizing the need to address common challenges together. It was the Forum process that started in Asia in Hong Kong that has led to this and we hope and pray that all over the world this process will result in something very special in each continent, to see what the Lord is doing and to respond to it.

It takes time. Ecumenical relations take a very long time. Trust does not develop overnight. But the centuries of suspicion and prejudice do fall apart if we have the will to see God at work in our continent, in our churches, and in our lives.

This is as far as Asia is concerned. I would like to add a few words about India. In India the Catholic Bishops' Conference of India, the National Council of Churches of India and the Evangelical Fellowship of India have jointly initiated the National United Christian Forum. Archbishop Vincent Concessao, who is the president, is here with us. We thank God for the process which has begun and that will bear fruit as time goes on.

## AFRICA

## Rev. Daniel Bitrus

*The Rev. Daniel Bitrus is a minister of the Church of Christ in Nigeria and is Secretary of the Africa Continuation Committee on the Global Christian Forum.*

The Africa regional meeting on the Forum took place in Lusaka, Zambia in August 2005, under the theme: *Jesus Christ in Africa - our Journey with Him.* About sixty of the more than seventy participants were from Africa. The programme of the meeting was designed on the model of various previous Forum consultations. It provided ample time for sharing among the participants, plenary presentations, and plenary and group discussion on the Forum as a framework for Christian unity and common witness. There was a sense of ownership of the programme and a sense of progression from one item building up to the next. Two keynote speakers spoke on the theme. Dr. Brigalia Bam, chairperson of the Electoral Commission of South Africa and former general secretary of the South African Council of Churches approached it from the ecumenical perspective, and Dr. Kwabena Asamoah-Gyadu, associate professor at Trinity Theological College, Ghana, and sub-regional co-ordinator of the Africa Theological Fellowship from an Evangelical – Pentecostal background. The two presentations helped the group to uphold in all the discussions the need for the churches to be involved in moral and socio-political issues while also giving clear attention to personal evangelism and spiritual renewal. There was really no serious controversy in this gathering on the issues of evangelism against social action, liberal versus conservative views, ecumenical versus evangelical positions, despite the wide diversity of churches and organisations that were present and despite the fact that many had never met with one another prior to this consultation.

Towards the end of the meeting a discussion evolved on the significance of the Forum concept for Africa, and on a possible follow-up. There was a shared view that a beginning had been made with something new and relevant and that it should be continued. One of the participants compared the Lusaka experience with the experience of the disciples on the mountain of transfiguration, where they wanted to build tents and remain. The temptation to build tents and stay in Lusaka was, however, graciously resisted and we went home. Emanating from a sense of accountability to the faith communities they represented, some participants said they were going back with the intention to convene national consultations. That was encouraging to hear, but I am yet to receive reports on such initiatives.

Serious concern was expressed to not allow this process to end in Lusaka. Therefore, a task force was formed to work out the modalities of setting up a Continuation Committee for Africa, as well as its mandate. This was done and it was agreed that a committee of eight was formed representing the African Instituted Churches, the Orthodox, Catholic and Pentecostal Churches, the Association of Evangelicals in Africa, the All Africa Conference of Churches, the United Bible Society – Africa Region and Youth. The mandate of the committee can be summarized as maintaining and sustaining the vision of the Forum on the continent. One of the tasks entrusted to it was to explore the possibility of hosting the Global Forum event in Africa. At its meeting in November 2006 in Nairobi, the committee set up a highly powered local organising committee under the chairmanship of Rev. Julius Karanja, the chairman of the Continuation Committee (the members of the local committee were asked to stand up and received a warm applause).

In conclusion, I would like to share some personal observations. I am convinced that the Global Christian Forum has been attractive to so wide a range of Christian traditions and has come to stay because it is not another organisation but a Forum, not with a board of trustees but with a Continuation Committee, not with a constitution but a purpose statement, not with members but with participants, and it does not issue resolutions but simply a statement or a message. It is a Forum that creates space where we respect our differences but are willing to listen to one another as we share our experiences of our journey with Jesus. Our differences are on temporal issues – what binds us together are eternal values: one Lord, one baptism, one Spirit, one hope. May the benefit of our coming together this week in Limuru take us towards realizing the priestly prayer of our Lord Jesus Christ that we may be one.

## EUROPE

The European regional consultation was held in June 2006 in Warburg, Germany. The participants were inspired by the example that came from Norway and emphasised strongly the importance of the Forum in the national and sub-regional contexts of Europe.

### Rev. Ornulf Steen

*The Rev. Ornulf Steen is General Secretary of the Christian Council of Norway.*

In Norway we have established one council with member churches of all the Christian traditions in our country. It came into being as a merger of the former Christian Council of Norway and the Council of Free Churches. The new body, which has kept the name Christian Council of Norway, thus consists of the following churches: Anglican, Baptist, Catholic, Church of Norway (Lutheran, the majority church), Independent Charismatic, Lutheran Free Church, Mission Covenant, Orthodox, Pentecostal, Quaker, Salvation Army and United Methodist and the Seventh-day Adventist as an observer. The Evangelical Alliance of Norway is also present as an observer.

A very important aspect in the formation of the new council has been the relationship between the majority and minority churches. The Church of Norway is still a state church with 85% of the population as members. This means that all the other churches are numerically small. In such a situation it is a real challenge to develop structures that facilitate relations and allow the majority as well as the minority to have a sense of ownership and commitment. The Church of Norway has repeatedly said that the council is useful to the extent that it is for all the churches. That is an approach which helps to reduce the negative effects of tensions that sometimes occur between a majority and a minority and we have been able together to develop structures accordingly.

Another important question has been how to deepen the relationships while at the same time maintaining the broad representation of the council. Or to put it differently: can we continue to be truly representative of such a broad spectrum of traditions without deepening our bonds? We run the risk of not moving beyond nice conversations if we do not seek to dig deeper, both in terms of our service together and in the ways we relate to one another. In asking ourselves these questions we have seen that it is necessary to continue to affirm one another as Christian churches, as we clearly did through the merger process. We have to be very open to one another and to respect our differences, for instance through the consensus procedures of decision making that we have adopted. Being in the same council does not mean that we agree on all theological and other issues. Sooner or later we will be confronted with some painful questions in our relationships. Ecumenism without dealing with such issues is not true to our calling to make unity visible. Ecumenism is more than a coalition of the willing because we are in fact by God's acts given to one another. You cannot choose your brother or your sister, you receive them. How will we act if one member church makes a decision contrary to the others on an issue that is perceived as crucial and very basic? Will the council then still be able to continue as a common platform and meeting place for all its member churches? Will we then have a history of building trust and fellowship that will carry us through? For the moment these are open questions because we have not been there yet. What I can say is that we have moved from a sense of superiority on both sides – majority and minority – to mutual respect and recognition.

One way of deepening relationships is that church leaders not only meet around the board table but also engage in a spiritual journey together. Learning from the experience of the Christian Council of Sweden we have invited our church leaders to a spiritual retreat. We will continue to work for a spirituality that nurtures our unity and is also expressed in our common service and witness. We are at the beginning of a long journey.

## Dr. Terje Hegertun

*Dr. Terje Hegertun is a Pentecostal scholar and one of the leaders of the Norwegian Pentecostal Movement, of which he has also been President.*

I am the first Pentecostal scholar working at the main Lutheran theological institution in Norway, and I am here representing the leadership of the Norwegian Pentecostal Movement. It is no secret that the Pentecostal Movement has had an ambivalent and sceptical attitude towards church structures and the organised ecumenical movement. So also in Norway. The time when the majority churches ignored us and put restrictions on us is still in the memories of our people. Therefore, it is so important after many hesitations that the Pentecostal Movement in Norway has become a full member of the new Christian Council to allow the fellowship to grow deeper. From my point of view the new council is still a delicate and weak plant. It must take all the time it needs to build a state of confidence. That is a crucial point at the beginning of this new journey. We must show that ecumenism is not something threatening but that it strengthens and confirms our identity as Pentecostals. At the same time it must make us more humble as we get to know the great variety within the body of Christ. We must facilitate meeting places other than board tables, to share our common faith and to meet face to face. The Global Christian Forum has helped us to discover that many ecumenical wonders are hidden in our testimonies. That must also happen at the local level in the real church life. We need many local Christian forums. It is also necessary for the new council that Pentecostals take time among themselves to reflect theologically on unity. We must learn that unity is a call from Christ our Lord and a commitment for each Christian who wants to be a friend of the Holy Spirit. We need to take time for reflections inside our denominations. In my research project I want to show that the first Pentecostal leaders regarded Pentecostalism as a movement of unity, love and reconciliation. So the key words are time, patience, Biblical reflections, and intercession from all of you in the majority churches.

## LATIN AMERICA

## Rev. Dr. Gloria Rojas

*The Rev. Dr. Gloria Rojas is President of the Evangelical Lutheran Church in Chile.*

Our meeting took place at the end of June 2007 in Santiago, Chile. As churches confessing the Triune God we gave ourselves a space to be together during four days. I would like to highlight the following points:

- The methodology that was used was a discovery for most of the participants. It was a methodology of listening to one another with respect and being open to get to know each other.
- The willingness to recognize one another as being part of the plan of God's mission and to know each other as co-workers in that mission.
- The willingness to recognize one another more as persons than as bearers of a title. It was very important to leave our titles behind in order to really listen to one another as persons and to hear from each other how we came to our churches, how we received that calling.

The methodology of personal testimonies is not part of the liturgy of many of our traditional churches. It is not part of our on-going work. For that reason it was a very important discovery for us, for our lives, to know that the other has a faith story, that his or her life of faith has an origin. It was very important to discover that we were either former Catholics who had come to the Evangelical or Protestant churches, or Evangelicals and Protestants who had come to the

Catholic Church. That is to say that there was no difference between us in respect to God's call. Each one discovered that on this common journey as women and men we are called to serve the ecumenical cause and the mission of God. At the end of our meeting we issued together, as participating churches and organisations, a message with respect to our ecumenical responsiblity.

And I believe that each participant felt the presence of the Lord among us, inasmuch as we left behind us the concerns of management and recognized each other as persons, as women and men in the service of the Lord.

## Mgr. Julio Terán

*Mgr. Julio Terán is the Bishop of Ibarra, Ecuador and a member of the Episcopal Conference of Latin America.*

There was an extraordinary communication and communion in the whole group. This was of course facilitated by our common bonds rooted in the history of our Latin American culture. Our languages, Spanish and Portuguese, also made it easy for us to communicate. Underlying all of this is our history of the faith in Latin America, which meant that we had to do away with the confessional walls of separation, the prejudices and facts of history that make our coming together in the Lord difficult. Really from my point of view the most important was this new spirit of beginning the meeting by speaking about our own faith stories and sharing them with our brothers and sisters. This is a spirit that is entirely different from the one that prevails in other inter-confessional and ecumenical dialogues which we have had, even with the best intentions, in our continent. Therefore, the Global Christian Forum presents itself as a great opportunity for us in Latin America.

A special moment in this meeting was to participate one evening in the worship service of a community in a local Pentecostal church in one of the poor neighbourhoods of Santiago. It was another occasion to express our faith and to take part in our very communicative Latin-American way of prayer and celebration. It was also another impulse for our meeting.

Finally, as a representative of the Catholic Church I would like to mention that there was a very helpful presentation of the conclusions of the assembly of the Episcopal Conference of Latin America that took place last May in Aparacido, Brazil, under the theme *Disciples and Missionaries of Christ.* This theme is also related to our meeting here in Limuru.

## North America

# Rev. Wesley Granberg-Michaelson

*The Rev. Wesley Granberg-Michaelson is General Secretary of the Reformed Church in America and one of the Presidents of Christian Churches Together in the USA.*

In his paper Wonsuk Ma said that churches together is not only a dream but also a possibility. The possibility of Christian Churches Together in the USA began in 2001 when a group of Christian leaders from a wide variety of traditions was hosted by Roman Catholic Cardinal Kheeler. They asked themselves whether the time had come for a new initiative. They said:

> We lament that we are divided and that our divisions too often result in distrust, misunderstanding, fear and even hostility. We long for the broken body of Christ to be made whole, where unity can be celebrated in the midst of our diversity. We lament that we have a diffused and diminished voice in matters critical to the gospel in our society, and we long for more common witness, vision and mission, as well as for strengthening the prophetic public voice of the Christian community in America. We lament that none of our current organisations reflects the full spectrum of Christians in the US. And we long for a place where our differences could be better understood and our communalities better affirmed.

It was out of that lament and that prayer of longing that CCT began to emerge. Its mission was stated simply: to grow closer together in Christ in order to strengthen Christian witness in the world. We decided early on to organise ourselves according to Christian families. In the case of North America, that meant the Catholic family, the Orthodox, the historic Protestant, the Evangelical – Pentecostal family and the family of those churches who are defined by racial and ethnic bonds. In our context in the USA with the history of race, this is very important for what are called the historic Black churches as well as other churches that are defined by their particular ethnicity. Over the years we came to see that there should be seven central purposes in what we would do, and they are:

- to celebrate a common confession of faith in the Triune God
- to discern the guidance of the Holy Spirit through prayer and theological dialogue
- to provide fellowship and mutual support
- to seek better understanding by affirming our communalities and understanding our differences
- to foster evangelism faithful to the proclamation of the gospel

- to speak to society with a common voice wherever possible
- to promote the common good of society in engaging other related activities.

The first four of these purposes,which focus on deepening our fellowship and our relationships with one another seem to echo what you have just heard about the Christian Council of Norway. The last three have to do with outward mission and witness. We also decided that we would make all decisions by consensus, and that in our membership there would be up to 20% of Christian organisations. It was felt that in order to recognise the ecclesiastical reality in America, particularly for some of our traditions, organisations were necessary along with denominations and communions. In 2006, after a process of about five years, we had come to the place where in each of our families there was enough representation to allow ourselves to be formally organised. So we have been functioning for only about a year and a half. We have two areas of focus. One is on the issue of poverty, particularly poverty in the USA. We discovered that we could all come together in a common commitment to combat poverty. We came to a statement that we all agreed to, the first time that such a breadth of Christians had ever done so. The second area of focus we have identified is evangelism. We have shared from our various traditions how we each understand evangelism.The next step will be how to implement action in these two areas.

The model of CCT is designed to have the focus on what the churches and organisations themselves do and to have the lightest possible structure in staffing and budget. No one in the US wants another ecumenical agency to which they would have to give a lot of resources. We have five presidents, one per family. A couple of months ago we hired our first and probably only staff member, the executive administrator. So this model is quite different. It is also very clear that many of our members are members of the National Council of Churches and are fully supportive of the NCC, which is a strong witness for its churches. Many of our other members belong to the National Association of Evangelicals and that organisation also continues strongly, as of course does the US Conference of Catholic Bishops. We have stressed repeatedly that CCT is an initiative that defines a new space allowing this breadth of fellowship to come together that has not previously existed, and to do so in an organised committed way, in order to grow closer together in Christ and to strengthen our witness in the world. It is one example of the possibility of Christian churches being together.

## Bishop James Leggett

*Bishop James Leggett is head of the International Pentecostal Holiness Church, President of the Pentecostal World Fellowship and one of the Presidents of Christian Churches Together in the USA.*

The formation of Christian Churches Together (CCT) in the USA has been a blessed experience. It has been my privilege to be involved almost from the start as a part of the formative Steering Committee. There was hesitancy in the beginning for most Pentecostals have not been involved in ecumenical movements. We have not and could not be a part of the National Council of Churches. Yet, involvement in Christian Churches Together, the broadest gathering of churches in the USA, has been a remarkable journey. It has been a tremendous learning experience. Other Pentecostal churches have joined in the journey. God has blessed our time together. It is a time of dialogue, much like we have had here, yesterday and today. This interaction between Evangelical/Pentecostal, Orthodox, Mainline, Catholic, and Historic African American Churches has broken down walls of misunderstanding and opened up avenues of genuine fellowship in the faith. Each of us has been enriched by the other families' traditions. We are stronger Christians by sharing our traditions of worship. I have learned much from each of the other families of faith, and I think they have learned as well from the Evangelical/Pentecostals. My own life has been broadened by this journey of togetherness. I am amazed at the way God is blessing His church.

This is what is happening in Christian Churches Together. We believe that God is graciously directing us. As Pentecostals, He is calling us to look afresh at the social call of the gospel. This was evident this morning in the presentation, and it was a great paper. I want a copy to take home with me. For too long we have been hesitant to focus on that part of the gospel message. We have focused on personal salvation and personal relationships, and we hope to share this emphasis with our brothers and sisters. Yet, we need to look more closely to our social responsibility as Christians. This is what I mean by mutual sharing, so that each of the families of faith are enriched.

I look forward to the future for what God is doing in CCT in the USA. We come together—Catholic, the Mainline, the Orthodox, the historic African American, and the Evangelical Pentecostal families—to declare that Jesus Christ is Lord to the glory of God the Father. We believe that God is working by His Holy Spirit in the church around the world. The work does not depend on us. It depends upon the presence and power of the Holy Spirit. God is at work by His Spirit, and He is doing marvellous things. Let us follow Him and do His will.

## Rev. Dr. Karen Hamilton

*The Rev. Dr. Karin Hamilton is General Secretary of the Canadian Council of Churches.*

The Canadian Council of Churches was founded in 1944 and is now one of the most inclusive councils in the world. It includes the Anglican, Roman Catholic, Protestant, Evangelical, Eastern and Oriental Orthodox church families. Since 1997 the council has been working with the consensus model, which means that every voice around the table has equal weight. This has enabled the Canadian Conference of Catholic Bishops and several other denominations to join the council. In our experience the consensus model works. It is not without its challenges to be sure. Sometimes things do not move as quickly as we would like, but the ability to have all of the voices has added richness and we appreciate very much our diversity in unity. To be a member of the CCC requires a centering in Jesus Christ and a Trinitarian confesssion. We work in the areas of faith witness, justice and peace, and bio-technology. A specific issue we are involved in with others is how religious leaders can challenge the G8. Last summer a summit of religious leaders took place in Cologne, Germany, in parallel with the G8. A statement was issued on just participation. This action will go on in the future, on behalf of God's people and especially the poor, to challenge the G8 on the millenium goals, debt cancellation, climate change, development aid etc.

The CCC has a privileged working relationship with the Evangelical Fellowship of Canada. One of the most recent areas of co-operation is a gathering of the denominations that belong to both the CCC and the EFC. There are six who have full membership and two who have observer status in both councils. The purpose of the gathering is to discuss what it means to be in such a dual relationship, and what are the challenges and the benefits.

## Mr. Bruce Clemenger

*Mr. Bruce Clemenger is General Secretary of the Evangelical Fellowship of Canada.*

The Evangelical Fellowship of Canada is a fellowship oriented towards mission and public witness. Our membership includes 40 denominations and church networks, 85 ministry organisations both with domestic as well as international focus, 34 institutes of higher education, and individual churches, some of which are related to our member denominations, some Anglican, United Church of Canada, Presbyterian etc. Evangelicals are a movement within the broader

Christian community that cuts across many denominations. Among the interesting projects between the EFC and the CCC is one called *Gifts of the Earth* that dealt with questions of food security, genetically modified food and the decline of the family farm system in Canada. Another endeavour was a joint intervention before the Supreme Court of Canada on the issue of a genetically engineered mouse for cancer research. The question was whether one could patent a mouse because if so, one could also patent other higher life forms. We won ! Yet another area of co-operation has been the Micah Challenge in which a commission of the CCC joined us. There are also strong links between the EFC and the Canadian Conference of Catholic Bishops. We have worked together on a variety of issues, also in a joint action before the Supreme Court, and are now in the process of considering a formal dialogue. Last year a statement was issued on the definition of marriage which was signed by the CCCB, several Orthodox churches and a whole range of evangelical denominations. So there is quite a vibrant engagement in Canada. Because of the scope of the CCC and the EFC, what is accomplished in the US by CCT can probably be accomplished in Canada through these two structures. It really depends on how much time we as executives have for working together.

## Rev. David Wells

*The Rev. David Wells is Chair of the EFC Board and Regional Superintendent of the Pentecostal Assemblies of Canada, of which he became General Superintendent in 2008.*

I want to share with you an interesting initiative that has to do with the upcoming Winter Olympics in Vancouver in February 2010. It goes back to the Winter Olympics in 1988 in Calgary. At that time it was primarily the evangelical community that came together for common witness. This time it is the broader Christian community representing the spectrum of traditions we have been talking about here today. It is interesting to note the evolution that has taken place towards a shared commitment of working together on things that we hold together, while allowing for a diversity of expressions when it comes to witness and social service. We have a formal arrangement with the Olympic organisers. We are working with them on concerns such as sustainability and care for the poor and the homeless, so that we will leave Vancouver a better city when we are done than when we began. We are working in areas related to hospitality at the homestay, arranging for 750 homes within the Christian community where international guests will be housed. We allow for diverse forms of mission and witness, each in our own distinct way as we understand it. Already the media in Vancouver are picking up that the Olympics are providing an opportunity for Christian unity. None of us sees this as something intended for 2010 only. We will continue to build on this platform of shared mission and shared concern, so that together we seek the peace and well-being of our city and for God's kingdom to be known and felt throughout our entire region.

*The plenary in prayer at Limuru*

## From The Participants
## Church Voices

During one of the evenings the participants met in their respective church and confessional groupings to share their impressions and look at the Forum from the perspective of their own particular tradition. Two of the groups, the Pentecostals and the Baptists, took the initiative to to put their comments in writing. An Anglican appraisal was received from a commission of the Anglican Communion that met shortly after the Limuru gathering.

### Visions and expectations of the Pentecostal delegation

As the Pentecostal delegation, we want to express our gratitude to the Continuation Committee of the Global Christian Forum for inviting us on a journey of uniting with the extended family of God worldwide. Thank you also for creating an environment in which we Pentecostals feel safe and do not feel intimidated by the historical mainline churches and their representatives.

You have challenged us indeed as is written in the GCF vision statement "To move out of the familiar ground to celebrate together, enter in dialogue together and act together to the glory of God the Father, Son and Holy Spirit".

In some national situations e.g. in the Netherlands, we already have several years of experience in dialogue with other traditions such as the Roman Catholic and Reformed Churches.

Our early leaders of the Azusa Street Revival prayed and hoped that the blessing of the outpouring of the Holy Spirit at that time would touch the whole church worldwide and would empower the whole church to reach the world with the Gospel of Jesus Christ.

We, as the Pentecostal delegation, have evaluated our experience in this Global Christian Forum and have collected a few remarks and comments of how we feel about the GCF process and we have some suggestions about the future of the Forum. In random order:

1. We have concluded that we can learn a lot from each other.
2. It would be helpful to us if possible to find another name or expression for the word ecumenical or ecumenism. Almost all of our constituencies at home are very allergic to that word. Forum, dialogue, exploring or journey for unity and mutual understanding would be better and more acceptable.
3. We would like to know how the GCF conceives of the number of total members of the Pentecostal movement worldwide, since a growing part of that number belongs to the Charismatic movement which is a part of the mainline churches. Do you count the number of Charismatics with

our numbers or do you count them as your own members or do you have a double count?

4. In the perception of the Pentecostal delegates we felt that the focus in the reports given so far was aimed too much on us and the issue of proselytism. We wonder if we could find a better way to talk about these matters in the GCF, more in dialogue instead of accusations and confrontations.

Would it be possible for us to question each other about this matter in a more exploratory way so we can learn from each other and explore matters like:

- when is someone a Christian or does one become a Christian?
- what does it mean to be a Christian?
- what is the nature of the church?
- what does it mean to make disciples?
- wat does it mean to go into all the world and make disciples?
- how can we become a missional church together?
- how can we evangelize together?
- does everyone in this world have the right to personally know the Lord Jesus Christ as his or her saviour?
- does everyone in this world have the right to grow in God and the things of God?
- does everyone in this world have the right to social justice?

We discovered that you brothers and sisters in Christ are as passionate as we are for God and the things of God. We can learn from your passion for the unity of the church of Jesus Christ. We need forgiveness for our arrogant, exclusive, triumphant and disqualifying attitudes. There are things that we feel ashamed of that hurt the body of Christ.

Joh. 17 … That we all may be one so that the world may believe.

**Perspectives from the group of Baptists attending the Forum**

1. The opportunity for such a diverse group of Christians coming together for fellowship and for discernment of what God is doing through our participation in this Forum is one to be cherished. The very fact of our encounter as Christians from so many traditions is something of a miracle for which we offer praise and thanks to God.
2. We celebrate the safe and open space that this Forum has provided for mutual exchange through the gift of speaking and listening and for the joy of new friendships in Christ. That the Forum is unconnected to entrenched institutional structures and that it does not seek to become another global organization have been major

factors contributing to the sense that what participants experience this week is a moment of hope enabled by the Holy Spirit.

3. We are concemed that an inclination could develop to institutionalize the movement, making it subject to authoritarian structures that define membership and set criteria for its life. We should resist this temptation and hold fast to the intention not to become another global church organization.
4. Yet we believe that the experience and the promise of this Forum suggest a longer life for the Forum than just this week. The challenge is to discern a way to continue to appropriate the gift of the Forum, while ensuring that it does not become a prisoner of institutional structures that have a life of their own.
5. We appreciate the efforts made at the Forum to show due regard for the various organized expressions of Christian living represented in our midst. We anticipate that even greater success can be registered in developing a balanced fare, informed by familiarity with the various ways in which churches and Christians seek to fulfil the mission of God in the power of the Holy Spirit. In this context, we evince sensitivity to the multiplicity of Christian traditions whose perspectives are addressed appropriately when issues are being discussed in major presentations.
6. The Forum should convene from time to time as a resource for the churches, addressing issues that are germane to the mission of the Church as an agent of God's reconciling purpose in the world. The Forum should convene from time to time as a centre of sharing, where participants take account of, and celebrate, the movement of the Holy Spirit in creating patterns of co-peration in the life of Christians and churches all over the world.

## Resolution of the Inter-Anglican Standing Commission on Ecumenical Relations

The Commission

1. rejoices at the culmination of the Global Christian Forum process with the meeting in Limuru, Kenya, in November 2007, of an "unprecedented broad gathering" of Christian leaders under the theme of 'Our Journey with Jesus Christ the Reconciler,' and the issuing of their 'Message to Brothers and Sisters in Christ throughout the World'
2. congratulates the Continuation Committee on the success of their work, and thanks the Rev. Sarah Rowland Jones for the significant contribution she has made

3. endorses the 'Proposals for the Future of the Global Christian Forum' produced by the Limuru Meeting for evaluating and continuing the work of the Forum, particularly at the regional level
4. affirms the Anglican Communion's continuing support for the role of the Forum process in extending, strengthening and supplementing existing encounters between Christian communities, and in bringing affective and spiritual dimensions more fully alongside cognitive approaches to ecumenism
5. encourages Anglicans to engage with future expressions of the Forum process
6. commends the method of the Global Christian Forum which places at its heart the sharing of individuals' accounts of their journeys of faith as a means of deepening our understanding of one another, "our ability to recognise how God is graciously at work among us", and our fellowship in the gospel.

(Quotations in this resolution are taken from the Message of the Global Christian Forum issued at the Limuru Meeting, November 2007).

*Part of the Pentecostal participants at Limuru*

# CHAPTER 3

## FROM THE PLENARY SESSIONS

*This second set of papers comprises the input provided in plenary sessiosn that was built into the programme of the gathering as part of the planning process. It includes the full texts of the presentations made by the plenary speakers as well as a few shorter contributions. Although the Bible studies were not the subject of a plenary presentation as such they were part of the material that was prepared beforehand and are therefore added to this chapter.*

## WELCOME

### Rev. Dr. Judy Mbugua

*Rev. Dr. Judy W. Mbugua is Team Leader of the Association of Evangelicals in Africa and a member of the Committee on the Global Christian Forum.*

Habari: As a Kenyan, I would like to welcome you to my home country. It is such a privilege to have the Christian world leaders gathered here. It is also such a joy to attend a meeting where I do not have to come by air! Kenya is a beautiful and peaceful country and we pride ourselves in hosting the 8th wonder of the world at the Maasai Mara game reserve. Those of you who are coming here for the first time we recommend that you take a safari and see what a beautiful country this is.

I would also like to welcome you on behalf of the Association of Evangelicals in Africa (AEA) which has its headquarter here in Nairobi. AEA started 40 years ago and claims over 70 million followers in its constituency. We have 33 National Evangelical Fellowships, 30 associate and 11 special members. We are also members of the World Evangelical Alliance (WEA) and again we are very proud and happy to have hosted the WEA International Council and some commissions here, in this very conference centre. Some of them, including the International Director Rev. Geoff Tunnicliffe and AEA President Rev. Ndaba Mazabane, are here with us.

The AEA has 7 commissions and 5 projects. These are making a difference in and beyond Africa. The Relief and Development Commission is based in Kampala (Uganda), the Communication Commission in Abidjan (Ivory Coast) and the Ethics, Peace and Justice Commission in Bulawayo (Zimbabwe). Others, like the Youth and Sports Commission and the Pan African Christian Women Alliance (PACWA, the Women Commission) are in Nairobi.

The Women Commission which I head works with women all over Africa on issues that affect African women like HIV/AIDS, poverty, domestic violence and the general empowerment of the African woman.

One of our projects is the Nairobi Evangelical Graduate School of Theology (NEGST), which in 2008 will mark 25 years of existence. It has produced and continues to produce some of the top theologians, partners and researchers in Africa. In July 2007, NEGST graduated the largest class yet, comprising of 140 students. These became part of the over 700 NEGST graduates making their impact on societies in Africa and around the world.

The rapid growth of the church in Africa means that many of the faithful are now found in countries where poverty is common and where human rights are lacking. We need to ask ourselves if the role of the church is purely spiritual. To what extent should it have a social agenda and engage in politics? By following the mission of Jesus, as a friend to the poor, we are encouraged to take this opportunity and preach a "practical" gospel to the people of Africa and around the world. The time has come when we as the Church of Christ cannot divorce ourselves from development issues. Especially now when in the present process of reconciliation and development the world is undergoing drastic and profound changes, and with scourges such as HIV/AIDS, acute poverty, war and its consequences, it is imperative to mention that limitations like inadequate leadership commitment and capacity have hindered the efficiency and effectiveness in combating these vices. We are in a unique position to instil moral and spiritual values in the lives of people and we have the ethical obligation to strive towards and embrace those things which will bring us together and not those which separate us, so that we can celebrate our differences with self-respect and self-assurance.

I pray that at the end of this confrence we will come up with resolutions that will help us make a differenceand also that our vision will be sharpened because where there is no vision, the people perish. Vision for the people of God means a penetrating supernatural insight and understanding of the nature, attributes and activities of God that shape the destiny of humankind! Is there anything worse than blindness? Yes, having sight but no vision.

Thank you and God bless you.

## FROM THE PLENARY SESSIONS
## WORDS OF ENCOURAGEMENT

# Rev. Dr. Samuel Kobia

*Rev. Dr. Samuel Kobia is the General Secretary of the World Council of Churches*

Brothers and sisters in Christ, I find it an exciting privilege and personally inspiring to participate in this gathering of believers from so many regions, cultures and expressions of the Christian faith. This is a remarkable opportunity for us to bear witness to the ways in which our own lives have been shaped by the good news of Jesus Christ, and to explore how our communities and ministries relate to one another in our calling as members of Christ's one body on earth.

The dream of sharing our testimony more directly and of interacting across traditional boundaries has arisen in a wide variety of places and circumstances throughout the history of the churches. If these humble beginnings of ours mature, if a renewed relationship bears fruit through conversations such as these, the question may arise as to who deserves credit. The only answer, I think, is that given by the apostle Paul in regard to the Corinthian congregation: "I planted, Apollos watered, but God gave the growth" (1 Cor. 3:6). In verse 9, Paul goes on to say that the one who plants and the one who waters have a common purpose, "for we are all God's servants, working together".

For some time, I have been engaged as a Methodist minister from Kenya in ecumenical ministries, with the aim of serving churches in their common witness to the gospel of Jesus Christ. At this time I happen to be general secretary of the World Council of Churches but today I am here first and foremost as a brother in Christ, one who desires to be God's servant, to plant, water and tend the crop as opportunities present themselves. And I want to tell you something of the faith journey which has brought me here.

Standing here in this hall for me invokes memories. In 1987, in this very hall, I was installed as the second African general secretary of the National Council of Churches of Kenya. Presiding over that service was the Rev. Byron Mkoha, head of the Church of God in East Africa. Preaching the message was the Rev. Dr. John Gatu, who was then the moderator of the Presbyterian Church of East Africa but who is known to many of you as a very active member of the Lausanne Committee for World Evangelisation. Across the fence from here is St Paul's Theological College where I was trained as a theologian. Two months ago St Paul's was awarded a charter and became St

Paul's University, and I was honoured to be appointed the first chancellor. So that is why this places invokes so many memories for me.

I was brought up as a Methodist, grounded in Methodism with its emphasis on personal spirituality and social holiness. My parents and those who surrounded me were Christians of the East African Bible movement that swept through these lands in those days, and who had the zeal of being new Christians. Later on I discovered that there were other Christians besides only the Methodists and Catholics of the place where I grew up. This was enriching to me. I got exposed to life in Kenya, to situations that challenged us to embrace the faith in a united way, so that the world may believe. That is how my faith was deepened and enriched and I embraced Jesus Christ as my personal saviour.

My father influenced my life very much. He was a Methodist who became a Pentecostal and a street preacher in Mombasa. When he retired and came back to Nairobi he continued as a Pentecostal lay preacher, preaching in the market place. He bequeathed part of the family land to the Pentecostal Assemblies of God. He called me as his eldest son and said "this is what I have decided". I said "Hallelujah!" and added that I would be prepared to lead a fundraising event to help the Pentecostal Assemblies build a church on that piece of land, on that Methodist land, in Meru.

So I stand here, not so much because of who I am, or what I am, but because of those with whom I interact. So many brothers and sisters in Christ have touched me and made an impact on my Christian faith. In my ecumenical ministry, I have stood on the shoulders of many giants of faith. Therefore, I am so grateful to the people with whom I have interacted in my life and ministry. To follow Paul's imagery, some have planted and others have watered and, providentially, God has given whatever growth I have experienced. Like the faithful people who have influenced each of us on our way, we Christians are called to be agents of transformation in the lives of men and women, and in the life of the world. One of the fourth-century Cappadocian church fathers, St Gregory of Nyssa, recognized the Christian experience in this life as "ever changing for the better and transforming from glory to glory through daily growth…without ever reaching the end of perfection. For true perfection means that one never ceases to grow towards that which is better and never reduces perfection to any limit." While perfection must await the coming of a new heaven and a new earth, in God's good time, the Christian continues daily to serve as an agent for transformation, and to bear witness to that transformation in so many people's lives, as well as in churches, society and the world as a whole.

One may plant, and another may water. Transformation and growth rely on interactive relationships. God has been revealed to us within the context of relationship. The Trinity of Father, Son and Holy Spirit interact as one, joined in the bond of love. The Trinity, "God in communion," calls us into communion with God and with one another. This act of salvation is accomplished not in some other-worldly manner but by entering our world, by becoming one with us, as one of us. God incarnate is *Emmanuel*, “God with us”, in the richest relationship any of us may know. I am called to be with you; you are called to be with me; we are called to learn, through encounter with one another, what it means to be one in Christ. The well-being of the church, the spread of the gospel, depends on meaningful relationships rooted in love and respect. It is only by lowering barriers, by coming fully into each other’s presence and confronting our prejudices, that we may come to better understand each other. And in such growth, we may discern the hand of God.

My purpose in these remarks has been to encourage you as this phase of our conversation begins. Let me conclude by sharing my hopes and my prayer as we risk closer relationships.

First, it is my sincere hope that Christian unity may be strengthened quite apart from the self-interest of any one institution. In some circles, we speak of “the one ecumenical movement” made up of all who wish to gain insight, to support practical steps towards unity and to express solidarity among the many members of the body of Christ. The World Council of Churches tries to foster coherence within the broader ecumenical landscape, but we do not see ourselves as identical to the movement as a whole, much less as the inspiration for growth.

Secondly, I am moved to hope by this unprecedented event and the potential inherent in the fact that this is a remarkably representative gathering of the body of Christ. Our faith in a common Lord and saviour brings us to this table – a common table where we pray together, read scripture together, eat together, learn together, and talk of future possibilities. Some would have said that this event was not possible, but here we are and the world wonders what will come next.

Finally, I hope that we will take the risk of working together as God’s servants, planting, watering, nurturing…and praying for the growth that is God’s gift. In the divine dance of the Trinity – the “choreisis” described by several church fathers – the Holy Spirit seems to have taken the lead in bringing us to Limuru. Now it is my prayer that this same Spirit of loving communion may cause our eyes and ears to open, make us ever more aware of God’s will for us, and challenge us to forge new relations – among ourselves and between our churches – that God may be served, and the good news proclaimed, in word and action. This I pray in Jesus’ name. Amen.

# From The Plenary Sessions
# Discerning What God is Doing Among His People Today

**Rev. Dr. Wonsuk Ma**

*Rev. Dr. Wonsuk Ma is a Korean Pentecostal pastor and scholar. He and his wife served as missionaries to the Philippines, engaging primarily in tribal church planting and leadership training. Dr. Ma is the Executive Director of the Oxford Centre for Mission Studies, Oxford, United Kingdom.*

## 1. Introduction

If we are to reflect on our journey as individuals and as people corporately, it would reveal how the human race has made amazing progress in every aspect of human life, particularly in the past one hundred years or so. From a distinctly Christian perspective, God has also revealed his own plan for his creation as well as his will to fulfil this plan. In this divine economy, the people of God, called collectively the church, has been graciously invited by God to join God's own journey of restoring his creation.[1]

My own reflection will look back at the last one hundred years (but I am not that old, to be sure) and highlight what God has been doing with his people as his "mission partners." I will begin with myself and then extend to others, and I will also begin with the past and move to the present. I do this as a second generation Christian, having grown up in a family where Christianity was always viewed as "weird" and abnormal. This was also a common experience for many of my friends from the non-western world. At the end of each section, I will add comments of what I have learned about what God is doing with his people. As my personal stories are incorporated in this reflection, my own cultural and ethnic orientation as a Korean and my Christian experience as a Pentecostal will be part of the stories. This particular reflection will take an oral form.

I am keenly aware that this reflection comes with some serious limitations. The first is that some church traditions such as Catholic and Orthodox will not be part of the reflection, primarily because of my limited contact with these traditions. This omission in no way implies the lack of their unique contribution to church unity and mission. Secondly, due to the broad sweep that I am taking of modern mission history, generalization is inevitable, with some details not

---

[1] My statement of "Mission as the Restoration of God's Creation" is found in Wonsuk Ma, "The Spirit of God in Creation: Lessons for Christian Mission," *Transformation* 24:3 & 4 (July & Oct 2007), pp. 222-230, esp. p. 227.

being discussed. It is possible that for some terms, the precise definitions are not given, assuming a general consensus of their meaning. The main purpose of this reflection is the sharing of my own journey of gradual awakening into God's call for mission and church unity. I hope that my own stories and reflection will invite my fellow Christians to join in the common walk of fellowship and partnership to fulfil God's call for mission.[2]

## 2. What Have We Learned?

What have we observed in God's work with his people in the last one hundred years? What have we learned from this observation about his intention and our response?

### *2.1 Christ: The Best Thing that Can Happen in Life*

My first encounter with Christian truth was extremely personal and real. I had been a "good" Sunday school boy, and church events were all part of my "fun" life, as I hardly remember what the Korean War was like, not to mention the harsh Japanese colonial rule which predated the war. When I was a teenager, one day my mother decided to take my younger sister, who had suffered from polio, to a healing crusade in a nearby town. Mom asked me to get up early in the morning (5 a.m.!) and join the dawn prayer meeting at the good Presbyterian Church. My first reaction was, "She can't be serious, that God could heal my sister, who had been given up by my own uncle, who was a surgeon!" Then, I realized that all the things I had learned from the Sunday school class might not be "just old stories" at all; they may be real, if Mom is taking my sister to the same God. I had never before heard of a God who can, and will, do such a thing, and much more than that, who gave Christ to die in my place. Although my sister did not experience a radical healing as expected, my conversion process was well under way. Christ's coming into my life had become the crucial experience for the rest of my days.

Christian mission begins with this conviction of the uniqueness of Christ and his offer of salvation. That explains why my Mom was so zealous in bringing the people around us to the church. Even though she struggled as the only Christian in a practically non-religious family by marrying my Dad, she thought all along that she was the only person in the family with "real life." The first fruits of her missionary engagement were all five of us, and then my cousins, and later my Dad and my Grandma, both of whom used to be the fiercest critics of her faith. For her and us, this was a sure proof that this God was supreme and we were among the lucky few in this Buddhist country. We had eternal life and we were the children of God! This God continued to prove

[2] I am trying to avoid excessive academic terms and expressions and maintain the oral feature of the presentation.

his love and mercy as my Mom regularly resorted to him when everything else failed.

It was one of the critical moments of my life, when I gave up my hopes to go to university, and temporarily stopped my high school studies to help my younger siblings to continue their studies, when both my parents became gravely ill. The only "lifeline" my Mom had was a small Pentecostal church which was known for "weeping in prayer." Desperate (and dedicated, I supposed), these people braved the cold winter and a dark path to "hang on" to the only hope for their daily survival. After the dawn prayer meeting, my Mom would tread the still dark path back home, worrying about what to cook for her five children. She recalled, having started the fire "by faith" with water in the pot, she heard something drop outside the door. She ran out to the doorstep and saw a sack of rice. Two shadows hurriedly disappeared under the cover of darkness. For her, they were, and are, the angels, and God had miraculously provided for her needs. Such stories as this were repeated throughout her life.

The reality of the Christian message as Christ's good news to the poor (Luke 4:18-19) is particularly felt among the marginalized. The humble and yet desperate desire of my parents for their children was for them to receive an education much higher than elementary education, which they could only attain under Japanese colonial rule. There are millions of the "poor" in the world to whom Christ's good news has been offered. Some of them are the millions of Indian Dalit parents, who struggle so that their children will be able to break the chain of oppression, poverty and social stigmatization; also the ever-increasing refugees in various parts of the world, dislocated from their homes by force; hundreds of thousands of children, who are enslaved in city brothels and industries, deprived of their basic rights to be children under care and protection; and millions of people under oppressive rulers, who fight for their freedom, as seen recently in Myanmar. This list goes on endlessly.

The steady and exponential growth of churches in the global south (or "southern church") has been in part attributed to the "poor" hearts finding the unique "good news" offered by Christianity. There is no doubt that such growth, for example in Korea, owes much to the missionary efforts of the western church (that is from Europe and North America, as well as Oceania), in spite of some criticisms, particularly as Christianity often came as part of a colonial enterprise. Even then, it was the "poor" who responded to the gospel. As experienced by the Pentecostal movement in the twentieth century, the "poor" are the most eager recipients of the gospel.

### *2.2 Mission: So Natural for God's People*

Someone has brilliantly defined evangelism as "a beggar telling another beggar where to get bread." Then it is not difficult to follow my Mom's reasoning, that sharing any good news with those who are in need is natural, whether at "home" or "out there." She was a genuine "Great Commission" Christian, although she never spoke about the Great Commission. According to her, sometimes people simply do not know what they so desperately need. This simplistic and deep conviction has made many first-generation Christians extremely zealous in their faith, be they Koreans, Chinese, Brazilians or Nigerians. Often their speeches are neither politically correct nor religiously tolerant, nor is their behaviour culturally refined or properly informed. In fact, they may appear religiously imperialistic and culturally arrogant, with their uncompromising dedication and overflowing energy. The recent hostage incident involving the Korean short-term mission group in Afghanistan is a case in point. However, I became one of them: a Korean missionary to the Philippines.

Church history is a history of missionary work, be it good or bad. The missionary instinct of Christianity has been recently confirmed by the "Back to Jerusalem" missionary movement of the Chinese house church movement.[3] This modern laboratory case of Christianity went through an entire generation, with almost no outside interference, under the extreme persecution of a brutal totalitarian political system. When the world finally had a chance to glance at the Chinese church, the big surprise was that the church had not only survived, but that it had also grown. An even bigger surprise has been its resolute commitment to "reach back to Jerusalem," while still struggling to survive in the midst of persecution. The understanding of the nature of the church ("ecclesiology") cannot be complete without this outward mission to the world.

The Edinburgh Missionary Conference of 1910 was a co-ordinated effort among Protestant churches to bring this intuitive mission into a carefully crafted plan to evangelize the world in their own generation. As almost all the non-western world was under the political control of the western "Christian" nations, there was optimism to finally complete the great commission. Plans and resources were at their disposal and they earnestly believed that they could "finish the job."[4] But within that generation, two of the greatest world wars humans have ever known were fought among "Christian" nations. The second half of the century witnessed the weakening of the western churches, while new churches emerged in the non-western world. Accordingly, the missionary mobilization was initially from the north and west to the east and the south. However, the last quarter of the twentieth century witnessed an increasing missionary movement from the south to the south (such as Brazilian missionaries to Malta). This can be seen as the result of the missionary success

---

[3] David Aikman, *Jesus in Beijing: How Christianity Is Transforming China and Changing the Global Balance of Power* (Washington, DC: Regnery, 2003), pp. 193-205; Paul Hattaway, *Back to Jerusalem: Three Chinese House Church Leaders Share their Vision to Complete the Great Commission* (Waynesboro, GA: Authentic Media, 2003).

[4] The conference theme, "The Evangelization of the World in This Generation," was indeed the watchword of the missionary community in the western world.

of the western church with many lives willingly given to share the very "good news" of Christ.[5]

What have we learned from this? The missionary call of the church begins with the uniqueness of Christ, and only those who affirm him as the way of life can obey Christ's invitation to join in God's ultimate goal of restoration. Although viewed as problematic in the religiously pluralistic world, this mission is carried out by those who believe and experience that Christ is the best thing that happens in life. Often God raises his people from the margins, be it in the church world (ecclesiastically) or in society (socio-economic context). In fact, it is the "beggar" who values the good news as well as the piece of "bread" he receives and is then willing to share this good news with other "beggars." The second half of the last century demonstrated incredibly diverse missionary dynamics: laity as well as clergy; evangelism as well as social engagement; western as well, as non-western; preachers as well as professionals. The Pentecostal movement has forcefully presented what is called the "prophethood of all believers," arguing that every believer has a missionary call.

### *2.3 Divided Body in the Name of Mission I: Which Life?*

A "Korean missionary" was as strange a concept to me as to my hosts. Until then, at least according to the common perception, "missionaries" were white and lived in a large compound away from people in the country, eating food they had brought from home. A missionary who needed to learn to speak English did not fall into the existing stereotype. However, this was not the first time that my unique value was not recognized: I saw it happen to my Mom long ago.

However, I quickly learned that "not all mission is created equal," and not everyone means the same thing when they talk of mission. The biggest divide I soon encountered was the emphasis on human life in reference to death: one group has a mission to preach "life after death," while the other has a mission to work for "life before death." This divide was particularly evident among the normal (or western) missionaries, and soon I also realized that "mainline" churches are distinguished from "evangelical" ones by their mission emphases.

These groups started together in the Edinburgh Missionary Conference in 1910 when carefully crafted theological agendas were presented for Christian (at least Protestant in this case) mission. Championing the marginalized and oppressed masses in society, particularly in the developing world, the "life before death" camp purported to prepare God's people and its church to play an

---

[5] I have personally been impacted by a young woman single missionary Ruby Rachel Kendrick (1983-1908) who died in Korea within a short time after her arrival. Her tombstone reads, "If I had a thousand lives to give, Korea should have them all." Taek-bu Jun, *Yanghwa-jin Missionary Biographies* [in Korean], rev. ed. (Seoul: Hongsung, 2005) includes many such records of early missionaries in Korea.

important role to create a just society. The move from Edinburgh to the formation of the World Council of Churches (WCC) caused the "life after death" group to gradually drop out. To mainline Protestant missiology, issues that hinder the creation of a just society are all mission topics: oppressive political systems, unjust socio-political structures, wide-spread poverty, the HIV-AIDS pandemic, ethnic genocide, human trafficking, among many others. The famous liberation theology from Latin America with its variations is but one example of the mission engagement of this group.

My early missionary life in the newly adopted country of the Philippines was during the time of the Marcos dictatorship. Home-grown (mostly Catholic) liberation theologians often led the armed resistance movement called the New People's Army. Many political "enemies" of the Marcos regime found this movement to be the only "home" for their social and political life. Such an approach often requires its missionaries not only to be in sympathy with the victims, but also to be involved in the struggle with them. Such solidarity with suffering fellow humans is indeed a noble cause, although sometimes the absence of "Christian-ness" is criticized.

The other "life after death" camp, to which I considered myself to belong, is extremely committed to the "soul saving" business. Having correctly diagnosed that human problems have their roots in sin and the spiritual severance from the Lord of all lives, Christ the Saviour is the answer to all human needs. Over the decades, this camp has strengthened its commitment to evangelism and church planting, just as the "before" camp has concentrated its efforts on issues in "this life." This evangelical mission was further reinforced by the surge of Pentecostal-Charismatic Christianity, resulting in the rapid growth of evangelical Christianity, particularly in "southern" countries. Theologically some topics on the "liberal" agenda, such as church unity, inter-religious dialogue, and social engagement, were left to the other camp. The Lausanne Congress on World Evangelization (1974), commonly viewed as the best expression of an organized evangelical mission, was a watershed event in that it positively embraced social service as an integral part of Christian mission.[6]

What is logically apparent (without even mentioning the Biblical teaching) is that these two approaches are complementary to each other, as we need to live our life both before and after death. My eager church planting among mountain tribal groups quickly taught me that the presentation of the Christian "good news" meant very little when many children were losing their lives because there was no adequate medical facility available. The "good news" has to include this earthly aspect as well as the heavenly one. At the same time, generous humanitarian aid without the presentation of Christ cannot be called Christian mission. Several years into this missionary journey, my wife and I

---

[6] Lausanne Committee for World Evangelization, "The Lausanne Covenant" (July 1974) found, among others, at http://www.lausanne.org/lausanne-1974/lausanne-covenant.html, accessed on Sept 11, 2007.

came to conclude that each "life" camp has part of the whole truth. This does not make their claim only a half truth. It is part of the full truth. However, each does not represent the full truth. Both are equally credible works of God's mission, but each is never complete without the other.

### *2.4 Divided Body in the Name of Mission II: Which Church?*

Our family's move from a small town to a nearby city was also a move from a one-church community to a many-church setting. In the new city, by my Mom's choice, we all moved to a small Pentecostal church under a woman pastor. In Korean society this is by no means a respected congregation even among fellow Christians. This "weeping church" so aptly described, because of various emotional expressions freely displayed, was where desperate youths, mothers and families came to weep and find hope for life. Even my Christian uncles (on my mother's side) urged us to get out of this "cultish and indecent" church, where nonsensical claims of healing and miracles were regularly made, not to mention the controversial "speaking in tongues." But my mother weathered the years of hardship, and this time criticisms from fellow Christians were added to the struggles with non-believing in-laws and other family members. I used to think that we needed to overcome the "world," but this time I also found out that we needed to overcome our fellow believers! With hindsight, I can see that there were doctrinal issues that divided the church. But I have also experienced enough cases to realize that small differences (often relational) or utterly "worldly" cravings for power and control have divided local congregations. From one Presbyterian church (in fact, only one "Korean Church" as early Presbyterian and Methodists decided) in Korea about 120 years ago, there are now more than 100 Presbyterian denominations, some due to "imports," but most are due to domestic divisions. Each group's claim for authenticity and truth, at the cost of others, is blatantly un-Christian.

My Pentecostal "table" was turned around as the Pentecostal movement spread its wings globally. By the time my wife and I were deeply involved in tribal areas in the northern Philippines, my Pentecostal denomination was the biggest and strongest, and still is the fastest growing. When we opened a church in a deep mountain village some years ago, one existing "liberal" church simply died, and we "praised" the Lord for his wonderful work. We thought that Christ's "full gospel" had finally arrived in this place. However, I quickly realized that there were hundreds of small villages in the mountains without a single Christian family, let alone a church. As most zealous missionaries from "new" (or "southern") churches would do, we were busy trying to evangelize everyone, including other Christians. In fact, we seem to have spent more energy in "converting" other Christians into our form of Christianity than we did non-believers. (Local) church growth was equated with the Kingdom growth, even if sheep-stealing is part of the strategy. The extremely individualistic nature of "evangelical" Christianity has spent much time and energy trying to figure out who is in and who is out. Anyone who is out should be "evangelized," be they Catholic or otherwise.

It was only when I began to meet with brothers and sisters from other Christian churches did it become apparent that I was not only ignorant, but also arrogant. In fact, when I saw a good post-Pentecostal scholar enjoying his cigar, my confusion was at its height: how can the mouth which smokes speak "heavenly language" (or tongues)? I was genuinely worried about the Holy Spirit who might have to look for fresh air. My understanding of church (ecclesiology), the Holy Spirit (pneumatology) and mission was hopelessly shallow and narrow. Later I also realized that the gift of the Holy Spirit in the twentieth century was intended for the whole church. Only a few courageous Pentecostals like David du Plessis understood the mind of the Holy Spirit and took this very good news to other Christian churches, while they received severe criticism from their own churches.[7]

It is also noticeable that the ecumenical movement which has worked to bring various Christian churches together has created, ironically, an environment for some churches to find it simply impossible to approach the network. It has inadvertently formed a "game plan" to know which belong to the "in church" and which are "outside" of the circle. How the Catholic Church has defined a genuine church and a second class church is a similar practice.

My "evangelize-everyone" attitude began to change when I started meeting wonderful new friends who dress and worship differently than I do. After all, I found out that I must look quite strange to them as well. This "church unity by fellowship" (*koinonia*) has been something I have observed from my youth: average Christians care very little about denominations. I also noted that from diverse orientations, common experiences of the Holy Spirit bring together God's people for celebration. This "spontaneous ecumenism"[8] was noted from the Azusa Street Mission, the very birthplace of the modern Pentecostal movement. My own experience of working with various church traditions in mission settings suggests that common commitment to mission is another platform where church unity can be experienced. This still leaves a legitimate place for a structural effort to create church unity.

### *2.5 A Tale of Two Siblings*

My first exposure to the Edinburgh Missionary Conference (1910) was almost by accident. I was a mission practitioner whose academic training was in Biblical study. Even the second Lausanne Congress on World Evangelism in Manila (1989) was not of interest to me, even if it did take place in the same country where I was working. Only when I was invited to participate in the

---

[7] David du Plessis, *A Man Called Mr. Pentecost: The Story of a Legendary Missionary to the Church* (South Plainfield, NJ: Bridge Publishing, 1977).

[8] This term was used in describing an unexpected ecumenical phenomenon among Pentecostals and Catholic Charismatics by Koichi Kitano, "Spontaneous Ecumenicity between Catholics and Protestants in the Charismatic Movement" (PhD dissertation, Centre Escolar University, Manila, 1981).

preparatory conference for the Edinburgh centenary (2005), did I become aware of this historic event and its enduring effect since then. As a Pentecostal, this was a new discovery. The following is a story of the two global missionary movements of the twentieth century, the Edinburgh Conference and the Pentecostal movement, born in the same decade (1900s), but with very little contact with each other. Yet both have exerted an enormous influence on Christianity today, like a tale of two siblings who never met each other.

The Edinburgh gathering in 1910, primarily a western "mainline" Christian gathering, was filled with optimism. After the two world wars shattered the optimism, many "heathen" nations gained their independence, and the tradition crystallized into an ecumenical movement so giving birth to the WCC, although a mission commission, the heir of the Edinburgh Conference, joined the body a few years later. The second half of the century was a story of ecumenism.

The WCC was born out of a missionary movement, which recognized that church unity is an integral part of, or prerequisite for, mission. To an outsider of the WCC circle, to be truthful to the original idea, church unity should always be explored in the context of mission. But in reality, discussion on church unity seems to have overridden mission. Some believe that this is one reason why the traditional "mainline churches" (particularly in the West) have steadily increased their influence in mission, membership and resources.

By contrast, the Pentecostal movement began as a marginalized fringe Christian phenomenon in the downtown of Los Angeles. Although mockery from the society was harsh, the most unbearable attacks were lodged by fellow Christians.[9] In every aspect, they were the powerless, as the Azusa Street Mission was headed by an African-American preacher William J. Seymour.[10] The marginalized and "poor" were attracted to the message of God's immanent presence by manifestations such as healing, miracles, and religious ecstatic experience (or "baptism in the Holy Spirit"). With its missionary fervor instantly recognizable,[11] the Pentecostal movement was predominantly a revival phenomenon. This "religion of the poor" survived both through its endless divisions and doctrinal controversies and also the never-ending external marginalization and criticisms. Thus, for the first half century of its existence it remained as a fringe movement.

However, its adherents hold a strong conviction that the "best thing" (Christ) in their life was even bettered by the empowerment of the Holy Spirit, and they

---

[9] Cecil M. Robeck, Jr., *The Azusa Street Mission and Revival: The Birth of the Global Pentecostal Movement* (Nashville, TN: Thomas Nelson, 2006), p. 134 reprints such a cartoon ridiculing the Pentecostal movement.

[10] Robeck, *The Azusa Street Mission and Revival*, esp. pp. 87-128 describes the pivotal role of Seymour in the Mission.

[11] For example, Allan Anderson, *Spreading Fires: The Missionary Nature of Early Pentecostalism* (Maryknoll, NY: Orbis, 2007), pp. 149-190 notes that as early as 1906 (the same year when the Azusa Street Mission began), a Pentecostal missionary was present in the "Bible Lands" (p. 152-53).

were extremely eager to spread the good news to the fellow "poor." This "fired-up poor" brought the movement during the second half of the last century into a global expansion in various shapes and forms. This movement of "primal spirituality" has had a particular appeal to those who are "poor" in many ways (economically, socially, politically etc.), and who live in destitute societies. Many "indigenous" types of Christianity, closely resembling the Pentecostal spirituality, but without any historic tie to the North American "springhead," have been "discovered." This spiritual and renewal movement, without any global structure or umbrella organization, has become a powerful missionary movement, evident in its exponential growth.[12] In its zealousness for mission, however, church unity was completely ignored, even though the Azusa Street Mission demonstrated the powerful potential of the Spirit for church unity and social reconciliation.[13]

These two most powerful mission movements of the twentieth century are especially comparable and contrasting in their origins. What is equally noticeable is their ethos of mission: the ecumenical initiative is a "gathering into" movement (centripetal), while the Pentecostal-charismatic movement is a "spreading out" movement (centrifugal). Now with a century of experience behind them, each one has begun to reflect on itself: recognizing its own strength and achievements as well as being self-critical about its weaknesses and mistakes. Understandably the WCC proceeds in a more organized way, while Pentecostals do so in an informal and "spontaneous" way. The recent general assemblies of the WCC highlighted the person and work of the Holy Spirit,[14] and took steps to intentionally include some Pentecostal delegates. Its latest Conference on World Mission and Evangelism in Athens (2005) is another case in point: its theme was "Come Holy Spirit, and Heal and Reconcile."[15] The presence of Pentecostal Christianity in the gathering was evident not only in the plenary speeches, but also in the workshops and worship programmes. The creation of a more neutral and new space such as the Global Christian Forum, although not organizationally connected with the WCC, is an indication of this growing awareness.

---

[12] Patrick Johnston and Jason Mandryk, *Operation World*, 21st century edition (Carlisle: Paternoster, 2001), p. 3 predicts close to one billion Pentecostal-Charismatic believers by 2010.

[13] The inter-racial and ecumenical nature of the Azusa Street Mission has been well documented. For the recovery of this tradition, specifically for Asian Pentecostals, see Robeck, Cecil M., Jr. "Pentecostal Ecumenism: An Introductory Essay for Asian Pentecostals." *Asian Journal of Pentecostal Studies* 2:1 (1999), pp. 87-103

[14] The most obvious is the theme of the 7th general assembly in Canberra, Australia (1991): "Come Holy Spirit, Renew They Whole Creation." The theme of the latest 9th general assembly still maintains the emphasis, although less explicitly: "God, in your grace, transform the world."

[15] "Conference on World Mission and Evangelism" (http://www.mission2005.org/, May 19, 2005), checked: Oct 25, 2007.

From the Pentecostal perspective, some churches, particularly from the "southern" continents, have slowly joined various gatherings of the WCC or its national councils. Often this move comes with much criticism from their fellow Pentecostal churches, sister organizations and their own constituencies. Ecumenical dialogues are in progress with the Roman Catholic Church,[16] the Reformed Churches,[17] and the Lutherans as well as the WCC at the global level, while growing national or local dialogues also take place. Unlike their dialogue partners, Pentecostal delegates are all individuals without any authority as representatives of their Pentecostal churches.

This self-critical reflection and growing awareness of each other through various (and sometimes courageous) contacts has led the two siblings much closer to each other than was possible decades ago. As the Edinburgh centenary celebration is being planned, this may be the historic opportunity to bring the divided church together for its mission. Even the 2010 Edinburgh conference is correcting its mistakes by becoming as inclusive as possible, ecclesiastically (as now Catholics, Orthodox, evangelicals and Pentecostals are included) and geographically (with an intentional effort to reflect the current global Christian status with the "southern" majority).[18] We have to confess that this divided history was not the Lord's intent, but human short-sightedness and failure to recognize the divine intent. In spite of human failure, the Spirit who with his creativity and graciousness brought forward God's mission now brings his church together for the same mission.

### *2.6 Huge Fringe: "Southern" Christianity*

Earlier we discovered that one division among the churches was between the "mainline" and evangelical churches. The former was generally regarded as "liberal" in their attitude toward the scriptures, mission and the world (including other religions), while the latter was "conservative" in the same areas. The former is generally found in the fold of the WCC, while the latter is "outside" of it. Regardless of their theological stance, however, in earlier days the western churches were the missionary-sending entities (benefactors, thus "Christian" as they were "missioning"), while the nations and states of the global south were considered the mission field (beneficiaries, "heathen," thus, "missioned"). This global divide was the setting one hundred years ago (e.g. in

---

[16] For example, "Evangelism, Proselytism and Common Witness: The Report from the Fourth Phase of the International Dialogue 1990-1997 between the Roman Catholic Church and some Classical Pentecostal Churches and Leaders," *Asian Journal of Pentecostal Studies* 2:1 (1999), pp. 105-151.

[17] For example, "Word and Spirit, Church and World: The Final Report of the International Dialogue between Representatives of the World Alliance of Reformed Churches and Some Classical Pentecostal Churches and Leaders 1996-2000," *Asian Journal of Pentecostal Studies* 4:1 (2001), pp. 41-72.

[18] Towards 2010, "Edinburgh 2010—Mission in Humility and Hope" (http://www.towards2010.org.uk/int_June_2005_doc.htm): checked: Oct 25, 2007.

the time of the Edinburgh Conference).

Now the rule of dividing the Christian world has changed drastically. The southward movement of the centre of the global Christian gravity means there are far more (almost four times more) Christians in the global south than in the north (or "west"). The rapid increase of "southern" missionaries is also a natural consequence, already outnumbering their traditional western counterparts. For example, Korea is the second largest missionary-sending nation after the United States, while the highest missionary-sending country per capita is surprisingly Mongolia.[19] The ambitious plan (but not at all surprising considering the huge Christian population that is still growing) of the Chinese house church networks to raise 200,000 missionaries in the near future to reach "Back to Jerusalem" can be a reality. These are just numbers. However, equally significant is what is "under the hood."

Southern Christianity has exhibited several important characteristics. The first is its holistic understanding of the Christian faith. It is not only the spiritual aspect of salvation that is important, but also the material and physical aspects as well. In a way "life before death" and "life after death" come together to form a complete spectrum of human life. In fact, a supreme God who cannot bring physical healing today, while promising an eternal life after one dies, is not convincing at all to people, who regularly expect their ancestor spirits to bring healing and good fortune. Equally holistic is the understanding of the natural and supernatural world. In the religious worldview where spirits, gods and demons are perceived to be extremely active in human affairs, it is no wonder that southern Christianity includes spiritual beings in religious life, and phenomena such as miracles and exorcism. Socially speaking, becoming Christian often comes with a high cost in many parts of the southern world, where Christianity is a minority "foreign" religion.[20] Only with the strong conviction that the best thing in life is Christ can Christians persevere in this hostile environment. Furthermore, generally speaking, these southern Christians take the scripture at its face value,[21] unlike western sophisticated methods of Biblical interpretation with their high degree of scepticism and suspicion. Unquestioned acceptance of religious teaching and scriptures is part of their culture. This explains why the same church (e.g. Anglican) demonstrates a remarkable difference between the West and the South (e.g. Uganda) over issues like human sexuality. Now the clearest divide in global Christianity is between the North and the South.

---

[19] It could be India in the total number, which includes many cross-cultural missionaries within a country. Johnston & Mandryk, *Operation World*, p. 6.

[20] A personal account of this sort is found in Wonsuk Ma and Julie C. Ma, "Jesus Christ in Asia: Our Journey with Him as Pentecostal Believers," *International Review of Mission* 94 (2005), pp. 493-94.

[21] Philip Jenkins, *The New Faces of Christianity: Believing the Bible in the Global South* (Oxford: Oxford University Press, 2006).

This too-good-to-be-true picture of southern Christianity is not without problems. There is a great danger for Christianity to be reduced to the old religion, for instance, where deities are "used" for human consumption. Nonetheless, southern Christianity has shown great potential to renew global Christianity, while deeply engaging in a completely non- or even anti-Christian society. This makes today's Christian mission extremely viable and effective.

## 3. Conclusion

The last one hundred years have shown us the remarkable work of God, as global Christianity has gone through unprecedented world crises and yet faced incredible opportunities. Christian unity will continue to remain a major challenge for Christian communities. There will be more reasons why divisions will further intensify, on the one hand, and more urgent and predominant reasons why the church should work together, on the other. The mission of God is to bring a complete restoration to his creation through the life-giving power of the Holy Spirit. If mission has divided the church, it is entirely due to human faults. In fact, mission will bring the church together.

Thus, our journey as fellow Christians has taught us that church unity is like riding a bicycle. We will fall unless we go forward. Church unity was rightly perceived within the context of mission, and this should continue. Called by one God, redeemed through the one Lord, and empowered through the presence of the one Spirit, church-together is not only a dream but also a possibility. There is a potential for spontaneous ecumenicity through loving fellowship and Spirit-led worship. Working together for the cause of God's kingdom is another viable arena for church-together. Furthermore we have sufficient experience to pursue this aim.

Then how can organic or spontaneous ecumenism be structurally regulated so as to perpetuate it? This represents a serious challenge as the history of ecumenism in the last half a century exemplifies. For this reason, we should not overlook the role of learning and reflection: the earnest desire to learn from the scripture and from fellow Christians should lead us to develop a desire to be one. Occasions like this have the potential to foster such authentic ecumenicity by combining open *koinonia*, Spirit-filled worship, and diligent learning to discern what the Lord is doing in different Christian communions. It is all for God's mission's sake that we are called together to be in one body so that the world may know that we are the people of God (John 17:21, 23). An African saying may encourage us: "If you want to go fast, go alone. If you want to go far, go together."

## FROM THE PLENARY SESSIONS
## WHEN EAST MEETS WEST AND NORTH MEETS SOUTH: THE RECONCILING MISSION OF GLOBAL CHRISTIANITY



### Dr. Cheryl Bridges Johns

*Dr. Cheryl Bridges Johns is Professor of Discipleship and Christian Formation at the Church of God Theological Seminary (Cleveland), USA. As a Pentecostal scholar she has participated in the work of Faith & Order in the USA and globally.*


This presentation is based upon two assumptions: first, that the "mainstream" ecumenical paradigm, which has served well the cause of Christian unity, is no longer viable for the challenges of the twenty-first century; second, that the gifts present in the global Christian movement when honoured as equal partners are adequate for the cause of unity and mission.

Most would agree that the structures built to create and sustain the cause of the visible unity of the church are in need of a major transformation in order to meet the current challenges and needs of the churches. This is not to say that these structures were not vitally important during the twentieth century. Through them many of the historic divisions between Christians were confronted and overcome. The modern ecumenical movement originating in the world missionary zeal at the turn of the twentieth century provided Christians with a common vision, a common witness and a deep fellowship. We are indebted to those who made the difficult sacrifices, breaking through the walls of fear and suspicion of the divided churches.

Through the efforts of both the conciliar and bilateral dialogues there has emerged a common understanding of baptism, Eucharist and ministry (i.e. BEM), and the recent "Joint Declaration on Justification" must be celebrated as a historic achievement healing the deep wounds of the Reformation. There are countless other no less significant advances that have been made through heroic efforts of women and men committed to the visible unity of the church.

However, it should be noted that the Christian landscape today is in many ways vastly different from that of a century ago. Over the decades, unnoticed by most in the North, the axis of Christianity has shifted to the global South and to the East. This shift is now so pronounced that it is almost impossible to ignore the new face of Christianity. It has been difficult for Christians in the West to keep up with these shifts and the ecumenical movement has struggled to do so, often assuming that the new forms of the one faith could be merged into the existing structures created for understanding and common witness. However, the current structures are proving to be old wineskins that cannot contain the new wine. The newer forms of churches, like David trying on Saul's armour, find themselves ill-fitted and uncomfortable with the form, language and structures of the modern ecumenical movement. Those who have invested their lives into building and maintaining these structures are at times blind to the challenges of the newer forms of Christianity, assuming that the newcomers, once they have learned the "ecumenical grammar" will fit into and contribute to the old ways. Furthermore, the old are often blind to their impotence, in spite of reduced budgets and vacant buildings.

It is my thesis, therefore, that a new form of ecumenism is needed in order to embrace the present challenges of world-wide Christianity. While many are aware of this need, there is little understanding and even fear of the forms of Christianity that are emerging in the East and in the South. Here we are today in a quandary where the words of Matthew Arnold seem most appropriate: We are living between a past that is dead and a future unable to be born. This time-between-times is frustrating but it is also pregnant with promise. As never before, we are in need of a rebirth for the sake of the visible unity of the church.

The World Council Assembly held in New Delhi (1961) articulated a vision of unity "made visible as all in each place who are baptized into Jesus Christ." This visible unity of the church has been difficult to achieve, but nonetheless it has sustained a generation of those who understood Christ's prayer for unity as expressing the longing for his body. This vision has endured conflict, misunderstanding and indifference. Today, it remains before us as a calling for a new generation.

The present generation faces new challenges. The conflict is not only between communions, but within communions there are ever deepening rifts, with battle-lines being drawn over human sexuality, the authority of Scripture and other matters. Deeper even than these rifts lie the fault-lines between the global South and the North, where each side represents very different forms of Christianity.

A point made at the New Delhi Assembly is worth noting: "the achievement of unity will involve nothing less than a death and rebirth of many forms of church life as we have known them...nothing less costly can finally suffice." No one at New Delhi could imagine the extent of the cost for this unity. Few could imagine the world as we now know it to be. Who at New Delhi could have imagined the demise of the Soviet Empire? Who would have dreamed of the ripple effects of the Second Vatican Council (1962-1965)? Could any of them understand the post-Christian West? Who at New Delhi could calculate the cost of death and rebirth as present to us today?

There are those who contend that the ecumenism of the twentieth century continues to be viable and eschew the language of "death." For them the modern ecumenical movement only needs fine tuning. Others, including myself, see the need for new forms for Christian unity, such as that found in the Global Christian Forum.

I do not pretend to have the answers as to the way ahead. There are only hunches from my limited vantage point as to how the Holy Spirit may be at work creating and re-creating God's original and real *oecumene.* If we are to take seriously the worldwide church we have to acknowledge that we face challenges.

In light of these challenges, Andrew Walls, as one of the first to point out the shifting axis of Christianity, notes that the church historian's work at the dawn of the third Christian millennium requires the dual tasks of *re-conception and re-visioning.* He also mentions the need for *conversion* but understands it to be a sub-category of *re-visioning.* However, if we make it a separate task, we can borrow from Walls, noting that the ecumenical work at the beginning of this century requires *re-conception, re-visioning and conversion.*

### Re-Conception of the Resources

Those desiring to construct a new ecumenical table must re-conceive the resources or gifts that are found within the world Christian movement. This means not only re-discovering the classical ecumenical heritage, but also taking stock of the resources found within the vibrant forms of Christianity in the global South. Re-conception would mean a blending of the old and the new in order to form a unique structure suited for the challenges ahead. There are "gifts" from the past that are to be honoured in the future, and conversely there are gifts in the newer forms of church that need to be equally valued.

### Gifts of the Global North

While not being the "privileged carrier" of the Christian faith, the churches of the North offer many gifts for the task of Christian unity. Foremost among these are the legacy of the Great Councils. From these Councils there has been preserved the apostolic faith of the church. The ancient creeds serve as standards for its life and witness. For that reason, there has been a resurgence of emphasis upon the Creeds as the ecumenical centre. Those advocating a "new ecumenism" see that a return to the ancient way is a way forward into the future.[1] While there are those who would disagree with making "Nicene Christianity" the heart of the contemporary church's life and witness, there is little doubt as to the richness found within the ancient ecumenical councils. The task of re-conception before us requires that we look deeply into the past for its wisdom and its standard of truth while at the same time seeking a vibrant

---

[1] Examples of "new ecumenism" can be found in the "Princeton Proposal for Christian Unity." See also Christopher Seitz, ed., *Nicene Christianity: The Future for a New Ecumenism* (Grand Rapids: Brazos Press, 2001).

witness in the present that honours the continuation of the revelation by the Holy Spirit.

Another resource found within the churches of the North may be described as "the gift of Christian humanism." This gift is derived from the ancient synthesis between Hellenistic philosophy and Christianity and bears the fruit of Christianity's elevation of reason and its quest for full "humanization". For some, such as Benedict XVI, this synthesis has been one of "decisive importance."[2] For Benedict, Hellenized Christianity is that which created the foundation of what "can rightly be called Europe."[3] The heritage of Greek philosophy, with its primacy of reason brought about a flourishing of culture, with an emphasis upon human rights and the rise of democracy. This legacy, while debated within Europe today, provided a template for the modern ecumenical movement. The "reasoned based" approach to dialogue, the work of Faith and Order and the quest for human rights are the results of this ancient synthesis.

The task of *re-conception* requires that the churches of the North re-examine their Hellenistic roots. Doing so may not mean agreeing with Pope Benedict's fervent desire to maintain the marriage of Greek philosophy and Christianity.[4] Instead, however, it may mean that while treating the legacy of Greece and Rome as a paradigm in honouring the important role of reason and philosophy, there would be an honest appraisal of its limitations.

This type of *re-conception* is represented in Robert W. Jensen's work on the Trinity. While Jensen understands that "Hellenic theology was from the beginning an exact antagonist of biblical faith," and that the triumph of Hellenism in the West resulted in a diminished Trinitarian understanding of God, he does not call for the "de-Hellenization" of Christianity. Instead, Jensen seeks its transformation:

> Throughout I have insisted on the clash of the gospel's and Hellenism's interpretation of God and have blamed Western theology's trinitarian enfeeblement on defeat in this battle. It is time to reiterate that I do not intend thereby to decry the "Hellenization" of Christianity or to propose termination of the metaphysical reflection in which the confrontation with Hellenism has

---

[2] Benedict XVI, "Faith Reason and the University: Memories and Reflections," Regensburg University, September, 2006.

[3] Ibid.

[4] Benedict laments Western civilization's "dehellenization." He sees this process occurring in three historical stages. The first was the program of the Protestant Reformation and its commitment to *sola scriptura,* the second took place with the advent of liberal theology in the nineteenth century. The third stage Benedict sees occurring at the present time in the "culture of pluralism." See his "Resensburg lectures." I am indebted to Dale Irvin for critiquing Ratzinger/Benedict's Hellenistic foundations. See his "Benedict XVI, European Christendom, and World Christianity," in William Rusch, ed. *The Pontificate of Benedict XVI: Its Premises and Promises* (Grand Rapids: Eerdmans, 2009).

> involved the gospel. On the contrary, the fault of Western trinitarianism was precisely a failure to carry on the meta-physical creativity begun by the Cappadocians, and so long as the Western church endures, it must be Hellenic.[5]

Also, re-conceiving would mean taking seriously the criticisms from the global South regarding the marriage between Greek philosophy/reason and Christianity. Here the question is the same as that of the great African theologian, Tertullian: "What Does Athens have to do with Jerusalem?" As withTertullian, the criticism from the global South regarding the marriage of Athens and Jerusalem can be biting as by the Nigerian Anglican bishop: "In spite of their pride in their wisdom (the Greek love of *sophia*) they had become utterly foolish."[6]

Hence there is a need for what Benedict calls the "purification of reason," noting that it was human reason that created the atomic bomb and it is human ingenuity that has made human genetics a matter of selection.[7] Southern Christians would want to add that reason must be purified by the critical agency of the Holy Spirit. After all, it is the Spirit who knows all things and searches the hearts of humanity. Many in the global South know all too well the "epiphanies of darkness" that dwell within the structures of social systems and that human reason alone cannot move the church into "all truth."

Therefore, while the churches of the North preserve the great legacy of Hellenized Christianity, they should offer this gift in the spirit of humility, knowing full well the temptation to be self-justifying.

Finally, within the churches of the North there are the resources of great educational institutions and organizations that have furthered the cause of Christian unity, and the financial resources for the continuation of the mission of the church. These resources, when used well, become means to power for the people and means whereby the hungry are fed, the poor are empowered, and the gospel is preached.

## Gifts of the Global South

Southern Christians are "citizens of Jerusalem," observes Philip Jenkins. As citizens of Jerusalem they offer unique gifts to the global church. The task of *re-conceiving* calls for incorporating these gifts without the Western assumptions that religion in the global South represents some form of "lesser

---

[5] Robert W. Jensen, *The Triune Identity: God According to the Gospel* (Philadelphia: Fortress Press, 1982; reprinted Eugene, OR: Wipf& Stock, 2002), p. 4.

[6] "The Church of Nigeria (Anglican Communion) and the Homosexuality Issue," online at http:www.anglicannig.org/hobstatementaug.htm. Quoted in Philip Jenkins, *The New Faces of Christianity: Believing the Bible in the Global South* (Oxford: Oxford University Press, 2006), p. 4.

[7] Jurgen Habermas and Joseph Ratzinger, *The Dialectics of Secularization* (Freiburg im Breisgau: Herder, 2005),p. 77.

developed Christianity" or "fundamentalist religion."

While the churches in the North hold the legacy of the Great Councils, the churches of the global South hold what Andrew Walls characterizes as the unique opportunities to witness the life of the apostolic church. Quoting his former professor, F.L. Cross, 'We know next to nothing about the ante-Nicene church," Walls asserts: "We now have better resources for understanding the patchwork of fragments of Christian literature that survive from before the age of the great councils by examining the recent histories of the churches of Africa and Asia than the Bodleian or the Vatican libraries can yield."[8] While Walls may be overstating the case for apostolic life being currently visible in the Southern churches, the evidence seems overwhelming that the life of these churches provides a dynamic hermeneutics for the interpretation of ante-Nicene Christianity.

Glimpsing into this window of opportunity we see a Christianity that takes Scripture seriously. Taking Scripture seriously is not the same as being fundamentalist. Many in the Global South are quick to point out that they are not "fundamentalists" in the sense that they hold to a rigid legal code. Rather, Scripture is viewed as a living word of the Spirit for the present time. This is especially true among Pentecostals where there is a fusion between Spirit and Word. Thus the Bible presents Christ "now present in the world and in their lives, manifesting the same divine power, and doing what he did in Galilee."[9]

"The ancient custom of hearing the Word is very much a living tradition in contemporary churches of the global South," observes Jenkins, "giving quite different quality to the reception and the impact of the text."[10] Furthermore, passages are shared, aurally and communally, with an audience with old-established expectations about the nature of oral tradition and communication. Also, communal reading occurs in a sacred setting, whether in reading and study groups or in the context of worship."[11] In this context "experiencing scripture communally promotes exalted concepts of the nature of the group that hears the sacred words, a sense that the religious community becomes the vehicle for the divine message."[12]

Any new ecumenical movement must re-conceive the role of Scripture in the life and witness of the churches. Taking seriously the dynamic, communal and Spirit-reading of the sacred text found in the global South means that Scripture is more central to the ecumenical task. It places a higher priority upon the present reality of the Holy Spirit in the text and within communities. The

---

[8] Andrew Walls, "Eusebius Tries Again," in Wilbert R. Shenk, ed. *Enlarging the Story: Perspectives on Writing World Christian History* (Maryknoll: Orbis, 2002), p. 4.

[9] Richard Shaull & Waldo Cesar, *Pentecostalism and the Future of the Christian Churches* (Grand Rapids: Eerdmans, 2000), p. 192.

[10] Philip Jenkins, *The New Faces of Christianity: Believing the Bible in the Global South* (Oxford: 2006) p. 26.

[11] Ibid.

[12] Ibid.

ecumenical journey includes more of what Jean-Marc Ela describes as 'a festival of language...which includes grasping the Word, searching for its meaning, questions and answers, prayers and chants."[13]

While the churches of the global South, for the most part, honour the legacy of Nicene Christianity, their "ante Nicene" life calls for the power of the apostolic witness to be that which validates the truth of the apostolic faith. While disconcerting to many Christians in the North, the South's emphasis upon the continuation of miracles, dreams and prophecy stands as a great gift to worldwide Christianity. Receiving this gift calls for the North to lay aside the old "social deprivation" readings of Christianity among the oppressed and to re-conceive the nature of the Christian witness.

The type of re-conceiving necessary to do this can be seen in the life and witness of Richard Shaull, whose address at the 1966 World Council of Churches World Conference on Church and Society called for a "conversion to the poor," and concerted action toward their liberation. His address captured the imagination of a rising generation of ecumenists. Shaull's later conversion to the "religion among the oppressed" is for the most part, an unknown story. This conversion came about as a result of years of studying Pentecostalism in Latin America. Here he found a form of Christianity that engaged the primal struggles between order and chaos. He described such Christianity as flourishing at "ground zero" of this struggle. Shaull identified this new paradigm of Christianity as a "reconstruction of life in the power of the Spirit."[14] This power to reconstruct life is most profoundly manifest in those places where "the most basic forms of life in the community- the family, local neighborhoods, social, economic and political structures are becoming unglued, leaving masses of poor people in both rural and peripheral urban areas without stable work, medical care, or opportunities for education."[15]

In these regions of the world, truth is experienced as an encounter of a power that is able to liberate people from evil. In the face of evil the power of the gospel brings direct divine intervention. When social institutions fail and political solutions become corrupt the Christian way often becomes the only source of liberation and the churches the only stable institutions. Into this chaos the gospel is preached to the poor offering healing for sick minds and bodies, the power to reorganize broken lives and to overcome addictions. Salvation is deliverance from the power of systemic evil. "It is," as Harvey Cox has observed, "the ability to lure anarchy into the sacred circle and tame it."[16]

This ability is not just a gift to the Southern churches, but becomes a worldwide ecumenical challenge. As such, it speaks to those churches in the

---

[13] Jean- Marc Ela, *My Faith as an African* (Maryknoll, NY.: Orbis, 1988), 45-46.

[14] Richard Shaull and Waldo Cesar, *Pentecostalism and the Future of the Christian Churches* (Eerdmans: 2000), p. 116.

[15] Ibid.

[16] Harvey Cox, *Fire From Heaven,* p. 120.

North who feel impotent in the face of terror, chaos and death. Thus the "sacred circles" drawn in the South can become protean for the rest of us who feel impotent in our ability to tame anarchy.

Another important gift or resource found within the South is the impetus to be the "militia Christi," advancing the kingdom of God throughout the world. While the missionary nature of the Church has historically been manifest in the Western churches, this is ceasing to be the case. Instead, the missionary force of the twenty-first century will be coming from the Southern churches. The task of re-conceiving the ecumenical movement will call for incorporating the new face of mission into its agenda while at the same time honouring the forms of mission developed in the West/North.

**The Task of Re-Visioning**

Constructing a new ecumenical movement means also a re-visioning of the journey toward Christian unity. This will require us to make some paradigm shifts. First, we will need to move away from the Western assumption that there is a single ecumenical model with a universal application. In the future, more effort will need to be made in taking into account local relevance "in the selection of themes and in judging what belongs to the foreground and what belongs to the background."[17]

Critics within and without the ecumenical movement have pointed out that the quest for the visible unity of the church has often been co-opted by social movements for human liberation. They point out the turn the World Council of Churches took in 1966 at the World Conference on Church and Society as an example of a move away from classical Christian teaching in favour of human utopias. Such critics are hesitant in regard to re-visioning.

However, in spite of these criticisms, re-visioning is necessary for the continuing viability of the quest for Christian unity and this quest must always take seriously the human condition. The Spirit's work among the marginalized and the conditions of oppression, hunger, poverty and human trafficking are not peripheral to the ecumenical calling. The intentions of the World Conference on Church and Society, namely to see God's presence and activity in the midst of human history, especially among the poor, is a call that should guide our present ecumenical calling.

Re-visioning the ecumenical movement would also mean that the churches of the North and the South are seen as equal partners in shaping the ecumenical future. Too often newer forms of churches are looked upon as exotic and under-developed. The result of such a bias is that in ecumenical gatherings participants from the Southern churches are asked to "flavour" the meetings with their worship, leaving the "real business" to the churches of the North. In the future the "real business" may include more testimony and more time for

[17] Walls, p. 14.

prayer and worship. Scripture may be more prominent as participants engage in a "festival of the Word."

The format of the Global Christian Forum is a hopeful sign towards a future in which the churches of the global South are encouraged to incorporate their worldviews into the task of unity. The inclusion of testimonies of faith journeys and the sharing of stories of ecumenical calling and vocation have brought to the Forum a deep sense of solidarity and equality among the participants. The leaders of the Forum are to be commended for their patient listening and their discernment as they attempt to move forward toward a viable future.

### The Task of Conversion

The tasks of re-conceiving and re-visioning cannot be accomplished without *conversion.* As Walls points out, "conversion means turning not substituting a new element for old- or adding a new element to the old, but changing the direction of what is already there."[18] The WCC Assembly in New Delhi called for death and re-birth. For a viable future there will need to be some death- like turning. This will require from all of us, those from the North and those from the South, both openness and humility.

On the part of Northern Christianity our conversion means that we soberly examine our gifts: the legacy of the Great Councils, the power of reason and critical thought, the institutions and resources. Conversion calls for examining how we have been guilty of making these gifts our own possessions. Have we been guilty of substituting reason and critical thought for life-giving faith? Do we have the legacy of the historic creeds without the authentic life they represent? Do we depend on our resources and our institutions rather than upon the power of the Holy Spirit?

On the part of Southern Christianity, conversion means that the gifts of apostolic power and faith, the living witness of Scripture and the passion for mission be soberly examined. All too often Southern Christians have imagined themselves as "true" Christians" over against an "apostate" or "post-Christian" North. This stereotyping fosters pride which deeply wounds the church's witness in the world.

The good news about conversion is that repentance and death prepare a path toward rebirth. True humility will bear the fruit of Christian unity. This unity is the distinctive mark of the people of God. So as we move toward a viable future, let us pray that we may be one: North embracing South, East embracing West, so that the world might believe.

[18] Walls, p. 21.

## From The Plenary Sessions
## Bible Studies

# Rev. Fr Thomas Michel

Each day, with the exception of the first day, began with a Bible study of thirty minutes in small groups, followed by a morning prayer in plenary. The overall theme was unity and the passages were taken from the Epistle to the Ephesians. Each group had a leader who had received in advance the texts and the study guides, prepared by Fr. Tom Michel, a Jesuit priest who served for many years as the secretary for ecumenical relations of the Federation of Asian Bishops' Conferences. The small group leaders had also a briefing session on the spot. The Bible study groups were formed by splitting in two the thirty participants that made up the eight discussion groups. In this way, the Bible study groups also reflected the diversity of the meeting while there was little pressure on participants to adjust and readjust to the interaction with different combinations of people. There had to be some slight modifications to the make-up for it proved useful to base the membership of two of the small groups on the use of languages other than English, i.e. French and Spanish. The careful preparations contributed in no small way to making the Bible studies one of the highlights of the event for many participants. Their only regret was that more time was not allotted to this part of the programme.

### 1. Learning from Paul to pray for one another (Ephesians 1: 15-23)

15 Ever since I heard about your faith in the Lord Jesus and your love for all the
saints, 16 I have not stopped giving thanks for you, remembering you in my
prayers. 17 I keep asking that the God of our Lord Jesus Christ, the glorious
Father, may give you a spirit of wisdom and revelation, so that you may know
him better. 18 I pray also that the eyes of your heart may be enlightened in order
that you may know the hope to which he has called you, the riches of his glorious
inheritance in the saints, 19 and his incomparably great power for us who believe.
That power is like the working of his mighty strength, 20 which he exerted in
Christ when he raised him from the dead and seated him at his right hand in the
heavenly realms, 21 far above all rule and authority, power and dominion, and
every title that can be given, not only in the present age but also in the one to
come. 22 And God placed all things under his feet and appointed him to be head
over everything for the church, 23 which is his body, the fullness of him who fills
everything in every way.

## Study guide Ephesians 1: 15-23

Our approaches to unity, which by necessity focus on dogmatic, historical, and organizational issues, can lead us to underestimate the availability of God's power to guide us on the path of unity, a power that is accessed through prayer. As a result, we do not pray enough for one another's churches and communities and allow that experience of prayer for each other to transform our attitudes and mutual relations. In this passage, Paul offers some directions for our prayer for one another's communities.

As we know, the words "in Ephesus" are lacking in some early manuscripts, and indeed, in this passage, Paul appears to be writing to Christians who are from his own community, but whom he appears to know from the information of others. He learns two things about them that lead him to keep on thanking God for them and remembering them in his prayers. One is their faith in the Lord Jesus, and the other is the love they have for all the saints. Do our churches continue this practice of Paul? How often do we thank God for the faith in Jesus Christ that we find in other Christian churches or the love for God's people that we see being lived out in other Christian groups? What specifically should we thank God for when we reflect on the Christian life lived by churches and communities other than our own? What aspects of their faith life and their loving *diakonia* are we especially grateful for?

But Paul also prays that God will bestow grace on these other communities. He asks God to give them a spirit of wisdom and revelation so that they know God better. [One could also translate this "that God give them *the Spirit* of wisdom and revelation," but it comes down to the same thing, that God sends the Holy Spirit to our fellow churches to make them wise and to reveal God's own will to them.} All of our churches need to grow continually in the knowledge of God and God's will, but this is only possible if God grants them the wisdom "that comes from above." If we really want other Christian churches to grow in the knowledge of God, we have to keep asking God to grant them wisdom. It is especially important to make this prayer when they have synods, elections, or important decisions to make, or when they are experiencing moments of crisis or confusion. Each of our churches must be able to count on the spiritual support of Christians from other churches.

Paul asks that "the eyes of their hearts" be illumined so that they know three things: 1) the common hope to which all Christians have been called, 2) the riches of the one Christian inheritance of which we are all heirs, 3) the incomparable power of God at work among all, the same power that God showed in raising Christ from the dead and in making him the source of all wholeness and unity. Our heart - that intuitive faculty of perceiving that transcends rational thought, and by grace attains to wisdom – has eyes to see, but usually so dimly that we fail to recognize the bases for unity among us. With Paul, should we not be praying that God enlightens the minds of all

Christians to know the one hope to which we have been called, the common inheritance of Christian faith and life in which we variously share, to bring us into unity and fullness in Christ? Perhaps one of the reasons why we seem to make so little progress on the path toward this full, visible Christian unity is that we do not have enough confidence in this "spiritual" side of ecumenism.

**Discussion questions.**

1. Failing to pray regularly for Christian unity, or limiting our prayers to the annual Unity Week, would seem to indicate a lack of deep commitment on the part of our Churches. Should a prayer for Christian unity be incorporated into every worship service?
2. What are some of the specific elements of faith and love that you find in other churches for which you want to thank God?
3. How would you describe the common hope to which all Christians are called? What is your hope?

## 2. Joining together to build God's temple (Ephesians 2: 11-22)

11 Remember that formerly you who are Gentiles by birth and called "uncircumcised" by those who call themselves "the circumcision" (that done in the body by the hands of men), 12 at that time you were separate from Christ, excluded from citizenship in Israel and foreigners to the covenants of the promise, without hope and without God in the world. 13 But now in Christ Jesus you who once were far away have been brought near through the blood of Christ.

14 For he himself is our peace, who has made the two one and has destroyed the barrier, the dividing wall of hostility, 15 by abolishing in his flesh the law with its commandments and regulations. His purpose was to create in himself one new man out of the two, thus making peace, 16 and in this one body to reconcile both of them to God through the cross, by which he put to death their hostility. 17 He came and preached peace to you who were far away and peace to those who were near. 18 For through him we both have access to the Father by one Spirit. 19 Consequently, you are no longer foreigners and aliens, but fellow citizens with God's people and members of God's household, 20 built on the foundation of the apostles and prophets, with Christ Jesus himself as the chief cornerstone. 21 In him the whole building is joined together and rises to become a holy temple in the Lord. 22 And in him you too are being built together to become a dwelling in which God lives by his Spirit.

### Study guide Ephesians 2: 11-22

It is perhaps the final verse of this passage that expresses the direction in which Paul's discourse is leading. In Christ, we are all being built together to become a dwelling in which God lives by His Spirit. The image is one of God building a house where God intends to dwell and be glorified through the Spirit. Clearly, the work of unity is God's own project, not something that we Christians have thought up on our own.

God has already brought us a long way along this path. We are the ones that the Jews, whom God had chosen to be His people, used to refer to as the uncircumcized, the "unchosen," the outsiders. Paul saw our "former" state as a sorry one in which we lacked every blessing by which the Jews could be distinguished: we were distant from Christ; we did not have the rights and privileges of citizens, but were merely tolerated as resident aliens; we were outside the promises God made to Abraham and his descendants; we did not share the hope of the Jews for a Messiah, and we were living in this world without God. There was bound to be hostility between those who had been given so much and those who were lacking so much.

But "now", in Christ, God has changed all that. First of all, Christ, embodying the Divine Word, preached the same message to those who were distant and to those who were near. Then, in Christ's death on the cross, God once and for all broke down the wall of hostility and made peace by making one new person for whom the old distinctions are irrelevant. By the Spirit we all have one Father and we all have direct access to that Father. We "outsiders" have now become insiders, members of God's own household, free to come and go as we please, with intimate access to God, the master of the house.

In this way Paul comes to his central image, that of God as a master contractor, building a temple for Himself of which we are the building blocks. If we magnify this image to try to see the project that God is engaged in right now, we see a great construction site, with our individual Christian communities and churches as the pre-fabricated parts that God is seeking to join together to build a temple dedicated to His own praise and glory. Each of our communities has its own unique qualities, its own gifts, to contribute to this project. We can either choose to take part enthusiastically in this building project of God, or else we can resist it and try to remain as isolated, useless, unused building blocks.

Christian unity is not something that we dreamt up for our own ends, but rather an integral part of God's plan of salvation. It is a participation in God's building of a holy temple for Himself; a project aimed at giving praise and glory to God. Should not we, who started out so far off and alien to God's activities, be grateful and enthusiastic about being "joined together and rising to become a holy temple in the Lord"?

**Discussion questions.**

1. What are some of the gifts with which God has blessed your church for the building of the one ecumenical Temple?

2. What are some of the spiritual gifts you have discovered in other churches that you feel are making important additions to the construction of the Lord's temple?
3. When our efforts at unity seem to stall and go nowhere, we forget that God is directing this project and taking initiatives, and that we are either co-operating or not as the case may be. What are some of the efforts at unity around the world that you feel can inspire and encourage others?

### 3. Growing to maturity in Christ (Ephesians 4: 1-6, 11-16)

1 As a prisoner for the Lord, then, I urge you to live a life worthy of the calling
you have received. 2 Be completely humble and gentle; be patient, bearing with
one another in love. 3 Make every effort to keep the unity of the Spirit through the
bond of peace. 4 There is one body and one Spirit—just as you were called to one
hope when you were called—5 one Lord, one faith, one baptism; 6 one God and
Father of all, who is over all and through all and in all. 11 It was he who gave
some to be apostles, some to be prophets, some to be evangelists, and some to be
pastors and teachers, 12 to prepare God's people for works of service, so that the
body of Christ may be built up 13 until we all reach unity in the faith and in the
knowledge of the Son of God and become mature, attaining to the whole measure
of the fullness of Christ. 14 Then we will no longer be infants, tossed back and
forth by the waves, and blown here and there by every wind of teaching and by
the cunning and craftiness of men in their deceitful scheming. 15 Instead,
speaking the truth in love, we will in all things grow up into him who is the Head,
that is, Christ. 16 From him the whole body, joined and held together by every
supporting ligament, grows and builds itself up in love, as each part does its work.

### Study guide Ephesians 4: 1-5, 11-16

In this passage St. Paul offers three ways that all of us can work for the unity that Christ desired for His disciples. The first is by actually living our Christian vocation in a way that is worthy of that call. When we act toward other Christians – and toward other Christian churches – with complete humility and gentleness, we make it easier for others to act that way toward us, and thus we bring Christian unity a step closer. Acting patiently when confronted with our own failings as well as those of others, and bearing with one another in love, especially at times of ecclesiastical crisis or on the occasion of hurtful statements, helps us all to maintain the bond of peace which the Spirit offers us.

Secondly, while not denying the real differences that exist, Paul invites us to reflect on what we have in common and proposes seven grounds for unity. 1) We form *one body*. There is only one body, one church of Christ, in which we all participate. By working for unity we seek to make visible the unity that Christ has already established among us. 2) There is *one Spirit* who is animating every Christian community. When we thank God for the faith and goodness we find in others, we are praising the Spirit that has produced that good. 3) We share a common *hope*. Christians profess a common goal. We all cry out "Come, Lord Jesus!" and we are all praying and working for the establishment of God's reign. 4) We all profess *one Lord* and Saviour, Jesus Christ. Since Christ is one, how can we allow ourselves to present such a divided witness to the world? Should we not repent of the scandal caused by our disunity? 5) We have *one faith,* a common appreciation of what God has accomplished and continues to accomplish in Christ Jesus. Even though our doctrinal formulations often differ, we are invited to go deeper, to explore the common faith that unites us. 6) We profess *one baptism*, the common experience of dying and rising with Christ, an experience that transcends disputes over baptismal formulae and rituals. Recognizing one another's baptism is an important step toward unity.

7) Most importantly, we acknowledge *one God and Father*. Just as our master, Jesus, was consumed with a desire to do the will of his Father, so also our churches exist to do the will of God. As there is One God, who is *over all*; so all our churches must stand before God in judgment and accept responsibility for how they have carried out their mission. We profess one God who works *through all*. Every church is called to be an instrument of God's grace. Seeing sister churches as God's instruments, through which God is working to reconcile the world to Himself in Christ, is also progress toward unity. We are conscious of the one God who is *in all*. An awareness of God's silent, loving presence in every Christian community will make us approach other confessions with the reverence they deserve.

A third step to attain unity is to reflect on the gifts that God has lavished on the various churches. While all confessions desire to embody the fullness of God's grace, each communion displays specific blessings. Some may emphasize their faithfulness to the apostolic message, others excel in communicating the prophetic message, still others stress evangelism, pastoral service, or teaching the faith. Recognizing that God has given these gifts, not for the glory and pride of any church, but rather for the building up of the one body of Christ in unity, is a mark of maturity. It is clear that for Paul, unity is a mark of maturity for the churches; disunity is evidence of a lingering immaturity. We will achieve mature unity by focusing always on Christ rather than being distracted by transient disputes. By "speaking the truth in love, we will in all things grow up into him who is the Head, that is, Christ."

### Discussion questions.

1. How many of our divisions and tensions can be traced back to a failure to act toward one another with humility and gentleness, to a lack of patience and love for one another? How can a humble and gentle

approach to doctrinal and organizational issues transform the discourse?

2. As we reflect on the grounds for unity offered by Paul (one body, Spirit, hope, Lord, faith, baptism, God and Father), do we agree that unity is different from uniformity? Can there be a true unity with a legitimate diversity?
3. Do you agree that growing toward greater unity is a sign of our churches' growing in maturity? Can we look forward to a day on earth when we will be more united and "attain to the whole measure of the fullness of Christ"?

*One of the Bible study groups*

## FROM THE PLENARY SESSIONS
## TRIBUTE TO DR. GEORGE VANDERVELDE

# Mgr John A Radano

*Mgr. John Radano was on the staff of the Pontifical Council for Promoting Christian Unity and was a member of the Committee on the Global Christian Forum until his retirement in 2008.*

Over the last decade, many persons have worked to develop the Global Christian Forum.

One person who worked hard on behalf of this forum process, but who is not here today at this important event, is Dr. George Vandervelde, a member of the Toronto Institute of Theology and of the Theological Commission of the World Evangelical Alliance.

For years George was a member of the Continuation Committee of the Global Christian Forum, and was very deeply committed to the development of the Forum. He participated in the planning meeting which the Continuation Committee held last November, 2006, in the Netherlands, which took decisive steps toward this global assembly in Limuru. But within two months of that meeting, after contracting a serious illness, he died in January, 2007. It was a great shock to all of us on the Committee.

I knew and worked with George for many years. I knew him in different settings. In 1990, he and I were part of a small planning committee representing the World Evangelical Fellowship (now Alliance) and the Pontifical Council For Promoting Christian Unity, of the Catholic Church, which worked toward establishing international dialogues between that Alliance and the Catholic Church. We both served on those committees which met from 1993-2002, and produced a report entitled *Church, Evangelization and the Bonds of Koinonia* published in 2003, which has been well received.

George was one of the fraternal delegates, representing the Canadian Council of Churches, participating in the 1998 Assembly of the Synod of Bishops in Rome, which focused on the region of America. When he arrived I recall bringing him into the Synod Hall in the Vatican, in which more than 200 Bishops were taking part where like the other fraternal delegates he was warmly greeted by Pope John Paul II. He enjoyed participating in that Synod.

A few years ago, Dr. Vandervelde took a leading role when his church, the Christian Reformed Church in North America, after dialogue with Catholic theologians representing the Bishops Conferences of Canada and the United States, made a statement acknowledging that Question and Answer 80 of the

Heidelberg Catechism, an important confessional standard, criticized a description of the Catholic mass which was inaccurate. When presenting that church's acknowledgement of the problem, I remember George saying, "we cannot confess what is not true."

But most of all, we need to remember George today for the contribution he made to helping this meeting of the Global Christian Forum come about. Perhaps we can do that best by concluding with a prayer.

Let us pray.

> Lord, we give thanks for the life and witness of George Vandervelde. We give thanks for his ecumenical vision, for his constant efforts to promote reconciliation between Evangelicals and Catholics. We give thanks for his efforts to promote mutual understanding, to break down the walls of hostility, and to promote healing over time. We give thanks for his commitment to the success of this Global Christian Forum.
>
> We remember him today, and ask you to bless his family.
>
> We ask all this in the name of Jesus Christ Our Lord, Amen.

ARCHBISHOP
OF CANTERBURY

November 2007

Message for the Global Christian Forum – Nairobi 2007

It gives me great pleasure to send you my warmest greetings and encouragement as you meet together in Nairobi for the Global Christian Forum.

The creation of this space of encounter for the broad range of churches encompassed by the Global Christian Forum is a significant and timely initiative. The call to unity and common witness requires us to develop new conversations as well as to build on the fellowship we already enjoy. In your encounters, may you discover fresh insights into how we can each be caught up into the reconciling love of Jesus, through whom "God has reconciled us to himself" (2 Corinthians 5 v18). I pray this will bear fruit in the deepening of our shared life in Christ and its outworking in imaginative co-operation in the years ahead.

+ Rowan Cantuar.

Lambeth Palace, London SE1 7JU

مجلس كنائس الشرق الأوسط

The Middle East Council of Churches

**Greetings Message to the Global Christian Forum in Nairobi**

We greet your meeting today united in our faith in Jesus Christ, our Lord and Saviour. You are meeting to renew the efforts to fulfil our common calling to give glory to our one God, the Father, Son and Holy Spirit. We applaud your standing together to strengthen the existing fellowship among our churches and the different associations, and to foster the bonds of co-operation among our people.

Since its founding, the Middle East Council of Churches (MECC) is committed to strengthen a sense of unity, confidence, continuity and purpose within the fellowship of its member churches. The MECC encourages its member churches to support and uphold each other as they help their people understand their faith and witness. Within the MECC, Christian dialogue takes place on all levels, from the pastoral grassroots to academic halls, from formal dialogue among church leaders to the day-to-day fellowship among Christians on the street. With greater maturity, they respond to the demands of their faith and witness.

If we look deeply at the situation in the Middle East region we see the many problems Christians face today. There are problems that make them feel worried, anxious about their future and the future of their children. We must stabilize the Christian presence in this region. We must find effective means for strengthening Christians to sustain themselves in these lands where they belong, where the Church was born, and in which they have the calling to proclaim God's grace and love.

Our readiness to engage in dialogue among ourselves must expand to encompass all human beings, seeking to appreciate in their spirituality the work of the Holy Spirit. In our region this priority focuses particularly on the Muslims in the full confidence that our Christian presence in society is given by God. In this regard, the MECC is developing and strengthening a systematic dialogue aimed at achieving mutual understanding for consolidating peace and creating good relations between people, for the benefit of humanity.

However, it is vital that the Christians of the Middle East revitalize their own cultural role that has characterized their modern history. It is no exaggeration to say that Christians of the Middle East are indispensable to a democratic and pluralistice Arab world. Thus, their presence is as important to the outside world as to their own fellow citizens.

Therefore, I hope these few days of the Forum will be the time to work for fellowship. Christians worldwide should remember that in ancient times, churches were founded in our region. MECC and the churches worldwide must be sensitive to current changes in the region, and be responsive to the changes and needs that affect and relate to Middle Eastern Christians.

May God Almighty bless your objectives and your good intentions, and may He grant you good health and peace.

Gurigis Ibrahim Saleh
General Secretary
The Middle East Council of Churches

November 6, 2007

*A break in the garden at the conference centre*

*A celebration of the African instituted churches*

# CHAPTER 4

## OUTCOME

*The purpose of the Limuru gathering was essentially to test out the Forum proposal with a large and representative group and, if it was well received, to provide some guidance for the future. The two documents that embody the results of the event in writing and that are presented here respond fully to these expectations. In the process, the text that had served as a* Provisional Purpose Statement *of the Forum since 2002 was affirmed as the* Guiding Purpose Statement *and included with the Proposals for the Future.*

## MESSAGE FROM THE GLOBAL CHRISTIAN FORUM TO BROTHERS AND SISTERS IN CHRIST THROUGHOUT THE WORLD

*"Our Journey with Jesus Christ, the Reconciler"*

Greetings to all those who call on the name of Jesus Christ as Lord!

As a wide variety of Christian leaders, men and women coming from 72 nations and six continents, from a broad range of churches, confessions and organizations, we rejoice for the unprecedented opportunity we have enjoyed in Limuru, Kenya, from 6th to 9th November, 2007. We, the 245 participants, have reflected on our journeys with Jesus Christ the Reconciler. We have been challenged in our time of Bible study to reflect on the words of the Apostle Paul: no longer to be aliens to one another, but "citizens with the saints and also members of the household of God... In whom you are also built together spiritually into a dwelling place for God" (Eph. 2:19-22).

For nearly a decade a compelling vision has empowered the Global Christian Forum process, whose participants have yearned to bring together church leaders and other Christians from all the families and traditions that lay claim to faith in Christ as saviour and Lord. This vision has also reflected the dramatic shift in the shape of Christianity in the 21st century, which is growing so rapidly in the global south. Representatives of the historic Protestant Churches, the Catholic Church, the Orthodox Churches, the Pentecostal Churches, the broader Evangelical movement and other Christian Churches and communities have discerned the need to be brought into relationship with one another for the sake of bearing witness to the Gospel. In regional meetings held in North America (2002), Asia (2004), Africa (2005), Europe (2006) and Latin American (2007), this vision has found strong affirmation. Now here in Limuru we have experienced an historic breakthrough by gathering globally as never before.

We give praise to the Father our Creator, to Christ our Reconciler and to the Holy Spirit our Comforter for the gracious emergence of the Global Christian

Forum. This process has encouraged us to develop a new awareness and understanding of one another, and to recognise that God is graciously working among us.

We have been invited to a common journey of faith with confidence under the guidance of Christ's life-giving Spirit. We have been encouraged to move out of the familiar ground on which we normally stand, to meet each other on a common ground where mutual trust might flourish and where we might be empowered to celebrate, enter into dialogue and act together to the glory of the Father, Son and Holy Spirit.

Our desire has been to create an open space wherein the representatives, from a broad range of Christian communities and inter-church organisations, who confess the triune God and Jesus as perfect in His divinity and perfect in His humanity, can gather together to foster mutual respect and to address common challenges.

We began by sharing personal testimonies of our encounters with Christ, and were enriched by a forum within which we could express our faith out of our respective confessional traditions and reflect on what it might mean to walk together in obedience to Christ. We acknowledge that we have differing views on substantive issues such as ecclesiology, the scope of evangelism and mission. Here a new beginning was made for encounter and dialogue.

Enjoying times of prayer, fellowship and Bible study, we participants have also discussed the challenges and opportunities we have in sharing the Gospel and in pursuing justice, loving mercy and walking humbly with God (cf. Micah 6:8). We have shared our experience of what God is doing in our churches and organisations, and how we participate in God's mission in the world by witnessing to the Good News of Jesus Christ in word and deed. We seek to show our love of God by also loving our neighbours (cf. Mat. 22:37-39), and working for the transformation of our societies in accordance with the example of Jesus and the truths of Scripture. We join with all people of good will in the pursuit of justice, peace and the care of God's creation.

We thank God for the unique breadth of this gathering, and for the opportunity it gave us to meet in an atmosphere of trust and openness in which we could acknowledge and repent of past failings to bear with one another in love. We acknowledge that we have often allowed prejudices to shape our understanding of different Christian traditions, and we welcome the opportunity as God's adopted children to encounter one another and to explore together the forgiveness and redemption found in Christ (cf. Eph. 1:5).

As Christians within our various traditions, we affirm the importance of being together to reflect upon the prayer of our Lord that those who believe in Him may all be one, so that the world may believe that God sent Him (cf. John 17:21). Recognizing that unity is first and foremost God's gift through the work of the Holy Spirit, our commitment is to press on in promoting ever greater understanding and co-operation among Christians, while respecting the diversity of our identities, traditions and individual gifts (cf. 1 Cor. 12). In so doing, we build on the basis of many ecumenical, inter-confessional and other historic initiatives to overcome divisions in the Christian family. We do not seek to replace these efforts.

The process of the Global Christian Forum, affirmed during these days in Limuru, must now continue. We will pray for one another and work to convene local and regional events, as well as other global encounters, in order to pursue this journey toward the goal of reconciliation.

Therefore, we call on all those who confess God as Father, Son and Holy Spirit, to raise their hearts with ours in the hope that all of humanity may come to know the fullness of life in Christ (cf. Mat. 28:19-20, Col. 2:10). We invite all brothers and sisters in the Lord to engage within their own settings the rich resources of the Global Christian Forum process in journeying together with Jesus Christ, who is the great Reconciler and the Hope of all ages.

"Now to Him who by the power at work within us is able to accomplish abundantly far more than all we can ask or imagine, to Him be glory in the church and in Christ Jesus to all generations, forever and ever. Amen." (Eph. 3:20-21).

Limuru, 9th November, 2007

**Churches, Church Families and organizations participating in the Global Christian Forum**

African Instituted Churches
Anglican
Baptist
Catholic
Churches of Christ
Disciples of Christ
Society of Friends
Holiness
Lutheran
Mennonite
Methodist
Moravian
Old-Catholic
Orthodox - Eastern
Orthodox – Oriental
Other Evangelical
Pentecostal (Assemblies of God, Church of God and others)
Reformed
The Salvation Army
Seventh Day Adventist
United and Uniting Churches

African Theological Fellowship
Campus Missions International
Christian Aid UK/Ireland
Conference of Secretaries of Christian World Communions
Edinburgh 2010
Forum Type Organizations
International Charismatic Consultation
International Fellowship of Evangelical Students
Lausanne Committee for World Evangelization
Organization of African Instituted Churches
Oxford Centre for Mission Studies
Pentecostal World Fellowship
Regional and National Ecumenical Organizations
United Bible Societies
World Council of Churches
World Evangelical Alliance
World Student Christian Federation
World Vision International
World Young Women Christian Association

A full list of participants can be found at www.globalchristianforum.org

Note: All Scripture quotations are from the NRSV translation.

*The message drafting committee*

# Outcome

## Proposals for the Future of the Global Christian Forum

The meeting affirmed the Guiding Purpose of the Global Christian Forum:

> To create an open space wherein representatives from a broad range of Christian churches and inter-church organizations, which confess the triune God and Jesus Christ as perfect in His divinity and humanity, can gather to foster mutual respect, to explore and address together common challenges.

In addition the Limuru meeting offered the following proposals to guide the further work of the Global Christian Forum Committee:

The meeting

1) affirmed the value of the Forum as an open space for developing new relationships and continuing conversations, and identifying common concerns, recognising that any resulting joint actions will be worked out through the participating churches and organisations
2) affirmed the need for the Forum to sustain its intentional commitment to gathering the largest possible representation of the Christian Churches worldwide around the table
3) affirmed that the Forum continue to be based on committed participation, rather than being a membership organization
4) proposed that the Forum process should continue to broaden and deepen the circle of participation (in terms of the numbers of individuals concerned, the breadth and inclusivity of constituencies, and with particular attention to under-represented groups, including women, youth, indigenous peoples and the physically challenged)
5) proposed that, to this end, the Forum should continue with the lightest structure possible, for example through a small secretariat at least at the current level,
6) requested participating church bodies to assume financial responsibility, as able, for this structure, and for the Forum
7) supported the GCF Committee in its efforts to establish a broad and sustainable financial basis for the Forum

In addition, the meeting

8) requested the GCF Committee to ensure a thorough evaluation is made of the Forum process after Limuru
9) proposed the GCF Committee facilitate a representative consultation to review the evaluation of the Forum process, and then reflect further on the future of the Forum
10) proposed that, in the light of these, the GCF Committee may facilitate further the Forum process and inter-church engagement at regional, national and local levels, as well as at the global level, and will encourage developments that promote the goals of the Forum at the regional and local level and within various traditions
11) proposed that the GCF Committee engage in dialogue with the church families and bodies represented in Limuru over the appointment of a new committee, ensuring both some measure of continuity and broad and inclusive representation

**Global Christian Forum: Guiding Purpose Statement**

To create an open space wherein representatives from a broad range of Christian churches and inter-church organizations, which confess the triune God and Jesus Christ as perfect in His divinity and humanity, can gather to foster mutual respect, to explore and address together common challenges.

In the spirit of John 17:21 " that all of them may be one … so that the world may believe that you have sent me" and because of our faith in a reconciling God (2 Cor.5: 18-21) a forum could pursue the following:

- Deepen our commitment to God's Word and mission in the world;
- Enhance our understanding of contemporary expressions of Christian mission;
- Pursue principles and practices that enable us to deal freely, responsibly and peaceably with our Christian differences and distinctive qualities;
- Engage in theological reflection in areas of mutual concern;
- Strengthen the wholeness of the church by encouraging communication and co-operation; and
- Foster relationships that may lead to common witness.

Limuru, November 2007

Explanatory note: This document was developed through discussions between leaders of the Orthodox Churches, the Pontifical Council for Promoting Christian Unity, the Evangelical and Pentecostal Movements, the World

Council of Churches and the Conference of Secretaries of Christian World Communions, and affirmed at the meeting of the Global Christian Forum, in Limuru from 6th to 9th November, 2007.

The Guiding Purpose Statement above repeats the language of the Provisional Purpose Statement adopted in Pasadena in 2002.

*The Kenyan opening celebration of the Limuru gathering*

*Lunch on the lawn*

*The cooks at work*

# CHAPTER 5

## CONFERENCE MATERIAL
## PROPOSED PROGRAMME

**<u>Tuesday 6 November</u>**
**Introduction to the Global Christian Forum**

First morning session

Brief welcome and introduction of the members of the Continuation Committee
Greetings
Morning prayers (led by the Local Committee)
Introduction to the Global Christian Forum (by Dr. Cecil M. Robeck, member of the Continuation Committee)
Brief presentation of the programme

Second morning session
Groups of 30 – Introduction to sharing of faith journeys and faith communities[1]
Sharing of faith journeys by the participants

First afternoon session
Groups of 30 – sharing of faith journeys by the participants

Second afternoon session
Finishing the sharing of faith journeys in groups if necessary
Plenary – Feedback from the groups
Greetings
*Words of Encouragement* – Dr. Samuel Kobia
Evening prayers (Lutheran tradition)

Evening – free

**<u>Wednesday 7 November</u>**
**Sharing our Discernment of what God is doing in our Churches and Organizations**

First morning session
Bible study in groups of 15
Plenary - morning prayers (Catholic tradition)
Presentation on *Discerning What God is Doing in OurChurches and Organizations*, by Dr. Wonsuk Ma[2]

---

[1] In the groups, facilitated by a member of the Continuation Committee and a participant who has had the experience at a previous meeting of the GCF.

Discussion
Second morning session
Panel presentation on progress of the Global Christian Forum process, highlighting results from the regional meetings and other examples.
Discussion

First afternoon session
Groups of 30 – discussion on the theme of the day

Second afternoon session
Groups of 30 – discussion continued
Plenary – Feedback from the groups

Evening prayers (Evangelical tradition)

Evening session
Meetings by regions; one group on global perspectives

**Thursday 8 November**
**Sharing our Discernment of our Place in God's Mission in the World**

First morning session
Bible study in groups of 15
Plenary - morning prayers (Pentecostal tradition)
Presentation on *New Developments and Trends in World Christianity*, by Dr. Cheryl Johns[3]
Discussion

Second morning session
Panel presentation on *Visions and Expectations of the Global Christian Forum,* by leaders of the main Christian traditions and global organizations
Discussion

First afternoon session
Groups of 30 – discussion on the theme of the day

Second afternoon session
Groups of 30 – discussion continued
Plenary – Feedback from the groups
First reading of the Letter to the Churches
Evening prayers (Orthodox tradition)

Evening sessions

---

[2] Director of the Oxford Centre for Mission Studies, UK/ Korea
[3] Professor at the Theological Seminary of the Church of God (Cleveland), USA

Meeting by traditions

**Friday 9 November**

**The Way Ahead**

First morning session

Bible study in groups of 15

Plenary - morning prayers (Anglican tradition)

Input by the group of leaders of the main Christian traditions and global organizations on the future of the Global Christian Forum

Discussion

Second morning session

Groups of 30 – discussion on the proposals for the future, guided by two questions:

how can we discern the Spirit leading us to overcome divisions and enter into new and broader relationships?

how can the Forum process can be taken forward globally, regionally, nationally and locally?

First afternoon session

Groups of 30 – discussion continued

Plenary – Feedback from the groups

Approval of the Letter to the Churches

Final Conclusions

Second afternoon session

Closing celebration

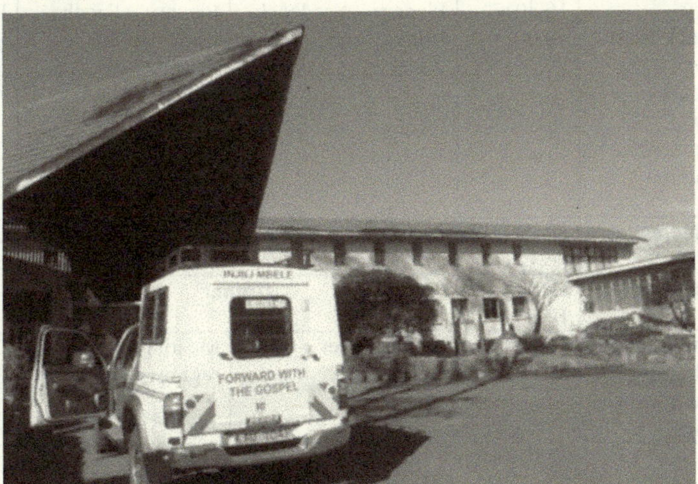


*The Jumuia Conference and Country Home*

# Conference Material
# Programme Schedule

| Time | Tuesday 6 November | Time | Wednesday 7 November | Thursday 8 November | Friday 9 November |
|---|---|---|---|---|---|
| 09.00 – 11.00 | Opening – Welcome<br>Greetings<br>Opening prayers<br>Introduction to GCF<br>Programme of the meeting | 08.30 – 09.00 | Bible study | Bibly study | Bible study |
| | | 09.00 – 09.30 | Morning prayer | Morning prayer | Morning prayer |
| | | 09.30 – 10.30 | Plenary – *Discerning what God is doing in our Churches and Organizations*<br>Dr. Wonsuk Ma | Plenary – *The Reconciling Mission of the Global Church*<br>Dr. Cheryl Johns | Plenary – *Proposals for the future of the Forum* |
| 11.00 – 11.30 | **Break** | 10.30 – 11.00 | | **Break** | |
| 11.30 – 13.00 | Groups of 30 – Introduction – Sharing of Faith Journeys | 11.00 – 12.30 | Plenary – *The Forum process ; the regional consultations ; other examples* | Plenary – *Visions and expectations of the Forum* | Groups of 30 – the future of the Forum |
| 13.00 – 14.30 | **Lunch** | 12.30 – 14.00 | | **Lunch** | |
| 14.30 – 16.30 | Groups of 30 Sharing of Faith Journeys | 14.00 – 16.00 | Groups of 30 – theme of the day | Groups of 30 – theme of the day | Groups of 30 – the future of the Forum |
| 16.30 – 17.00 | **Break** | 16.00 – 16.30 | | **Break** | |
| 17.00 – 18.30 | Plenary – Feedback from groups<br>Greetings<br>*Words of Encouragement*<br>Dr. Samuel Kobia | 16.30 – 18.00 | Plenary – Feedback from groups | Plenary – Feedback from groups<br>First reading of a Letter to the Churches | Plenary – Feedback from groups<br>Approval of Letter to the Churches<br>Final Conclusions |
| 18.30 – 18.45 | Evening prayer | 18.00 – 18.15 | Evening prayer | | Closing celebration |
| 19.00 | **Dinner** | 18.30 – 19.30 | **Dinner** | | |
| 19.45 | Departure of those being housed in nearby facilities | 19.30 – 20.30 | Meetings per tradition | Meetings per region | **Dinner** |

# CONFERENCE MATERIAL
# LIST OF PARTICIPANTS

The participants at the Limuru gathering had at their disposal a list by groupings according to the church, church family, organisation or movement under which they were invited (some represented more than one). They also received an alphabetical list. For the purpose of this book the list by groupings is reproduced here, with some slight modifications. The advantage is that it illustrates clearly the composition of the gathering and the breadth of the range of Christian traditions present, which would be much less visible if it were in alphabetical order by names of participants. On the other hand, this format has some limitations which should be acknowledged. The designations of the groupings do not all refer to comparable realities and some participants had an affinity with more than one grouping. This lack of tidiness is in itself a given and an integral part of what the Global Christian Forum is all about.

Note: Where two countries are listed the second is the country of residence.

| CHURCH / ORGANIZATION | NAME OF REPRESENTATIVE | COUNTRY |
|---|---|---|
| **African Instituted Churches** | | |
| Organisation of African Instituted Churches - OAIC | Rev. Nicta Lubaale | Uganda / Kenya |
| OAIC / Christ Holy Church | Most Rev. Daniel Okoh | Nigeria |
| Church of the Lord (Aladura) Worldwide | Archbishop Dr. Rufus Ositelu | Nigeria |
| Church of the Lord (Aladura) Worldwide | Venerable David A. Fabusoro | Nigeria / UK |
| OAIC / Kimbanguist Church | Rev. Zeyi Ndingambote | Dem. Rep. of Congo |
| OAIC / Africa Israel Church Nineveh | Archbishop John Mweresa Kivuli II | Kenya |
| Divine Healer's Church | Rev. John Okai Adjetey | Ghana |
| **Anglican** | | |
| Representative of the Archbishop of Canterbury / Church of England | Rt. Rev. David J.L. Hawkins | UK |
| The Anglican Communion – AC | Rev. Canon Gregory Cameron | UK |
| AC / Anglican Church of Kenya | Bishop J. Kanuku | Kenya |
| AC / Anglican Church of Canada | Rt. Rev. Victoria Matthews | Canada |
| AC / Anglican Church of Central America | Rt. Rev. Julio E. Murray T. | Panama |
| AC / Church of North India | Bishop Dhirendra Kamur Sahu | India |
| AC / St Paul's University | Rev. Anya Damary | Kenya |
| AC / St Paul's University | Rev. Joseph Wandera | Kenya |

| | | |
|---|---|---|
| AC / Council of Anglican Provinces of Africa | Rev. Joyce Kariuki | Kenya |
| **Baptist** | | |
| Baptist World Alliance – BWA | Dr. Denton Lotz | USA |
| BWA | Dr. Neville Callam | Jamaica |
| BWA | Rev. Dr. Fausto Vasconcelos | Brazil / USA |
| BWA / Caribbean Baptist Fellowship | Rev. Peter E. Pinder | Bahamas |
| BWA / Union Evangelical Christians-Baptists Russia | Rev. Vitaly Vlasenko and Mrs. Vlasenko | Russia |
| BWA / Union of Evangelical Free Churches Germany | Rev. Regina Claas | Germany |
| BWA / Baptist Union of Great Britain | Rev. Dr. Kate Coleman | UK |
| BWA / Asia Pacific Baptist Federation | Rev. Pushehu Bonny Resu | India |
| **Catholic Church** | | |
| Pontifical Council for Promoting Christian Unity – PCPCU | Bishop Brian Farrell | Ireland / Vatican |
| PCPCU | Mgr. John Radano | USA / Vatican |
| Symposium of Episcopal Conferences of Africa & Madagascar - SECAM | Most Rev. Theodore Adrien Sarr | Senegal |
| SECAM | Rev. Fr. François-Xavier Damiba | Burkina Faso / Ghana |
| SECAM /Kenyan Episcopal Conference Commission for Ecumenism | Rt. Rev. Philippe Anyolo | Kenya |
| Federation of Asian Bishops' Conferences - FABC | Archbishop Orlando B. Quevedo | Philippines |
| FABC | Archbishop Fernando R.Capalla | Philippines |
| FABC | Rev. Fr. Thomas Michel | USA/Vatican |
| FABC | Sister Dr. Clemens Mendoca | India |
| Council of European Episcopal Conferences - CCEE | Mgr. Aldo Giordano | Italy / Switzerland |
| CCEE / Focolare Movement | Ms. Mechtild Grosse-Venhaus | Germany / Kenya |
| Latin American Episcopal Conference - CELAM | Rev. Fr. Crisóforo Dominguez Pedral | Mexico / Colombia |
| CELAM | Bishop Julio Terán Dutari | Ecuador |
| CELAM | Most Rev. Donald James Reece | Antigua & Barbuda |
| United States Conference of Catholic Bishops - USCCB | Bishop Stephen E. Blaire | USA |
| USCCB | Rev. Fr. Ronald G. Roberson | USA |
| USCCB | Rev. Fr. James Massa | USA |
| Kenya Episcopal Conference - | Rev. Fr. Jan Lenssen | Belgium / Kenya |

| | | |
|---|---|---|
| Commission for Ecumenism | | |
| KEC - Commission for Ecumenism | Mr. Cosmas Maythia | Kenya |

**Disciples / Churches of Christ**

| | | |
|---|---|---|
| Disciples Ecumenical Consultative Council - DECC | Rev. Dr. Robert K. Welsh | USA |
| World Convention of Churches of Christ - WCCC | Rev. Jeff Weston | USA |
| DECC / WCCC - Associated Churches of Christ in Zimbabwe | Br. B.J. Mpofu | Zimbabwe |

**Evangelical**

| | | |
|---|---|---|
| World Evangelical Alliance International Council – (IC) | Rev. Ndaba Mazabane | South Africa |
| WEA IC | Dr. Geoff Tunnicliffe | Canada |
| WEA IC – Evangelical Fellowship of Canada | Mr. Bruce Clemenger | Canada |
| WEA IC – Evangelical Fellowship of India | Rev. Dr. Richard Howell | India |
| WEA IC | Mrs. Margaret Jacobs | Australia |
| WEA IC | Rev. Dr. Sang-Bok David Kim | Korea |
| WEA IC | Rev. John O. Smith | Guyana |
| WEA IC – Christian Endeavour Germany | Rev. Rudolf Westerheide | Germany |
| WEA IC – South Pacific Evangelical Alliance | Rev. Walo Ani | Australia |
| WEA International Leadership Team (ILT) – Micah Network | Ms. Jane Furniss | Australia |
| WEA ILT – Evangelical Alliance UK | Rev. Joel Edwards | UK |
| WEA ILT | Rev. Dr. David Parker | Australia |
| WEA ILT | Rev. Eileen Stewart-Rhude | Canada |
| WEA ILT | Mr. Bill Winger | Canada |
| WEA ILT – Integral Alliance | Ms. Fiona Wilson | UK |
| WEA ILT – Association of Evangelicals of Africa | Rev. Dr. Judy W. Mbugua | Kenya |
| WEA ILT – Evangelical Fellowship of Asia | Mr. Godfrey Yogarajah | Sri Lanka |
| WEA ILT – Evangelical Association of the Caribbean | Rev. Dr. Gerald Seale | Barbados |
| WEA ILT – European Evangelical Alliance | Mr. Gordon Showell-Rogers | UK |
| WEA ILT – Forum for Ibero - American Dialogue of Evangelicals | Mr. Alfredo Mora | Costa Rica |
| Federation of Evangelical Churches & Missions in Burkina Faso | Rev. Etienne Bazié | Burkina Faso |

| | | |
|---|---|---|
| Evangelical Churches Fellowship of Ethiopia | Rev. Alemu Shetta | Ethiopia |
| Evangelical Alliance of Kenya | Rev. Willy Mutiso | Kenya |
| African Theological Fellowship | Dr. Watson Omulokoli | Kenya |
| Church of Christ in Nigeria | Rev. Daniel Bitrus | Nigeria |
| Evangelical Church of West Africa | Rev. Anthony Omolewu Farinto | Nigeria |
| Alliance of Evangelical Churches & Missions in Tchad | Rev. Célestin Ngarndeye Bako | Tchad |
| Evangelical Fellowship of Zambia | Bishop Paul E. Mususu | Zambia |
| Evangelical Church of India | Bishop Ezra Sargunam | India |
| Indonesian Evangelical Fellowship | Rev. Dr. Roland Octavanius | Indonesia |
| Laos Evangelical Church | Rev. Dr. Kamphone Kounthapanya | Laos |
| French Evangelical Alliance | Mr. Frédéric Baudin | France |
| Norwegian Council for Mission and Evangelization | Rev. Rolf Ekenes | Norway |
| African and Caribbean Evangelical Alliance | Rev. Katei M. Kirby | UK |
| Latin American Evangelical Fellowship CONELA | Rev. Ricardo Luna | Ecuador / USA |
| South Sea Evangelical Church | Rev. Graham Tom Tohuwepo | Solomon Islands |
| Pacific Islands Evangelical Alliance | Rev. Manu Mafi | Tonga / New Zealand |

**Friends**

| | | |
|---|---|---|
| Friends World Committee for Consultation - FWCC | Ms. Nancy Irving | USA / UK |
| FWCC | Rev. Seth Chayuga | Kenya |

**Holiness**

| | | |
|---|---|---|
| Church of God (Anderson) | Rev. Dr. Donald K. Smith | USA / Kenya |
| Evangelical Church of the Nazarene | Rev. Oscar Medina Guzman | Peru |
| Christian and Missionary Alliance | Dr. Julio Pablo Rosas H. | Peru |
| Miracle Mile Mission/ Korean Evangelical Holiness Church | Mr. Kim Suk-hwan Brian | USA |

**Lutheran**

| | | |
|---|---|---|
| Lutheran World Federation - LWF | Rev. Dr. Ishmael Noko | Zimbabwe / Switzerland |
| LWF / Church of Sweden | Archbishop Anders H. Wejryd | Sweden |
| Church of Sweden | Rev. Christofer Lundgren | Sweden |
| LWF / Evangelical Lutheran Church of Chile | Rev. Dr. Gloria Rojas | Chile |
| LWF / Evangelical Lutheran Church of Zimbabwe | Rev. Dr. Chiropafadzo Moyo | Zimbabwe |

| | | |
|---|---|---|
| LWF / Ethiopian Evangelical Church Mekane Yesus | Rev. Iteffa Gobena | Ethiopia |
| LWF / Evangelical Lutheran Church in Bavaria | Prof. Dr. Joachim Track | Germany |
| Lutheran World Federation | Prof. Dr. Kathryn L. Johnson | USA / Switzerland |
| Church of Norway | Rev. Dr. Olav Fykse Tveit | Norway |
| LWF / Evangelical Lutheran Church in America | Bishop Jessica Crist | USA |
| LWF / Protestant Batak Christian Church | Rev. Dr. Bonar Napitupulu | Indonesia |
| International Lutheran Council - ILC | Rev. Dr. Carlos W. Winterle | Brazil / Kenya |
| **Mennonite** | | |
| Mennonite World Conference - MWC | Dr. Larry Miller | USA / France |
| MWC / Brethren in Christ Church | Bishop Danisa Ndlovu | Zimbabwe |
| MWC / Mennonite Church Colombia | Mrs. Patricia Urueña | Colombia / Ecuador |
| **Methodist** | | |
| World Methodist Council / Uniting Church in Australia | Rev. Prof. Robert Gribben | Australia |
| WMC / Korean Methodist Church | Bishop Shin Kyung Ha | Korea |
| WMC / Korean Methodist Church | Rev. Dr. Won-Jae Lee | Korea |
| WMC / Methodist Church Great Britain | Rev. Peter Sulston | UK |
| United Methodist Church - UMC | Rev. Dr. W. Douglas Mills | USA |
| UMC | Bishop Emilio J.M. de Carvalho | Angola |
| Methodist Church Ghana | Rev. Prof. Asamoah-Gyadu | Ghana |
| **Moravian** | | |
| Moravian Unity Board | Rev. Robert Sawyer | USA |
| **Old-Catholic** | | |
| International Old-Catholic Bishops' Conference | Archbishop Dr. Joris A.O.L. Vercammen | Netherlands |
| **Orthodox - Eastern** | | |
| Ecumenical Patriarchate | H.E. Metropolitan Makarios | Cyprus / Kenya |
| Russian Orthodox Church | Archpriest Vsevelod Chaplin | Russia |
| Russian Orthodox Church | Rev. Fr. Igor Vyzhanov | Russia |
| Church of Greece | Rev. Fr. Gabriel Papanicolaou | Greece |
| Greek Orthodox Patriarchate of Alexandria | H.E. Metropolitan Makarios | Cyprus / Kenya |

| | | |
|---|---|---|
| Orthodox Church in America | Very Rev. Leonid Kishkovsky | USA |
| Polish Autocephalous Orthodox Church | Mr. Jaroslav Charkiewicz | Poland |
| Romanian Orthodox Church | H.G. Bishop Sofronie | Romania |
| **Orthodox - Oriental** | | |
| Armenian Apostolic Church - Holy See of Etchmiadzin | H.G. Bishop Nathan Hovhannisian | Armenia / UK |
| Armenian Apostolic Church - Holy See of Cilicia | H.G. Bishop Nareg Alemezian | Lebanon |
| Coptic Orthodox Church | H.G. Bishop Serapion | Egypt / USA |
| Malankara Orthodox Syrian Church India | Fr. Dr. John Mathews | India |
| Syrian Orthodox Patriarchate of Antioch | H.E. Metropolitan Mar Gregorios | Syria |
| **Pentecostal** | | |
| International Pentecostal Holiness Church | Bishop James D. Legget | USA |
| Church of God in Christ, USA | Ms. Ephah Kondowe | Malawi |
| Pentecostal Assemblies of Canada | Rev. David R. Wells | Canada |
| Church of Pentecost, Ghana | Rev. Bright Senaya | Ghana |
| Ghana Pentecostal Council | Rev. Dr. Michael Tawia-Ransford | Ghana |
| Nairobi Pentecostal Church, Kenya | Rev. Stephen Kapachia | Kenya |
| Association of Pentecostal and Charismatic Churches | Rev. Randriaranaivoravelona | Madagascar |
| Assemblies of God Malawi | Rev. Dr. Lazarus Chakwera | Malawi |
| Apostolic Faith Mission of South Africa | Rev. Dr. Japie J. LaPoorta | South Africa |
| Assemblies of God, South Africa | Dr. Henry Bailey | South Africa |
| Church of God of Prophecy Africa | Bishop Dr. Stephen Masilela | Swaziland |
| Assemblies of God Zambia | Bishop Joshua H.K. Banda | Zambia |
| Zimbabwe Assemblies of God Africa | Rev. Washington Rupapa | Zimbabwe |
| Zimbabwe Assemblies of God Africa | Rev. Edward Christmas | Zimbabwe |
| Indian Pentecostal Church of God | Rev. Dr. K.C. John | India |
| Indonesian Pentecostal Churches Fellowship | Rev. Yesayas Tobing | Indonesia |
| Indonesian Pentecostal Churches Fellowship | Rev. Dr. Muljadi Suleiman | Indonesia |
| Yoido Full Gospel Church - Kenya | Rev. Dr. Ahn Tae-Kyung | Korea / Kenya |
| Calvary International Ministries | Rev. Dr. Prince Guneratnam | Malaysia |
| Assemblies of God, Malaysia | Rev. Dr. Peter Ong | Malaysia |
| Assemblies of God, Pakistan | Rev. Zia Paul | Pakistan |

| | | |
|---|---|---|
| Philippine Assemblies of God | Rev. Dr. Joseph Suico | Philippines |
| Asia Society for Pentecostal Studies | Dr. Julie Ma | Korea / UK |
| Open Bible Standard Churches | Rev. Dr. Kenneth Ragoonath & Mrs. Ragoonath | Trinidad & Tobago |
| Pentecostal Assemblies of the West Indies | Dr. Pat Philip Glasgow | Trinidad & Tobago |
| Church of God, Bulgaria | Bishop Alexander Todorov | Bulgaria |
| Association of Roma Pastors | Rev. Miroslav Atanasov | Bulgaria |
| Union of Evangelical Churches of the Revival | Rev. Daniel Thévenet | France |
| Pentecostal Federation of Italy | Rev. Michele Passaretti | Italy |
| Assemblies of God, Netherlands | Rev. Peter B. Sleebos | Netherlands |
| Pentecostal Movement of Norway | Dr. Terje Hegertun | Norway |
| Church of God in Romania | Rev. Dr. Ioan Tipei | Romania |
| Assemblies of God, Romania | Rev. Dr. Ioan Ceuta | Romania |
| Union of Pentecostal Christians of Evangelical Faith in Russia | Bishop Pavel N. Okara | Russia |
| Union of Pentecostal Christians of Evangelical Faith in Russia | Ms. Vera Okara | Russia |
| Pingst – Pentecostal Movement of Sweden | Rev. Lars-Ivar Nilsson | Sweden |
| New Testament Church of God, UK | Bishop Eric A. Brown | UK |
| Church of God | Bishop Richar Mendoza Vega | Ecuador |
| Theological Institute FIET | Dr. J. Norberto Saracco | Argentina |

**Reformed**

| | | |
|---|---|---|
| World Alliance of Reformed Churches - WARC | Rev. Dr. Setri Nyomi | Ghana / Switzerland |
| Reformed Ecumenical Council - REC | Dr. Richard L. van Houten | USA |
| REC | Rev. Dr. Douwe Visser | Netherlands |
| WARC / Presbyterian Church (USA) | Rev. Dr. Clifton Kirkpatrick | USA |
| WARC / Toraja Church | Rev. Dr. Henriette Hutabarat Lebang | Indonesia |
| WARC / Presbyterian Church of Trinidad &Tobago | Rev. Joy Evelyn Abdul | Trinidad & Tobago |
| WARC / Church of South India | Dr. Pauline Sathiamurthy | India |
| WARC / Independent Presb. Ch. Brazil | Rev. Clayton Leal da Silva | Brazil |
| WARC / Presbyterian Church of East Africa | Rev. Samuel Muriguh Njoroge | Kenya |
| WARC / Presbyterian Church of Ghana | Rev. Herbert Anim Opong | Ghana |
| REC / Reformed Church of East | Rev. Jonathan Kangogo | Kenya |

| | | |
|---|---|---|
| Africa | | |
| Reformed Church in America | Rev. John Ornee | USA |
| **Seventh-day Adventist Church** | | |
| SDA General Conference | Dr. John Graz | Switzerland / USA |
| SDA East Central Africa Division | Dr. John B.D. Kakembo | Kenya |
| SDA General Conference | Dr. William G. Johnson | USA |
| **The Salvation Army** | | |
| Salvation Army International Headquarters | Commissioner Linda Bond | Canada |
| Kenya Territory | Lt.Colonel Kenneth Hodder | Kenya |
| Kenya Territory | Major Tira Mbaja | Kenya |
| **United and Uniting Churches** | | |
| Evangelical Church of Germany | OKR Rev. Jens Nieper | Germany |
| Protestant Church in the Netherlands | Rev. Dr. Bastiaan Plaisier | Netherlands |
| **National Organizations** | | |
| Federation of Protestant Churches in Madagascar | Rev. Edmond Razafimanantsoa | Madagascar |
| Christian Association of Nigeria | Rev. Anthony Farinto | Nigeria |
| National United Christian Forum | Archbishop Vincent M. Concessao | India |
| French Protestant Federation | Rev. Claude Baty | France |
| French Protestant Federation - Churches of African Expression | Mrs. Victoria Kamondji | France |
| Christian Council of Norway | Rev. Ornulf Steen | Norway |
| Christian Council of Sweden | Rev. Sven-Bernhard Fast | Sweden |
| Canadian Council of Churches | Rev. Dr. Karen Hamilton | Canada |
| Christian Churches Together in the USA - CCT | Rev. Dr. Richard L. Hamm | USA |
| CCT - National Baptist Convention USA | Rev. Dr. William Shaw | USA |
| Christian Aid UK/Ireland | Ms. Karimi Kinoti | Kenya |
| **Regional Ecumenical Organizations** | | |
| All Arica Conference of Churches | Rev. Geoffrey Kayigamba | South Africa |
| Christian Conference of Asia | Rev. Dr. Kamphone Kounthapanya | Laos |
| Caribbean Conference of Churches | Mr. Gerard A.J. Granado | Trinidad & Tobago |
| European Conference of Churches | Rev. Dr. Bastiaan Plaisier | Netherlands |

| | | |
|---|---|---|
| Latin American Council of Churches | Rev. Israel Batista | Cuba / Ecuador |
| Middle East Council of Churches | H.G. Bishop Nareg Alemezian | Lebanon |

**International Organisations**

| | | |
|---|---|---|
| Campus Missions International | Rev. Dr. Kim Chung Il John | Korea |
| Edinburgh 2010 | Dr. Daryl Balia | South Africa / UK |
| International Charismatic Consultation - ICC | Mrs. Kim Catherine-Marie Kollins | Germany |
| International Fellowship of Evangelical Students – IFES | Mr. Calisto Odede | Kenya |
| Lausanne Committee for World Evangelization – LCWE | Mr. Gideon Para-Mallam | Nigeria |
| LCWE | Rev. Dr. Judy Mbugua | Kenya |
| Oxford Centre for Mission Studies - OCMS | Rev. Dr. Wonsuk Ma | Korea / UK |
| OCMS | Dr. Damon Wai Kwan So | Hong Kong / UK |
| United Bible Societies – UBS | Dr. Philip H. Towner | UK |
| UBS | Mr. David Ayi Hammond | Togo / Kenya |
| World Council of Churches - WCC | Rev. Dr. Samuel Kobia | Kenya / Switzerland |
| WCC | Rev. Dr. Walter Altmann | Brazil |
| WCC | Rev. Dr. Robina Winbush | USA |
| WCC | Mr. John Taroanui Doom | French Polynesia |
| WCC | Rev. Dr. Martin Robra | Germany / Switzerland |
| World Student Christian Federation – WSCF | Mr. Maxwell Omondi | Kenya |
| World Vision International – WVI | Dr. Valdir Steurnagel | Brazil |
| WVI | Mr. Gordon Roger Gandiya | Zimbabwe |
| World Young Women's Christian Association - YWCA | Rev. Pirjo-Liisa Penttinen | Finland |

**Speakers**

| | | |
|---|---|---|
| Dr. Cheryl Bridges-Johns | Theological Seminary Church of God (Cleveland) | USA |
| Rev. Dr. Wonsuk Ma | Oxford Centre for Mission Studies | Korea / UK |

**Continuation Committee**

| | | |
|---|---|---|
| Rev. Wesley Granberg-Michaelson | World Council of Churches | USA |
| Rev. Fr. Michael Gundiaev | Russian Orthodox Church | Russia / Switzerland |
| Rev. Dr. Sang-Ehil Han | Church of God (Cleveland) | Korea / USA |
| Rev. Dr. Richard Howell | WEA/ Evangelical Fellowship of India | India |
| H.E. Metropolitan Mar Gregorios | Syrian Orthodox Patriarchate of Antioch | Syria |

| | | |
|---|---|---|
| Rev. Dr. Judy W. Mbugua | Association of Evangelicals of Africa | Kenya |
| Mgr. John Radano | Pontifical Council for Promoting Christian Unity | USA / Vatican |
| Dr. Cecil M. Robeck | Pentecostal | USA |
| Rev. Sarah Rowland Jones | Anglican Communion | UK / South Africa |
| Rev. Dr. Fausto Vasconcelos | Baptist World Alliance | Brazil / USA |
| Mr. Huibert van Beek | Global Christian Forum - secretary | Netherlands / Switzerland |

**Local Committee**

| | | |
|---|---|---|
| Rev. Julius Karanja | African Christian Church & Schools | Kenya |
| Mr. Oliver Kisaka | National Council of Churches in Kenya | Kenya |
| Mr. Nelson Makanda | National Council of Churches in Kenya | Kenya |
| Rev. Willy Mutiso | Evangelical Alliance of Kenya | Kenya |
| Rev. John Gichimu | Organisation of African Instituted Churches | Kenya |
| Mrs. Miriam Mnarobi | Association of Evangelicals of Africa | Kenya |
| H.E. Metropolitan Makarios | Greek Orthodox Patriarchate of Alexandria | Cyprus / Kenya |
| Rev. Dr. Judy W. Mbugua | Association of Evangelicals of Africa | Kenya |
| Rev. Geoffrey Kayigamba | All Africa Conference of Churches | Kenya |
| Mr. David Hammond | United Bible Societies Africa Area | Togo / Kenya |
| Rev. Fr. Jan Lenssen | Kenyan Episcopal Conference | Belgium / Kenya |

**Staff Team**

| | | |
|---|---|---|
| Mr. Douglas Chial | Administration | USA / Switzerland |
| Ms. Lona Lupai | Administration | Sudan / Switzerland |
| Mr. Juan Michel | Communication | Argentina / Switzerland |
| Rev. Theo Gill | Communication | USA / Switzerland |
| Ms. Maria McKay | Communication | UK |
| Ms. Christina Fertis | Interpretation | Uruguay / Switzerland |
| Rev.Carlos Sintado | Interpretation | Argentina / Switzerland |

# Part III
# Towards the Future

# CHAPTER 6

## EVALUATIONS

## INTRODUCTION

### Mr. Huibert van Beek

The Limuru gathering requested the Committee on the Global Christian Forum to ensure that a thorough evaluation of the Forum process be made in the period following the global meeting (see point 8, Proposals for the Future, page 120). The Committee understood this to mean that any future planning of the Forum should be preceded by such a review, so that the findings and recommendations of the evaluation would be fully taken into account. It was decided, therefore, that the evaluation should be carried out in the period from March to September 2008 and that a representative consultation would be convened in November 2008 to do future planning (see Proposals for the Future, point 9). The review should cover the Forum process from the very first consultation in August 1998 until the end of 2007 i.e. including the Limuru global gathering.

The Committee was of the opinion that the evaluation should be entrusted to a qualified and experienced research institute, study centre or other agency which should be independent of the Global Christian Forum and the main participating churches and organisations. Some degree of familiarity with world Christianity and inter-church relationships would be an asset. Terms of Reference were established, advice was sought from competent resource persons and approaches were made to a number of institutions.

In response, the Committee received several proposals out of which three were selected for further consideration: the Oxford Centre for Mission Studies (OCMS, Oxford, UK), the Centre for Intercultural Theology, Interreligious Dialogue, Missiology and Ecumenics (Centre IIMO, Utrecht Universtity, The Netherlands) and the International Faculty of Theological Education (FIET, Buenos Aires, Argentina).

The proposals from OCMS and Centre IIMO were similar to a large extent but differed in the sense that OCMS aimed primarily at collecting responses from individual participants in Forum activities, in particular the Limuru gathering, whereas Centre IIMO emphasized the importance of feedback from participating churches and organisations as institutions. The Committee saw this as complementary and, therefore, invited the two Centres to do the evaluation jointly. In doing so it also took into consideration that OCMS has its roots in the evangelical movement while Centre IIMO is more at home in ecumenical circles, which was another enriching aspect. At closer examination it turned out, however, that a joint evaluation presented some considerable practical difficulties. Given the rather tight time-line it was therefore agreed that each Centre would proceed with its own review and would produce its own report.

Because of the specificities of Latin America as a region, and the interest of a regionally based evaluation in addition to the two others, the Committee also accepted the proposal of the FIET Institute to do a review within the Latin American region.

All three evaluating agencies presented their reports within the given time-line. The main parts[1] of these three reports are reproduced hereafter because they provide a comprehensive assessment of the Forum process up to and including the Limuru gathering, and at the same time offer a very important set of directions towards the future of the Global Christian Forum.

[1] Full reports are available on request from the Secretariat of the Global Christian Forum.

# THE GLOBAL CHRISTIAN FORUM 1998-2007, AND BEYOND

## AN EVALUATION REPORT BY OCMS (OXFORD CENTRE FOR MISSION STUDIES)

## CHAPTER 1: INTRODUCTION

In January 2008 OCMS was invited by Global Christian Forum (GCF) to tender for an evaluation of GCF, to be completed by October 2008. A costed proposal was tendered in February, which was accepted alongside another proposal from IIMO, University of Utrecht. It was suggested that we work together, with OCMS as the leading agent, but after due consideration, we agreed that this would not be a sensible use of time and that we would work independently, with IIMO doing two parts of the original proposal (see Appendix Aa) and OCMS doing the rest, {parts 1-4, and 7}. GCF would thus receive two independent reports, by September 30th 2008. The proposal that was submitted is included in Appendix Aa.

Brian Woolnough, a Research Tutor at OCMS, developed, executed and wrote up the evaluation on behalf of OCMS.

### The OCMS Research Evaluation Programme.

The case study evaluation has used a combination of qualitative and quantitative methods.It has sought to answer the questions; What is the GCF? Who is the GCF? How has it been managed? What has it done? Why has it done it? What has it achieved? and What are the possible, and the preferable, ways forward?

Data has been collected from a number of sources.

1. Copies of the GCF papers have been provided by the Secretariat, including minutes of all the Continuation Committee meetings and their membership, reports of the different Consultations, lists of the participants at the Nairobi Forum, various Action Plans, a report of the Story of GCF written by Huibert van Beek, various background papers from early stages of the GCF process, along with a full set of management papers and financial statements for GCF. Huibert van Beek, at the Secretariat, has always provided these background papers, and answers to any specific requests, with enormous efficiency.

Information has also been derived from the book *Global Christian Forum, Transforming Ecumenism* ed. Richard Howell, the GCF publicity brochure *One faith, many voices*, and the GCF website. Other information has been found from reports and comments on GCF on different pages on the web. The story of GCF has been reported in Chapters 2, 3 and 6, and Appendix Ab.

2. The Continuation Committee has been at the heart of GCF throughout its life, and its members are a prime source of personal data about GCF. A qualitative questionnaire was designed and sent to each member of the Continuation Committee to establish their perception and aspirations for GCF. Their responses have been analysed and reported in Chapter 4.

3. The largest GCF gathering, and the culmination of its nine years of existence, was held at Limuru, in Nairobi, at the end of 2007. A second questionnaire was designed, influenced by the responses to the first questionnaire and the information gathered to date and sent to the 236 attendees at this Forum. Their responses have been analysed and reported in Chapter 5.

4. A series of questions was specifically addressed to the Secretariat concerning the Management Structure of GCF; questions relating to the personnel, the structures and office arrangements, and the financial arrangements. These answers have provided the basis for an analysis and evaluation of the management arrangement supporting GCF's programme, which is reported in Chapter 6..

On the basis of the data received and after careful and prayerful deliberation, conclusions have been drawn, (Chapter 7), and recommendations made, (Chapter 8), as to how we believe GCF might best progress. We hope and trust that this evaluation will be useful to GCF as it continues to seek God's will in the future.

# CHAPTER 2: THE STORY OF GCF, SO FAR

### Aim

The aim of this first section was to find out what GCF had done and what it has sought to do - what it's aims and objectives were.

### Sources of Data

This section seeks to obtain a picture of GCF from written and published material. I have the Minutes of all the GCF committee meetings and reports of, and press releases from, each of the GCF regional and global meetings as provided by the GCF secretariat. Huibert van Beek was an excellent, and very prompt, source of very comprehensive records of the work on GCF throughout its existence. Searches have been made of other references to their meetings and influence, especially from the world wide web, and though this has produced some illuminating references from external sources many of the references on the web have been written by those directly involved with GCF itself as members of the Continuation Committees. Helpful information has been found in the printed material available (e.g. the book on *'Global Christian Forum; Transforming Ecumenism'*, edited by Richard Howell, 2007, and the GCF flier *'One face, many voices'*).

### 2.i. The beginnings of GCF and its programme of meetings

The Global Christian Forum grew out of dissatisfaction with the World Council of Churches in the late 1990s in that the WCC was representing only a relatively small part of Christendom. Many Christian traditions, especially the Roman Catholic Church and the growing Pentecostal, Evangelical and new churches in Africa had stayed outside of the WCC. The idea of a 'forum of Christian churches and organisations' had been first suggested in the mid-1990s by the Rev. Dr. Konrad Raiser, then General Secretary of the WCC. Subsequent discussions lead the WCC to propose that a group be set up to further possibilities for getting all the major Christian traditions meeting together in fellowship. Huibert van Beek, then working as Programme Executive in the Office on Church and Ecumenical Relations for WCC, was given the task of furthering this goal. The first meeting was held in Bossey in 1998, at the end of which a Continuation Committee was set up from those at the meeting to carry forward the set of proposals approved. It was intended that the new grouping should be quite independent of the WCC, in view of the historical antipathy that had grown up between some denominations and the WCC. The aim was to hold meetings in the different regions of the world leading up to a grand global gathering. The original time scale was aiming for a 'high-level, global forum meeting of 150-200' within 2 years, but in the event it took nearly ten years. The movement was originally known as the 'forum proposal' but agreed to use the name Global Christian Forum in September 2000. Throughout the life of the GCF its membership stressed that it should be seen as a *process*, not as an organisation or a series of meetings. It is not appropriate here to attempt a full history of the GCF, rather to highlight the key events and the underlying personnel. For fuller descriptions readers are referred to Huibert van Beek's authoritative account included as Appendix Ab and the excellent chapter *'The Global Christian Forum: a narrative history'* by Sarah Rowland Jones in the book *'Global Christian Forum, transforming ecumenism'*, ed. Richard Howell.

The initial meetings were of a consultative nature with the relevant church leaders in the region, who were specifically invited by Huibert van Beek on behalf of and what became known as, the Global Christian Forum. The Continuation Committee met in between and at the regional consultative meetings a regional planning group was set up to plan each Regional Meeting.

The following meetings were held:

| Location | Date | Nature of meeting | Region | Number attending |
|---|---|---|---|---|
| Bossey, Switzerland | August 1998 | Initial discussions and production of formative document | | 28 |
| Pasadena, USA | Sept 2000 | Continuation Committee met with Evangelical and Pentecostal leaders | | 21 |
| Pasadena, USA | June 2002 | First regional consultation with all main Christian traditions | USA | 60 |
| Hong Kong | May 2004 | Consultation with all the main Christian traditions | Asia | 47 |
| Lusaka, Zambia | August 2005 | Consultation with all the main Christian traditions | Africa | 59 |
| Warburg, Germany | June 2006 | Consultation with all the main Christian traditions | Europe | 51 |
| Santiago, Chile | June 2007 | Consultation with all the main Christian traditions | Latin America and Caribbean | 58 |
| Nairobi, Kenya | Nov 2007 | Culmination of consultations, the global gathering | The world | 226 |

*(n.b. It has been noted that the figures attending the meetings differ slightly in different reports. The figures given here are those quoted in the Huibert van Beek account)*

# CHAPTER 3
# THE GCF CONTINUATION COMMITTEES, THE HEART OF GCF

## 3.i. The Committees

Since its conception in 1998, the GCF has been driven forward by a core group of men and women representing the different church traditions and denominations. Whilst certain of the committee members served for only a short period, leaving largely for personal and professional reasons, there has been a core of eight or so people who have been the driving force for most of the life of the Forum. This group has been lead throughout by the inspirational and outstanding Huibert van Beek, of whom more later.The membership of the Continuation Committees and the periods for which they served are noted in the tables below.

**Membership of Continuation Committees**

| Name | Affiliation | Country |
|---|---|---|
| Rev. Dr. Hilarion Alfreyev | Russian Orthodox | Russia |
| Fr. Mikhail Gundiaev | Russian Orthodox | Russia |
| Met. Gregorios Y. Ibrahim | Syrian Orthodox | Syria |
| Rev. Canon David Hamid | Anglican | UK |
| Rev. Dr. Sarah Rowland Jones | Anglican | UK/SA |
| Rev. Canon David Perry | Episcopalian | USA |
| Rev. Wesley Granberg-Michelson | WCC and Reformed Church in America, | USA |
| Dr. Fausto Vasconcelos | Baptist | Brazil/USA |
| Rev. Richard Howell | Evangelical Church of India | India |
| Dr. George Vandevelde | Evangelical WEF and Christian Reformed Church in America | Canada |
| Ms. Kuzipa Nalwamba | Evangelical IFES | Zambia |
| Rev. Dr. Judy Mbugua | Evangelical AEA | Kenya |
| Mgr. John Radano | Roman Catholic | Rome/USA |
| Mgr. Jean-Claude Perisset | Roman Catholic | Rome |
| Rev. Dr. Cecil Robeck | Pentecostal Assemblies of God | USA |
| Rev. Dr. Han Sang-Ehil | Pentecostal Church of God | USA |
| Dr. Musimbi Kanyoro | YWCA | Kenya |
| Huibert van Beek | Reformed | Dutch |

**Period of service on Committees**

| Name | Service | 98 | 99 | 00 | 01 | 02 | 03 | 04 | 05 | 06 | 07 |
|---|---|---|---|---|---|---|---|---|---|---|---|
| Rev. Dr. Hilarion Alfreyev | 1998-2000 | | | | | | | | | | |
| Fr. Mikhail Gundiaev | 1999-2008 | | | | | | | | | | |
| Met. Gregorios Y Ibrahim | 1998-2008 | | | | | | | | | | |
| Rev. Canon David Hamid | 1998-2002 | | | | | | | | | | |
| Rev. Sarah Rowland Jones | 2004-2008 | | | | | | | | | | |
| Rev. Canon David Perry | 1998-2000 | | | | | | | | | | |
| Rev. Granberg-Michaelson | 2005-2008 | | | | | | | | | | |
| Dr. Fausto Vasconclos | 2007-2008 | | | | | | | | | | |
| Rev. Richard Howell | 2002-2008 | | | | | | | | | | |
| Dr. George Vandervelde | 2000-2007 | | | | | | | | | | Died |
| Ms. Kuzipa Nalwamba | 2002-2005 | | | | | | | | | | |
| Rev. Dr. Judy Mbugna | 2007-2008 | | | | | | | | | | |
| Mgr. John Radano | 1998-2008 | | | | | | | | | | |
| Mgr. Jean-Claude Perisset | 1998 | | | | | | | | | | |
| Rev. Dr. Cecil Robeck | 1998-2008 | | | | | | | | | | |
| Rev. Dr. Han Sang-Ehil | 2002-2008 | | | | | | | | | | |
| Dr. Musimbi Kanyoro | 1998-2005 | | | | | | | | | | |
| Huibert van Beek | 1998-2008 | | | | | | | | | | |

Perhaps the most remarkable feature of this analysis is the continuity of service throughout the life of GCF of a small number of committed individuals. In particular, Fr. Mikhail Gundiaev (Russian Orthodox), Metropolitan Gregorios Y Ibrahim (Syrian Orthodox), Richard Howell (Evangelical Church of India), George Vandervelde (Evangelical. WEF) until his death in 2007, Mgr. John Radano (Roman Catholic), Rev. Dr. Cecil Robeck (Pentecostal, Assemblies of

God), Rev. Dr. Sang-Ehil (Pentecostal, Church of God), and Dr. Musimbi Kanyoro (YWCA), and more recently Rev. Sarah Rowland Jones (Anglican), and Rev. Granberg-Michaelson (Reformed Church in America), have served alongside Huibert van Beek (Reformed) whilst at the same time holding full time, highly demanding, jobs at a high level in their employing organisations.

Though the committee was small, they genuinely represented much wider constituencies. They were each in their own church traditions and in their professional lives holders of very senior positions, their personal vision for the church matching the vision of GCF and thus their promotion of GCF and their normal work were intertwined. Thus their influence both for the work and the vision of GCF was significantly greater than their numbers. As an illustration, the principle posts of those most involved with GCF through membership of the Continuation Committee was:

Fr. Mikhail Gundiaev: Archpriest of Moscow Orthodox Patriarchate and parish priest of the Moscow Patriachate in Geneva

Mar. Gregorios Ibrahim: HE Metropolitan of the Syrian Orthodox Church

Rev. Richard Howell: General Secretary of Evangelical Fellowship of India and Vice-Chairman, World Evangelical Alliance

Dr. George Vandevelde: Professor at Toronto School of Theology, Secretary of WEA dialogue with Vatican's Pontifical Council for Promoting Christian Unity

Mgr. John Radano: Head of the Western Section of Pontifical Council for Promoting Christian Unity

Rev. Cecil (Mel) Robeck: Professor at Fuller Theological Seminary, Director of David J. Du Plessis Centre for Christian Spirituality

Rev. Sang-Ehil: Ass Academic Dean and Ass Professor of Theology and Spirituality at Church of God Theological Seminary

Dr. Musimbi Kanyoro General Secretary of World YWCA

Rev. Sarah Rowland Jones: Research and Ecumenical Adviser to Archbishop of Cape Town, member of the Inter-Anglican Standing Commission on Evangelical Relations

Rev. Granberg-Michaelson: General Secretary of the Reformed Church in America

Huibert van Beek, formerly Programme Secretary for Church and Ecumenical Relations at the World Council of Churches

Thus the Global Christian Forum consists, in personnel terms, of Huibert van Beek, and the voluntary service of less than ten church leaders, plus voluntary support from many others to help with particular tasks such as the organisation of meetings. It has been a remarkable achievement from such a tiny team. The GCF has indeed fulfilled its aim of being a process and not an organisation. (See Section 3e for further details of the management 'structure' of GCF).

### 3.ii Aims of GCF

According to their latest publicity flier the Global Christian Forum seeks 'To create an open space wherein representatives from a broad range of Christian churches and inter-church organisations which confess the triune God and Jesus Christ as perfect in His divinity and humanity can gather to foster mutual respect, to explore and address together common challenges'. When the idea of a forum was first proposed the aims were spelt out in Proposals Regarding a Forum of Christian Churches and Ecumenical Organisations' as 'seeking to build more significant, more inclusive relations', it would 'transcend the limitations of existing frameworks, to think new thoughts, dream new dreams, and glimpse new visions.' It sought 'a more effective, a more sustaining, more inclusive network of relationships... to bring differences of understanding among the partners into a mutually committed dialogue so that all may find their way to a clearer discernment and a more faithful obedience.' It was clearly focussed upon building relationships between a wider range of Christian Churches and Organisations.

In the early years of the GCF the Continuation Committees and the consultations at Pasadena spent a considerable part of their meetings discussing the aims and purpose of the GCF - 'a Forum for what? What is the need?' Not only what should the Forum do, but also why? It was suggested that the forum should be 'a process for exploration, a place for listening to those who are not part of the established ecumenical structures, a space for those who are not at the table, a place of learning and participation, with a minimal structure as necessary.'

At the Pasadena consultation in 2002 a GCF Provisional Purpose Statement was produced:

> To create an open space wherein representatives from a broad range of churches and inter-church organisations, which confess the triune God and Jesus Christ as perfect in His divinity and humanity, can gather to foster mutual respect, to explore and address together common challenges.
>
> In the spirit of John 17v.21 "that all of them may be ones . . . so that the world may believe that you have sent me." and because of our faith in a reconciling God (2 Cor. 5 vv.18-21) a forum could pursue the following:
>
> Deepen our commitment to God's Word and mission in the world;
>
> Enhance our understanding of contemporary expressions of Christian mission;
>
> Pursue principles and practices that enable us to deal freely, responsibly and peaceably with our Christian differences and distinctive qualities;
>
> Engage in theological reflection in areas of mutual concern;

Strengthen the wholeness of the church by encouraging communication and co-operation; and

Foster relationships that may lead to common witness.

It was soon agreed that this statement of vision should not be submitted for further discussion but should be used as an ongoing framework. This is the statement which has been used until the present time. Subsequently the GCF has stressed that it should be a process, a journey, an open-ended journey together without preconceived objectives. Thereafter, the stated aims have not been changed: it was re-affirmed at the meeting of the GCF in Nairobi 2007.

### 3.iii. Who attended the meetings?

The GCF aimed to involve the full range of the Christian world. Attendance at the meetings was by personal invitation from the Secretariat, either as named individuals or as representatives of the particular organisation. Huibert van Beek, and the Continuation Committee discussed and agreed these, both the organisations and churches to be represented and the numbers from each, at the committee meetings. In the event the following churches and Christian organisations were involved, were represented at the final global meeting, and gave support to the work and aims of the GCF:

**Churches:** African Instituted Churches, Anglican, Baptist, Catholic, Churches of Christ, Disciples of Christ, Society of Friends, Holiness, Lutheran, Mennonite, Methodist, Moravian, Old-Catholic, Orthodox (Eastern), Orthodox (Oriental), Pentecostal, Assemblies of God, Church of God, Reformed, Salvation Army, Seventh Day Adventists, United and Uniting Churches.

**Inter-church groups:** African Theological Fellowship, Anglican Communion, Campus Missions International, Baptist World Alliance, Christian Aid, Conference of Secretaries of Christian World Communions, Edinburgh 2010, International Charismatic Consultation, International Fellowship of Evangelical Students, Lausanne Committee for World Evangelism, Lutheran World Federation, Methodist World Conference, Organisation of African Instituted Churches, Oxford Centre for Mission Studies, Pentecostal World Fellowship, Regional and National Ecumenical Organisations, United Bible Societies, World Alliance of Reformed Churches, World Council of Churches, World Evangelical Alliance, World Methodist Council, World Student Christian Federation, World Vision International and World Young Women Christian Association.

Of those invited only the Assemblies of God in the USA and the World Assemblies of God declined to be involved.

To get a feel of how the different church traditions have been involved in the GCF activities a breakdown of the churches into six main groupings has been made for those attending the different consultations and the forum. It is not easy to categorise churches into simple groupings, and it is recognised that this is a relatively crude classification.

Though some churches group together under formal structures, the church as a whole may be seen as more of a continuous spectrum. (Indeed two correspondents subsequently took exception to the proposed classifications, one wanted the Anglican church to be a distinct separate category and one (rightly) took exception to a single group having the exclusive use of the term 'evangelical'.) However it may be useful to make some broad groupings to see how the different church traditions were represented at the different meetings.

**Numbers attending the GCF, by church designation.**
Nb1. The designation of members carries some uncertainty-especially when the individual is representing a multi-church organisation.
Nb2.The numbers do not include the members of the Continuation Committees.

| Church Designation | Pasadena 2000 | Pasadena 2000 | Hong Kong 2004 | Lusaka 2005 | Warburg 2006 | Chile 2007 | Nairobi 2007 |
|---|---|---|---|---|---|---|---|
| Traditional Protestant | 8 | 11 | 12 | 18 | 16 | 9 | 68 |
| Pentecostal | 3 | 6 | 11 | 9 | 9 | 13 | 40 |
| Evangelical | 6 | 7 | 10 | 5 | 7 | 10 | 45 |
| Orthodox (Russian and Eastern) | 0 | 7 | 6 | 4 | 6 | 5 | 11 |
| Roman Catholic | 0 | 4 | 4 | 3 | 5 | 9 | 9 |
| African (AICs) | 0 | 4 | 0 | 9 | 2 | 0 | 12 |
| Inter-church/para-church orgns | 4 | 12 | 11 | 15 | 6 | 10 | 35 |
| Total | 21 | 51 | 54 | 63 | 51 | 56 | 220 |

It will be seen that the meetings were strongest in the representation of the traditional Protestant churches, the Pentecostals and the Evangelicals. Clearly the Pentecostals and the Evangelicals had been specifically targeted and their involvement is in strong contrast to the previous lack of enthusiasm for earlier forms of ecumenism, as demonstrated by their non-involvement with the work of the World Council of Churches. All meetings also had representatives from the Roman Catholic tradition, a group who also had been reluctant to join with the World Council of Churches. The emerging African Churches were involved in all of the meetings, except the Asia and the Latin American regional meetings. If we consider the attendance of the final forum at Nairobi we find the representation was as follows (overleaf):

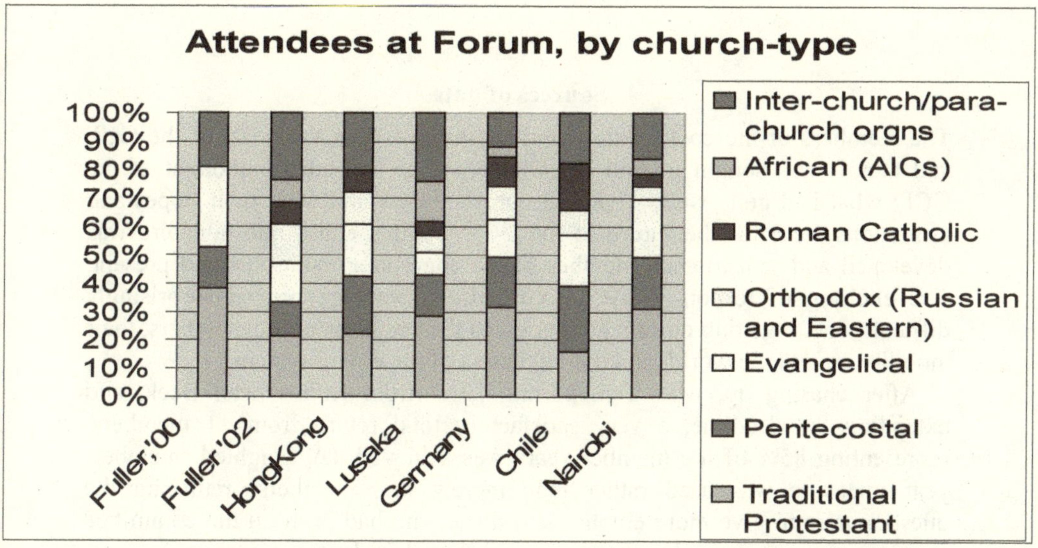
Attendees at Forum, by church-type
100%
90%
80%
70%
60%
50%
40%
30%
20%
10%
0%
Fuller,'00
Fuller'02
HongKong
Lusaka
Germany
Chile
Nairobi
Inter-church/para-church orgns
African (AICs)
Roman Catholic
Orthodox (Russian and Eastern)
Evangelical
Pentecostal
Traditional Protestant

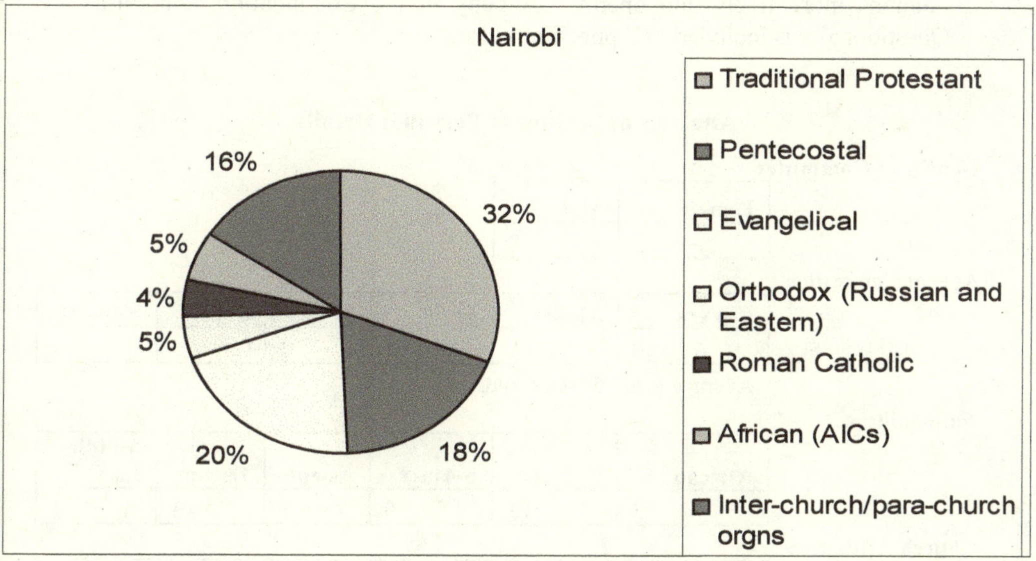
Nairobi
16%
32%
5%
4%
5%
20%
18%
Traditional Protestant
Pentecostal
Evangelical
Orthodox (Russian and Eastern)
Roman Catholic
African (AICs)
Inter-church/para-church orgns

# CHAPTER 4
# THE CONTINUATION COMMITTEE RESPONSES, WHAT DO THEY THINK?

### Sources of data

The members of the continuation committee have been the heart of the GCF and thus it was sought to find out what they, as individuals, thought of the GCF; what had gone well, what had not gone well and what their hopes and aspirations were for the future of the GCF. To this end a questionnaire was developed and sent to each member of the committee, both past and present. The eliciting of responses by the committee members proved surprisingly difficult, due to getting current addresses, to the busyness of the members, their mobility around the world, and the fickleness of the e-mail system.

After chasing up, with a supporting letter from Huibert van Beek, and extending the deadline, a very satisfactory total return from 11 members, representing 85% of the member-years was achieved. (A weighted 'member-year' measure was used rather than merely the 'members' returning the questionnaire to give more emphasis to those who had been on the committee for many years compared to those who had served for less).

The questionnaire was largely qualitative in nature to elicit the member's opinions more freely and openly. A copy of the Continuation Committee Questionnaire is included as Appendix Ac.

### Analysis of Section 1: Personal Details

**Gender of Committee**

| Female | Male |
|---|---|
| 3 | 8 |

**Age of Committee**

| <30 yrs | 31-40 | 41-50 | 51-60 | 61-70 | >70yrs |
|---|---|---|---|---|---|
| 0 | 1 | 2 | 3 | 5 | 0 |

Average age = 57 years old.

**Nationality**

| African | N Amer | S Amer | Asian | Europ | Middle East |
|---|---|---|---|---|---|
| 3 | 3 | 0 | 1 | 3 | 1 |

**Church Affiliation**

| Protestant | Pentec-ostal | Evang-elical | Ortho-dox | Cath-olic | African I C |
|---|---|---|---|---|---|
| 4 | 2 | 2 | 2 | 1 | 0 |

*The membership of the Continuation Committee consists of a mixture of gender, age, nationality and Church affiliation. There is however a predominance of elderly male protestants from the 'old world'. This is due to the nature and history of the committee; consisting of senior members of the churches well known in ecumenical circles.*

When asked why they served on the committee all spoke of their personal commitment to the vision of the GCF, whilst five also said that they had been asked to represent their particular church traditions: the Pontifical Council for Promoting Christian Unity, the Russian Orthodox Church, the International Fellowship of Evangelical Students, and the Anglican Standing Commission of Ecumenical Relations and the World Evangelical Alliance. The location of the GCF in Geneva was also mentioned as a convenient and economical reason.

The only reason given for ceasing membership of the committee was moving from the organization they were representing. No one mentioned any disillusionment with the vision of the GCF.

### Analysis of Section 2: Personal Visions for GCF

**2.i.** Express concisely (in one sentence) what your personal vision is for GCF, and whether it had changed over the years.

This question was asked to see whether the published aims of GCF matched the personal aims of those who were driving it forward. Their responses are recorded largely verbatim, though in some cases a slightly abbreviated version has been recorded.

> "To **provide space** for **contacts** among those Christians who have not wanted to be in contact with certain Christians before and to do so in the context of one ecumenical movement, hoping that all would see the importance of **seeking the visible unity of Christians."**

> "It should **become a space** for **the wide spectrum of Christians**, where they feel themselves **free** to have sincere **discussion on many burning issues** of the contemporary world and, possibly, be able **to express and all-Christian position** on some of them."

> "The GCF seeks to **gather the wide diversity** of the global Christian community together into **fellowship** in order to strengthen **participation in God's mission** in the world."

> "**Uniting** the Body of Jesus Christ for **more effective ministry**"

> "That it will continue to **bring all Christians** to the table **to pray** together and **to talk** together"

"Freedom could be one of the characteristics of GCF. Churches through their membership can participate, share, accept and receive their attitudes without feeling they are obliged to be linked totally or to change their attitudes, structures and other elements of their churches. Also the bilateral dialogue, contact and relationship, is always encouraged. This gives new dimension to the word friendship."

"My vision for GCF is a **space** where representatives of **all Christian traditions** come together to **promote visible unity** and **common witness.**"

"A **space** where people of different denominational affiliation can **talk together** and **shape a vision for unity** that will enhance **Christian solidarity** on matters we need to **act together**. To have a joint **witness** in our nations – **develop a common political theology** anchored in Christian orthodoxy."

"An old Heineken advert (almost) said – it refreshed parts other beers/ecumenical initiatives do not reach; ie **provide a unique opportunity for building relationship** between different Christian bodies that otherwise would be unlikely to have any depth of encounter. (Those relationships are then able to take on a life of their own outside the **catalyzing framework of the GCF**)"

"To give concrete **expression to unity** in the world-wide body of Christ."

"The GCF is **a *process*** through which **church leaders who would not otherwise have met or chosen to meet brought together** is such a way as to meet on more or less common ground and enabled to begin **to develop a sustainable and long-lasting relationship** with the hope that these relationships **will yield a greater measure of unity** between all Christians."

### *Conclusion*

Though there is much in common in the above responses different members emphasize distinct aspects. The main points arising are:

1. The concept of providing a 'space' for discussion, which is a free, un-threatening, safe place.
2. The aim of bringing together churches who in the past have kept themselves quite separate.
3. Seeking to promote, to create and then to demonstrate 'unity' within the different churches.
4. The importance of the GCF as a mechanism for strengthening 'relationships' between individuals and churches.
5. The concept that the GCF would be a 'catalyst' that would prosper and develop on-going, self-sustaining relationships and action into the future.
6. The stress that the GCF should be a 'process' and not an organization.

7. That the GCF should also prosper specific 'action', particularly mission, but also for witness, for ministry and developing a political theology.

To the principle aim of bringing people together to develop relationships, for some there is a second aim: that the GCF should have as an objective some action, in mission, in witness and for meeting the needs of the world.

These different aspects were taken into the second questionnaire to ask those who had attended the Nairobi Forum how they rated the different aims.

It may be worth commenting on 'the dogs which did not bark.' No one mentioned the aim of bringing different Christians together to discuss and resolve their differences, and no one mentioned a goal of setting up a single, global ecumenical organization. This was not to be a World Council of Churches expanded to include the whole of Christendom. Also, only one person referred to the final aspect of the published vision for the GCF "to explore and address together common challenges."

**2.ii.** Has your vision for GCF had changed over the years, if so how?

> "I have **become more convinced** that the Forum process should be absolutely independent from the World Council of Churches and other ecumenical organizations."

> "My own vision has not changed. The strategy and **timing have changed**: it took a decade to arrive at Nairobi, with regional consultations a careful process that has produced remarkable initial fruitfulness."

> " After being an active member in different ecumenical organizations for more than 25 years I feel that these (GCF) changes could bring new visions in the world of ecumenism."

> "At the early stages of the process my vision was **more in terms of building bridges** between the ecumenical movement and the evangelical/Pentecostal movements."

> "I've become **more confident in its ability to deliver** what it aimed to achieve. To begin with I thought the Limuru (global) event might be too ambitious. But the core ideal remains the same – I experienced some of the power of new relationship building in Pasadena and have seen that replicated and expanded in succeeding meetings."

*Conclusion*

The majority of the committee said 'no', their vision had not changed, rather had become stronger and that it was possible. The time required to build the process had been longer than anticipated.

## Analysis of Section 3
## The achievements and disappointments of the GCF

In this section members were asked to think critically about the GCF's progress over the last nine years, and to focus on what they were asked to respond to; what they felt had been the main achievements of the GCF, what had been their greatest disappointments, what had hindered the GCF from making more progress, and what they would do differently if they had had the time again.

**3.i.** What has been the best thing that GCF has achieved so far?

"GCF has shown that, with patient hard work, it is possible to find ways of **breaking down barriers** between those Christians who have refused to speak to each other before."

"It succeeded to create really **brotherly atmosphere** at its meetings **amongst those participants who had never had any practice of meeting each other before**"

"**The Limuru (Nairobi) meeting**, where more people came and understood the vision."

"Getting evangelical churches and the WCC related churches and the Roman Catholic Church to **share a forum** through their leaders and to welcome each other gracefully."

"An **historically unprecedented** (at least in modern history) **global fellowship** that has brought leadership from the major Christians "families" – Orthodox, Catholic, Evangelical/Pentecostal/historic Protestant – **into a real spiritual encounter and genuine relationship with one another** as followers of Jesus Christ."

" The positive response of the churches **who were out of the ecumenical** scene and their agreement to be part of the GCF, the **boundaries** which were obstacles in the way of those churches **does not exist any more**, the Holy Spirit **broke the walls between all churches** ands between south north, east west."

"It **demonstrated** to an increasing number of people from all the traditions **that it *is* possible to find common ground."**

"To get the various protestant **'factions' to the table."**

**"The Limuru (Nairobi)event.** It could not have happened without all that went before, particularly, I think, in terms of generating confidence within the World Evangelical Alliance and then (which took a little longer) the Pentecostal constituency. Both the WEA Gen Sec and the Pentecostal World Fellowship President attended and both signed up to the "Message" that was agreed at the end, as did senior Roman Catholic and Oriental and Eastern Orthodox participants

– **quite amazing**. Now we have institutional commitment it should give a stronger green light to future events and initiatives. If one were to answer the question in the abstract, I would say that the most important dimension has been to **reintroduce/strengthen the 'affective' component of faith in encounter between Christians,** rebalancing the cognitive faith/order, doctrinal/ecclesiological approach that has dominated so much of ecumenical meetings in recent decades, and contributed to some of the stagnation that is being felt."

"**Visible expression of belonging to the world-wide body** as expressed in Nairobi conference. Particularly the official **coming together** in Asia of the Catholics and Ecumenicals and Evangelicals as a result of GCF Asia meetings."

"The GCF has managed to do two complementary things. 1. It has **brought to the table** for the very first time, a significant number of **people who would traditionally never darken the door of an ecumenical meeting** because they viewed ecumenicists as uninterested in their agenda or unworthy of their interest. 2. It has brought to the table ecumenical veterans who at times had written the others off either as uninterested in the ecumenical agenda or as unworthy of their interest. It has **introduced these two groups of people to one another,** facilitated a conversation between them, and allowed them the freedom to speak candidly with one another."

*Conclusion*

The strongest response, in one form or another, was that the greatest achievement of the GCF had been the Nairobi Forum itself, and the consultations leading up to it. That it had happened! The grandiose, excessively ambitious, goal of bringing all the Christian traditions together had actually happened. Orthodox and Catholics, Evangelicals and Pentecostals, traditional Protestants and Africans had actually met together in harmony, and shared their faith journeys. "Quite amazing!" Through hard and careful work over the years, barriers between the churches had been broken down. Though it might be understandable hyperbole to claim that boundaries between churches "does not exist anymore" and "that the Holy Spirit had broken the walls between *all* churches, and the north and south", clearly the committee saw, and were proud of the real, remarkable progress which had been made over these nine years.

At a deeper level, the comment that there had been a shift away from organizational, ecclesiastical, doctrinal ecumenical efforts to Christians re-asserting the importance of the affective in their own lives and relationships is very significant, though how much this can be attributed to the GCF alone or as part of a global, postmodern trend is debatable.

**3.ii.** What has been the greatest disappointment with GCF?

"There is still need to bring others into the process, and also to assess the opportunities for the next steps. For example, **when can a deeper dialogue** begin to take shape among those who have participated so far."

"It is **too early** to speak about real disappointment at this point. The one thing, which can be disturbing until now the Forum process was too focused on widening the circle and, especially, attracting representatives of Pentecostals and all those who normally do not participate in the ecumenical movement. Sometime it resulted in **impairing of participation of Orthodox Churches** and paying less attention to their interests and problems."

"**Not selling its vision more** and faster."

"One of the original aims was to concentrate effort on laity but the Forum is once again becoming **very clergy and leadership dominated**."

"The GCF has **not yet established an "institutional" framework** – its more like an emerging exploration and movement – and it **hasn't identified common purposes** around which we might say and do together."

"I feel that **some churches are not always aware** of the fact that the new dimension in the ecumenical movement **is not only a continuation of our togetherness**; but it is a new discovery that those who were in and those who were out can be together IN; **not only to shake hands but to promise to work together."**

"It has **failed so far to bring to the table the leadership of the Assemblies of God** in the USA and of the **World Assemblies of God** where the USA leadership has a big say."

"None I can think of."

"We are **not good as we might be at communication** in many of its dimensions – getting word of the Forum out beyond immediate participants. We also need to work at **encouraging those who have participated to 'take more ownership'** ie to take their own initiatives to use GCF methodology in their own regions/contexts etc and not passively expect events to be driven from the centre. Some regional 'continuation committees' need rather more hand-holding than others – we would like them to be more self-driven."

"**No disappointments,** ecumenical endeavors **are slow and delicate** and GCF has progressed slowly but surely."

"My deepest disappointment is grounded in the **inability of the GCF to communicate** its purpose in a manner that is sufficiently clear and compelling to allow it the time necessary to accomplish this purpose without outside interference, or **the unwillingness of ecumenical veterans to grant it space** to accomplish its purpose – I haven't yet decided which. I believe that some folk, particularly among ecumenical veterans view the GCF either as an organization that is intent upon competing with existing ecumenical structures, or that it is an organization they need in some way to control. I am disappointed that we have to expend **energy defending what we are about."**

*Conclusion*

1. Some disappointments are general, the lack of communication to inform a wider proportion of the church about the existence and purpose of the GCF. Some hint at a disappointment at other churches and ecumenical organizations entrenched in resistance. It is recognized that change on this scale is a slow process and this softens some of the lack of impact.

2. Other disappointments are more specific and point to some tensions that need to be addressed:

a. An emphasis on involving the Pentecostals has been at the expense of the Orthodox churches.

b. A specific disappointment has been a lack of involvement of two large Pentecostal bodies, the Assemblies of God in the USA and the World Assemblies of God, but does this emphasize the bias towards the Pentecostals?

c. A lack of 'depth' in the dialogues, but has this been deliberate in avoiding theological differences in the search for unity?

d. A lack of any institutional framework for the GCF, and a lack of specific objectives which churches could work on together, but has that been deliberate in developing the GCF as a process, an open journey together?

e. A lack of regions taking their own initiative in following up the GCF vision in their own areas. This is a serious issue if the GCF is to be seen as a catalyst only, and not just a provider of stimulating events. If the vision is valid it must be self-sustainable. (*n.b. my understanding is that there is evidence of regional events being furthered in Asia and Latin America. BEW)*

**3.iii.** What have been the main hindrances to the GCF achieving what you want for it?

"GCF is still not so well known, and has **limited resource**"

"Its **newness**"

**"Lack of staff/office"**

"It is difficult for churches to trust interfaith tables **without the leaders** of those faiths being present on those tables."

**"2000 years of church history**, plus, since World War 2, the institutionalized separation of the 'ecumenical movement' from the evangelical, Pentecostal and contextually indigenous churches (eg AIF). Also, the Vatican's relationship, while crucial, could be described as 'cautiously ambiguous, until more recently."

"The ecumenical voice was **not heard enough by many churches in Asia, Africa, and the United States.** I realized from the enthusiasm of those who were called anti-ecumenicists how they were interested, happy and active – a witness of their readiness to be with others. **The question on money** (budget, fees, membership etc) is not one of the priorities as it was in the past."

"a) **Finance,** if the GCF had funds at its disposal it could have moved faster and wider, b) **Human resources**, (same as above), c) **a clearer view of what its purpose** should be beyond 'creating opportunities to meet people who had not met before'."

"Not all **churches** have **communication channels** for procession invitation or even building consensus on issues tabled."

"**Lack of money**! While we have achieved a huge amount with minimal budget, and the **ad hoc nature** of funding (and to try to become more formal might have scuppered, or at least undermined, the entire enterprise) our lack of committed funding has not allowed any expansion of the **staffing** that would be necessary to do more."

"Some **more resources** for GCF, to carry on its ministry."

"Before I respond to this question, I want to **register my joy over the success** that the GCF has experienced so far. Church leaders on both sides are **extremely busy**, churches who have committed themselves historically to the ecumenical process are **weary** from too many meetings, and view GCF as **competition** – a 'cheap' form of ecumenism. Historical divides take time to build trust. Fears of some that ecumenicalism would **undermine their own focus on world mission and evangelism** and an unhappiness of being put into direct fellowship with those **they believe to be spiritually and morally bankrupt**."

*Conclusion*

Various difficulties were highlighted as hindering the GCF achieving its aims:
1. The historical traditions over 2000 years of different churches establishing their own type of Christianity, with the accompanying mistrust and suspicions of other church traditions and strong commitment to their own priorities, was recognized as a deep and non-trivial problem.. Thus it was recognized that the newness of the GCF was unlikely to bring in universal harmony over a single decade – though what had already been achieved was celebrated.
2. In addition to the deep distinctions between the churches, it was recognized that the individual church leaders were very busy and, in some cases, weary of more new initiatives. The role of the very top church leaders in leading the

way by personal involvement / recognition was recognized, and their absence noted.
3. The lack of resources, both in financial and human terms, was recognized with the reliance on *ad hoc* funding and the availability of only a tiny staff (basically one man) limiting the range and the timing of the GCF's work. On the other hand there was no call for a large increase in resourcing which might change the whole spirit of the GCF being a process rather than an organization.
4. One internal, intrinsic hindrance to progress was suggested; that the GCF should be clearer about what its actual purpose should be, beyond getting people together and building relationships.

**3.iv.** If you had your time with GCF over again what, if anything what would you do differently?

> "I would proceed the same way. The committee talked through each step, and did its best to assess the opportunities it had. I wish there had been **more assistance for Huibert van Beek,** on whom most of the burden fell."
>
> **"Nothing"**
>
> "**Help sell its noble vision**."
>
> "I realized by being on the committee that only those visions that are shared by all the expected participants can succeed, **I would shelf my ideas** and create space for ideas of Gods people to happen."
>
> "I don't think that much would change. The main problem early on was a lack of capacity and resource to explore this vision. The WCC gave assistance which was essential, but also limited. Little or no help from elsewhere. From the first consultation at Bossey to the two meetings at Fuller, almost four years past. **This could have moved more quickly** if resources and capacity were available from somewhere. Huibert van Beek with others did all they could during these early years, but this magnificent vision deserved far more resources and capacity than it initially could receive."
>
> "I think that from the very beginning the plans were well prepared and the aim was very clear; how to accommodate more Christians in a new organization (sic!)."
>
> "I would go over all of it again because I believe that GCF **had to go through this 'fumbling' process of finding its way,** gain step by step, trying out the next step without knowing exactly how."
>
> "**I would try to speak with as many leaders as possible**."

**"Try to identify someone who could have pushed harder on the financial side,** to strengthen out 'institutional' capacity, while nonetheless having kept the initial phase informal and flexible – maintaining the independence that was necessary to retain the 'inviting capacity.'

"Some **more concrete steps at continental and national levels.**"

"Not sure what, if anything, I would do differently. I believe the process is going forward pretty well. One concern, though I am not sure that we would go back and change things, is that **the committee might have been bigger and more representative.** Have we struck the right balance or leant too much on various institutional ecumenical bodies. We need a balance. The process we have engaged in has been a delicate one that requires an even hand. Personally I think that Huibert van Beek has done a marvelous job at following the committee's instructions and providing appropriate questions and advice."

*Conclusion*

1. There was no strong feeling that things should have been done differently. Though the speed with which the GCF developed was questioned, especially in its early years. It was recognized that the very process of working, of 'fumbling' on, of finding the way forward, was an important and necessary part of the development process which could not be hurried.
2. There were personal responses where folk felt they might have acted slightly differently, in the committees or in promoting the GCF outside.
3. Specific suggestions posited that:

a) A person might have been designated with a fund-raising brief.

b) A wider, more inclusive membership of the committee might have been considered, there being a possible imbalance towards the existing ecumenical organizations.

c) More attention might have been given to continental and national development, as distinct from the centralized structure.

d) Once again the contribution made by Huibert van Beek was highly commended.

### Analysis of Section 4: The Purpose of the Forum

This section sought to elicit from the committee members what they thought of the main purpose of the forums, and what they hoped would have been achieved at each forum. It sought to move from the general aims and vision to a more specific purpose and outcomes. The intention was to refer to the actual forum gatherings, both in the regions and, especially, the global forum in Nairobi. In the event, the question was ambiguously phrased, some interpreted the 'forum' as the whole GCF process, and so the responses were less helpful than anticipated.

**4.i.** What do you see as the main purpose of the forum?.

"**Bringing a spirit of reconciliation** between Christians who have been divided from one another, so that more and more Christians can see the importance of the one ecumenical movement as a response to the prayer of Christ for the unity of his disciples (cf Jn 17:21)"

"Common Christian witness to the world, which is becoming more and more non-religious."

"Uniting different Christian Denominations."

"A welcoming table **for Christian fellowship**, it is not for church unity but church solidarity."

"In the New Testament we read *' For just as the body is one . . . and we were all made to drink of one Spirit'* 1Cor 12: 12-13. The main purpose of the GCF is to **discover how this** startling truth – we are all made to drink of one Spirit – **can be experienced and embraced as a growing reality** within the wide global diversity of the Christian community."

"**To bring more churches together** and **to find ways of how to work together** on different global, regional and local levels. The new challenges in the world need a new vision for the future. An individual church cannot do it alone. Churches together can bring new solutions for those challenges."

"To contribute to **putting in place** at the global, regional and local levels **concrete mechanisms that enable all the Christian traditions to work** towards greater unity and common witness."

"To **facilitate dialogue** without becoming too enshrined as an institution."

"To catalyse, and contribute to the **deepening, of relationships** across the full spectrum of the Christian family, especially among those who might otherwise not have the opportunity for such encounters."

"To create space for **deepening of understanding of each other's traditions, developing relationship** and **maturing of dialogue.**"

"The main purpose of the GCF is to convene and to **facilitate a safe conversation** in which people from diverse ecclesial backgrounds that would never seek out or find a natural way to meet, may embark upon a process that can **lead to a greater level of understanding, respect, cooperation and unity between them."**

*Conclusion*

Most of the responses related to the general aim of getting people together in a safe environment to facilitate dialogue, better understand each other, and develop relationships and respect between Christians who had had little contact in the past.

There was just one of producing any action beyond the forum, setting up a mechanism that enables Christians to work together towards greater unity and witness.

**4.ii.** What do you hope that each forum would achieve? (Please describe specific intended outcomes.)

"Christians who have never intended to have such contacts and begin to **build new relationships** with them for the sake of the Gospel of Christ."

"**Get to know each other better**. See how they could work together emphasizing areas of agreement."

"The one and most important outcome so far has been to get **all the people** at the table and **feel welcome** to the conversation. I think that this has been achieved and it is a very big achievement."

"I am not sure I understand what is meant by 'each forum.' If we look at the regional consultations, my hope would have been that in each context, **new relationships** of fellowship would have been established between parts of the Christian community that previously were unfamiliar, distrustful, or hostile towards one another. Further I would hope that such **relationships would be sustained** and **empower expressions of cooperation in common witness and mission.**"

"The plan of each forum gathering should **tackle one of the challenges and big issues** which are obstacles in the way of human unity. **Peace and justice could be one of the issues where all churches can work together**. Up till today, some churches believe that there is a just war. Another challenge could be **poverty**, which is developing and already developed in many societies. The GCF can bring out some **practical of how to diminish poverty** on different levels: universal, regional and local."

"So far there were **no other specific intended outcomes than enabling the gathering** of the largest possible representation of all Christian traditions in each forum and enabling a real encounter. Each forum could have been more representative than it actually was."

"**Get leaders** across the denominational spectrum **at the table**. That regional and national **leaders replicate that** in their regions and nations."

"First , **that relationships** made at forum meetings **might be sustained between individuals** concerned, and also **overflow into relationships between their respective institutions**, whether in cooperation in mission of various sorts, or in increased dialogue. Second, that where **regional continuation committees** have been set up that these might **take on significant ownership of the process**, initiating future events/ their own fundraising etc. The (global) continuation committee do not have sole ownership rights over the process / metyhodology / name etc. It is a gift for all God's people."

"Some **more concrete steps** at continental and national levels."

"1. The right people at the highest level were present. 2. The agenda was sufficiently defined to facilitate conversation, without micro-management. 3. The committee was able to facilitate conversations with grace without becoming heavy-handed. 4. Space was made available for private conversations, meetings that were in keeping with GCF's purpose. 5. A **sense of hope and encouragement for continued participation**. 6. The methodology used **opened up the reality of faith in one another**. 7 The recognition of this faith was sufficient to begin a process of conversation **that lead to greater trust and appreciation for the other**. 8. Participants look back on the process and affirm its value. 9. That **participants will encourage others to participate in future**.

*Conclusion*

Three groups of responses derived from the question about what specific outcomes had been hoped for in the forum.

1. That the forum had been an end, an outcome, in itself. That the fact of bringing so many folk together from different, often hostile, traditions to talk, to listen, to change attitudes and to build up positive relationships was the main and the intended outcome of the GCF.
2. Others saw the forum as a means to an end, hoping that the good relationships would continue both at the individual level and between the institutions that they represented. Also that the participants would take the GCF vision home with them and set up their own GCFs in their own regions, taking ownership of the process for themselves. This would be worked out in common witness and mission.
3. One respondent had hoped that an outcome would be the tackling of specific important, social and political issues. The challenges and issues that are obstacles to the way that humanity lives in the world such as peace and justice, and world poverty. This was a hope which had not, in fact, been addressed.

### Analysis of Section 5: The Distinctiveness of the GCF

The last fifty years has not been short of ecumenical initiatives. This section sought to find what, if anything, was distinctive about the GCF from those who had spent so much time and effort seeking to promote it.

**5.i.** There are many different ecumenical organizations around the world. What, if any, are the main features that make the GCF distinctive?

> "While there have been contacts between Pentecostals, Evangelicals with 'mainline' churches and with the WCC before, the distinction of the GCF is that it has **brought together a number of those** just mentioned, of all of the above, **who had not been part of these previous contacts**, and it has encouraged them to continue in this same direction."
>
> "The GCF **is not**, and should not become**, an organization** in the full sense of the word. It is better characterized as **a process**."
>
> "Their objective – Unity"
>
> "The uniqueness is the ability to let **testimony** and respect for each faith to be **the place to begin a conversation.** This forum is held together by spirituality rather than social action or dogma."
>
> "First, the GCF is distinctive because it **embraces such a wide range of participation** from all the major Christian 'families' that has not existed globally, at this level, in modern times. Second, the GCF is distinctive in placing a priority on genuine 'koinonia' among its participants through **the sharing and testimony of each person's spiritual journey** with Jesus Christ. This methodology is radically different than other ecumenical approaches."
>
> "The whole **structure of the GCF is different**. There are no offices, no employees, no budget, but there is a spirit of working together through emails, internet and other non-costly ways. For GCF the aim is not to collect money for programs, but it is to create programs to be implemented by churches."
>
> "GCF is **not an ecumenical structure**. It **avoids the word** ecumenical in its name so that those who mistrust ecumenism (rightly or wrongly) feel confident to join. It does not avoid the ecumenical discussion. Distinctive features are 1) **it is a process**, a movement, not an organization, 2) it has **an inclusive methodology** which consists of a**) sharing of the faith itineraries,** b) processes **allowing participants to bring their issues and priorities to the table,** and c) allowing participants to develop ways of discussing and dealing with the issues, and 3) It has **a very light operational structure**."
>
> "It is not organizational and **not lead by institutional leaders** of the churches and organizations. It gives an edge to potentially influence the rank and file."

> "That it is not so much an organization as a movement / **methodology!** Orthopraxy matters more than orthodoxy – 'see how these Christians love one another' etc – that we **build relationships** that allows us to **begin by recognizing one another as brothers and sisters in Christ,** members together in His body, and that this defines the point of departure from which other dialogues / activities can then be pursued."

> "It is not an organization or an institution. It has succeeded in **bringing on table traditions which were not in conversations** at the level which GCF has succeeded."

> "GCF is not now nor has it ever been an ecumenical organization. The committee has been very clear that GCF is **not an ecumenical organization** or **nor does it provides any competition** with those organizations that possess an ecumenical vocation. The GCF is **nothing more than a *process* of introduction**, **a convening table**, **a safe place** that brings people together at a relatively preliminary level. This process is a unique gift to the Church."

*Conclusion*

The main distinctives of GCF can be summarized as follows:

1. The GCF embraces a far wider range of Christian traditions than previous ecumenical initiatives. It seeks to include all branches of the Christian family, from the North and South, including Orthodox and Catholic, Protestant, Evangelical, Pentecostal and the African churches. It deliberately sets out to bring in many of those who had previously avoided all such coming together. It consciously avoids the use of the word "ecumenical" in its publicity.
2. The GCF is not an organization, but a process, a methodology. It is inclusive, starting with the assumption that all Christians are brothers and sisters in Christ. The methodology at its meetings have an introduction where all participants share their own faith journeys with each other, then allow each to bring their own issues and priorities to the gathering to be addressed safely, as appropriate.
3. It seeks to build relationships, not consensus doctrine or social action.
4. It deliberately has a very light structure of organization, with a minimum of staff and resources.
5. It seeks to be a stimulus, a catalyst for further meetings and action. One member even spoke of the GCF as 'nothing more' than a process of introduction, that brings people together in a safe environment.

## Analysis of Section 6: The Future for the GCF

One of the main reasons for this evaluation was to help the Committee to think through how it should seek to develop in the future. The Nairobi Global Forum was the event that the work of the GCF had lead up to over its nine or so years of existence. It had been the culmination of all the other consultations and meetings. Where to now? To this end each member of the committee was asked for their personal opinions independently. It is hoped that this data will reinforce the corporate discussions of the Continuation Committee that have been held since the Nairobi Forum.

**6i.** What would you like the GCF to do in the next decade?

> "To **arrange more meetings** which continue the characteristic of the last nine years. To begin to shape some of these meetings **to bring a greater contact with the instruments of the ecumenical movement** (such as the WCC, the WEA etc) and closer contacts with their official structure."
>
> "I would try to find new models of uniting Christians. One of the ways to achieve this will be **to make an analysis of different attitudes of various Christian groups** towards the moral issues and traditional values. **New cross-confessional alliances may appear** in the future along these lines."
>
> "**Share its vision** to different parts / continents."
>
> "Continue to nurture the faith of Christians and to remove fears of one another and most important **to help eradicate prejudices** that churches hold against each other."
>
> "I would like to see the GCF thrive and grow. This would include **establishing a regular encounter with leaders of the main Christina groupings and 'families'** through the world, perhaps in relationship to the WCC Assembly or else separately. I would like to see the **vision of GCF inspire regional and local expressions** that reflect the same inclusivity and spiritual / relational dynamic that has characterized this movement."
>
> "**Invite other churches to participate**, to encourage on both locals and regional levels **to work together and witness together** to the whole would, **to prepare for the second GCF with the issues of peace and justice** as one of the issues."
>
> "i) **Continue to widen the circle** (drawing in more people, multiplying Forum events in regional and local settings.)" ii) Begin **to focus on certain issues** common to all Christian traditions and experiment with the Forum methodology as a new way of dealing with those issues."
>
> "**Listen** to those who have attended this far and try and **shape an agenda** that reflects those needs, to sharpen a **focus on what is most important for dialogue**. Personally I think issues around political theology have potential for engendering support."
>
> "We probably need to return **to all the regions** (Middle East included) with a second meeting, and consolidate **the first round of encounters**. Perhaps some of these, after the initial 'getting to know one another', could **have particular**

**themes**, so that not only ecumenicists, but specialists / practitioners in other areas (eg mission / justice and public affairs / healing and health care support . . . ) might be drawn into new relationships with analogues from other parts of the Christian spectrum. Some of such thematic meetings might be global. We need **another global event for high level leadership** after another ten years, both as an endorsement of all that has been done and an affirmation that whatever needs to happen (which should emerge over the intervening period) should be pursued."

"Intentional efforts **at continental and national levels every year**, and **two global gatherings.**"

"Given the specific task of the GCF I believe that the **GCF should have a relatively limited life span.** It could accomplish much or all it intends to accomplish over a period of a single generation, say 30 years. **Hold regional and global meetings very two or three years**. Those who have already been to a GCF should be invited again to build up confident working relationships."

*Conclusion*

Perhaps the first conclusion is that there is no general consensus among members of the committee as to how the GCF should develop from here, indeed there are certain areas where there is a distinct difference of opinion. There are two main thrusts, 'more of the same' or do something different.

1. The main suggestion is that the GCF should continue, consolidate and develop its programme as before. It should hold more meetings, both at the regional and the global level. It should invite more partners of the church family. It should encourage local regions to take up the GCF vision and promote their own meetings and relationships.

2. There was the suggestion that the meetings should move on from the previous pattern, of meeting to develop understanding, trust and relationships, and start to focus on specific issues of common Christian concern such as peace and justice.

3. Continued efforts should be made to inspire the top leaders from the whole spectrum of Christian organizations to share the GCF vision, and to meet regularly together.

4. Others suggested that there should be an effort to build up stronger relationships with other ecumenical groupings, like the WCC, and develop structures to work together, so that new cross-confessional alliances might be developed. (This would be a change of direction from the current policy of keeping the GCF distinct from other ecumenical groupings, especially WCC, and keep the GCF as a process rather than a structured organization.)

5. It was suggested that the views of those who had attended the GCF meetings should be listened to, and an agenda for the future action developed (which it is hoped this evaluation is doing!)

6. One suggested that the GCF should have a limited life span, acting as a catalyst for others to take up the GCF vision. (but as such a life span was likely to be in the order of a generation, this is not an issue for the present.)

**6.ii.** What would you hope that the GCF would have achieved by the end of the next decade?

> "To have **held more meetings** and built **stronger relationships with ecumenical organizations**, and to have raised the general consciousness of the importance of seeking the visible unity of Christ's disciples."
>
> "The **GCF vision shared more widely**."
>
> "A **better witness** of the Christian faith and more prayers."
>
> "I would hope that the GCF would **have embraced an appropriate organizational / institutional framework**, while **maintaining its highly relational and non-bureaucratic character.** I would hope that the GCF's purposes and forms of common witness and mission would be formally embraced and expressed. Thus, I would hope that the GCF would become **not only a relational fellowship** but also **a witnessing community** during this period."
>
> "If **the establishment of peace** as a burning issue for some regions and local churches could be achieved through the efforts of the churches that would be a great victory for GCF. Peace would come out with a new atmosphere of being together. Avery complicated but important issue. It results with **justice for all** societies where conflict is the major issue."
>
> "A general acceptance that the coming together in each locality of all the Christian churches (the New Delhi 1962 concept of unity) and globally (the Nairobi 1975 concept of the conciliar fellowship) are of the essence of our calling."
>
> **"Churches speaking with one voice on major social issues**, cooperating and sharing resources beyond traditional denominational boundaries."
>
> "To be well on our way to **doing ourselves out of a role**, because GCF –type methodology would be increasingly taken for granted in existing and new ecumenical encounters. Christians across the whole spectrum would have **increasingly good relationships** at every level, from local to global."
>
> "Intentional efforts at continental and national levels every year, and two global gatherings. Resulting in **concrete developing relationships**."
>
> "I hope that the GCF will have been able to **build up a critical mass** of diverse Christian leaders so that they will continue **to interact and work in a complementary rather than competitive way."**

*Conclusion*

What members hoped would have been achieved by the end of the next decade matched, to some extent, what they had suggested should be done. It some cases they were still rather general aspirations, but they were certainly not SMART objectives!

1. General aspirations that the wider sharing of the GCF vision, and way of working, should have spread and be more widely practiced, were suggested; as were stronger relationships between individuals and organizations, less hostility between Christians, the establishment of peace and justice for all, and churches speaking together on major social issues.
2. That what the meetings suggested at both the regional and global levels should have taken place and consequent good working relationships developed.
3. It was hoped that a 'critical' mass of church leaders from the different traditions working together would have been established which would perpetuate, and accelerate, the GCF vision without further input. This could be an intentional aim, and would mean that certain leaders should be invited repeatedly to successive meetings, to build up confidence and relationships for such a critical mass to become established.
4. That the GCF should have become a witnessing community.
5. That the GCF should have established a stable institutional structure, whilst still maintaining its relational and non-bureaucratic structure.

**6.iii.** What resources do you believe the GCF needs to fulfill its objectives?

> "**Churches and organizations need to continue their levels of support**, financial and otherwise, and deepen their interest in this process. A key will be that **the secretary's office** (which Huibert van Beek has fulfilled so well up to now) will have the proper resources to function well."

> "**Human and financial**. Also a **central office**."

> "Needs more **money** to have **staff.**"

> "The GCF would need **a full-time 'ambassador**" who would be continually casting the vision and meeting with church leaders around the world to further knowledge, support and participation, and also **a full time executive staff person** dealing with all the implementing and organizing requirements. One administrative assistant would support this effort. Including travel and necessary infrastructure, my rough guess is that this would take about **$400,000 a year** to do this well, which would make it the best ecumenical bargain in the world."

> "**Good will. Qualified people. Active leaders. All with the guidance of the Holy Spirit**."

"**A secretariat with two or three staff** and **guaranteed annual funding** on the basis of successive three-year planning."

"**People, people** – those who can influence decisions in their churches and those who can bring dialogue to members."

"**Enough money**, and with it **the certainty that it will continue to flow in**, for at **a minimum two full time staffers.** One to do the admin, the other to do the vision / concept / theology (affective AND cognitive!) / relationship building / communication strategy / initiating and catalysing events / facilitating wider use of GCF methodology in other ecumenical relationships and meetings / fund raising / etc etc – and enough **funding also to support a continuing programme** of events under the GCF banner, mostly regional."

"More **staff / volunteers and advocates** for the vision at national, regional and global level,"

"i)The most critical resource is our **human resource**. Need to rebuild the secretariat to fill Huibert van Beek's role when he retires. ii) It needs to develop **more and regular funding**, GCF should continue to seek money form a wide range of organizations so that it should not be dependent or answerable to any one." iii) It needs **time** to spread its vision and activities."

*Conclusion*

The resources required for the GCF to continue and develop were personnel, cash and some 'base'. One member also suggested that the Holy Spirit would be an important resource too, presumably others would have agreed with this, and felt it implicit in all that they did.

1. The personnel required to run the GCF was seen as absolutely vital, especially in view of the fact that the inspirational and irreplaceable Huibert van Beek was about to retire. Different suggestions were made as to the number, and role, of the staff required. All suggestions were modest and did not imply a vast structure. A full-time executive person, possibly an 'ambassador' for the GCF with paid support staff, as well as volunteers, was required.

2. Funding, and funding guaranteed for a medium term programme (3years?) was required. The funding was required for both central administration and travel at the Secretariat and for the regional meetings. It was mentioned that the funding should not be coming from a single donor, to whom GCF would then be accountable. The actual funding required for the GCF was not normally mentioned, depending on the scale and size of the yet undetermined operation, though one member suggested that an annual budget of $400,000 would be a bargain!

3. One, only one, sought a central office. Clearly there is no taste for a big centralized organization.

## Analysis of Section 7: The global church

This final section sought to probe how the committee perceived the nature and role of the Church. It sought to see what underlay their motivation to work for the GCF. To this end, two questions were asked;

**7.i.** It has been suggested that there are two distinct ways of demonstrating the unity of the church; *either* by getting people from different churches together and talking about the commonality and the distinctiveness of their beliefs *or* by getting people from the different churches working together to tackle problems in the world, through mission, through campaigning or through addressing the problems of world poverty and injustice. How do you react to this dichotomy?

> "It is necessary to seek the visible unity of Christians who are badly divided from one another. To seek the unity of Christians, **it is necessary through deep theological dialogue to seek unity** in the one apostolic faith, sacramental life and ministry; it is necessary to find ways **to cooperate with each other in matters of mission**, which we are only able to do partially now because of our divisions. It is **important also for Christians to find ways of facing the problems of the world** together, problems such as poverty and injustice. **The quest for unity is multidimensional.**"

> "We have to use any chance to do together whatever can be done together. This practical expression of our faiths can lead us to a greater readiness to understand each other and respect our different traditions. I think that we should **not speak about 'demonstrating the unity of the Church'.** In orthodox ecclesial understanding, the unity of the Church is not something that already given to us and should be only demonstrated. We can speak **only about presence of many churches** at the table. **Some of them belong to the One Church, some of them are close to Her, others are more distant.** The role of reaching the full unity of the Church proved to be not very productive in the life and work of the WCC. **I feel that we should not place this idea in the centre of the Forum process.**"

> "By using **both**."

> "I believe talking and working together are **both important**."

> "This is essentially **the old ecumenical polarization** between Faith and Order and Life and Work. 60 years of ecumenical history, dominated by these two initiatives and hindered by the tension between them, has not moved a wider unity embracing evangelical, Pentecostals and other ecumenically marginalized groups, nor has it created fully engaged participation by the Vatican (ie membership in WCC). **A new dynamic**, not bound by the existing dichotomy, needs to be created, with **a focus on spiritual and relational and missional** dynamics. **That is what the GCF is doing.** It builds on past ecumenical achievements in this task, but is free from the limitations of existing categories, organizational structures and style."

"Church unity does not mean that churches loose their identity. Church unity does not mean to speak about, preach, read and write on it without living it. **Church unity today means that the doctrinal and theological obstacles should not remain obstacles. Church unity means that we should pray together, face challenges together, and give common witness of our faith and mission together**. An **agreement should seriously be taken into consideration** that the church is One, Holy and Apostolic Church; and that we believe in the Holy Trinity, in One God, in Jesus Christ our Savior: and that we have one source of our faith, teaching and strategies, which is the Holy Bible"

"Part of the failure of the ecumenical movement and the WCC is that it has **not been able to overcome this dichotomy.** Faith and Order and Life and Work came together in the 1930s to form the WCC for two reasons i) one could not without the other and ii) it should be a movement of the churches. All through the history of the WCC, F&O and Church and Society (later JPSS, JPIC etc ) have remained separated. The third component, Mission (the IMC, CWME) have almost gone lost. One of the lessons of the GCF is that **unity and mission have to be held together."**

"I think action that's theologically based and just a response to issues will have a strong missiological underpinning. That's why **unity for its own sake is not the issue**, rather the churches reflecting together on the role of the church in the world."

"We have a God of **"Both-And"!** Each is necessary, and each can draw energy from and feed it into, the dynamics of the other."

"It should **start with talking** but must **result in concrete steps to address issues.**"

"I do not believe that this dichotomy is legitimate. It seems that **both** things are necessary and that they are mutually beneficial. Both are extremely important. Currently the 'Life and Works' approach is considered 'sexy'. Many have decided that they won't bother with the issues that divided them historically and try and work together without doctrinal agreement. This may seem an easier approach, but it is not. **It may work well on issues such as peace, poverty**, education, human rights, humanitarian and disaster relief etc but **will run into problems when considering evangelism or missionary work,** sexuality, or right to life etc because the underlying theological issues have not been resolved. For these latter issues we simply must continue working on the theological underpinning."

### *Conclusion*

The question as to whether we should seek to demonstrate the unity of the church through talking together or working together, clearly touched on some raw and unresolved issues relating to the nature of the 'Church' and what we mean by, or hope for, in 'Unity'.

1. The most popular response was that we should do both, talk together about faith and order and also work together in the world. Some suggested that it was not, in practice, possible to do one without the other. Each can draw energy from and feed it into, the dynamics of the other. Others suggested that this was not quite so easy, and that the dichotomy, the conflict, between the two approaches was real and had never been resolved by the ecumenical movement over the last 60 years.

2. There is a distinction between 'mission' and 'social work'. The different churches can, and should, work happily together on issues such as peace and justice and relieving poverty. In areas such as mission and evangelism, even issues of sexuality and the right to life, underlying theological differences can become less tractable problems.

3. Different traditions have quite different perceptions about the nature of the Church, whether there is only one true Church or whether the Church consists of all those who declare their faith in, and seek to serve, the one triune God. Such deep theological distinctions will not be easily resolved, and still exist among members of the GCF Continuation Committee. The type of unity that the GCF is working for, through relationships, understanding and mutual respect has, so far, avoided the difficult problems that would be met if the members of the Forum sought to discuss the distinctions in 'deep theological dialogue'.

4. It was suggested that this dichotomy was an out-dated and unhelpful approach to bringing church members together. We needed a new, different approach; 'a new dynamic, not bound by the existing dichotomy, that needs to be created with a focus on spiritual and relational and missional dynamics'. That is what the GCF *is* doing, and the approach it should continue to pursue.

**7.ii.** It has been suggested that the cultures, and the problems, facing different regions of the world are so different that there is little point in trying to unify globally, that the GCF should concentrate on regional rather than global meetings. How do you react to this?

> "GCF should **take into account both** regional and universal concerns."
>
> "I feel the Forum should **try to be a global expression of Christianity** (non eccesial, of course). At the same time, regional meetings proved to be very productive and should be kept as a tool of **getting people interested to meet at the global level** as long as it is needed."
>
> "That is possible to unify globally but **start regionally**. Failure comes when they begin top down."
>
> "I don't believe you."

"Such a statement is a denial of the Gospel. Most pressing ecumenical task today is to **build bridges** between those churches that carry a strong sense of Christian 'tradition' and a commitment to the catholicity of the church with those that express contagious spiritual vitality and explosive growth. The former have their strength in the 'North', the latter are dominant in the 'South'. A regional approach hinders this most needed challenge of building these bridges."

"Yes. Regional consultations are important but we should **also think locally**. In the Middle East, we live this experience, all churches are active locally. **They create a network for living, working, feeling, being together, and giving witness together** – this is only an example."

"GCF should indeed concentrate on regional and local, but without neglecting the global. It is not a matter of unifying more or less but of having a **clear understanding of what is possible and necessary globally** and **what is possible and necessary regionally and locally."**

"To focus the discussion that would be necessary but to divide the world in those terms would be to **fragment the One Church**. With sensitive listening and understanding the differences we can stand together in one mission with **different strategies for different regions**."

"I suspect that where the rubber hits the road , in terms of **bad relations, tends to be at the more local / regional level** which is why **this is a priority area** for activity. However i) local activity **does not necessarily have to be managed by GCF** and ii) local activity is often **helped by having affiliation to the GCF and its global bodies** so that level of support needs to be maintained and nourished."

"In an age of globalization GCF should focus both on globally and locally. The bottlenecks are at the top and therefore **Global leaders need to meet first**."

"The task of the GCF is not unification, it is about facilitating relationships that can lead towards a genuine Christian unity. My understanding of the Church of Jesus Christ is that it **is both** global and local. There are different cultures and problems around the world. We can not be the Church for the world and not take seriously the local setting, nor can we be church at the local level and ignore the Church at the global level.

*Conclusion*

1. Most said that the GCF should address both the global and the regional and local levels, There was difference as to whether it is better to start regionally, leading up to the global regions, or to start at the global level with the global leaders meeting first and then influencing the regions.
2. It was recognized that the regional meetings and the global meetings were different, addressing different needs, and so the agenda for each meeting should

be planned differently as appropriate, to match what is possible and what is necessary

3. It was noted that problems of churches working together was often at the local rather than at the global level. The issues that the top Church leaders should be addressing at the global level are quite different, and of a different kind, to what local church leaders are facing with other churches in their locality.

4. It was stressed that the work of the GCF was not to bring about unity in the churches, but to develop good relationships between the churches so that they might, in mutual trust, work, pray and worship together.

**Analysis of Section 8: Further comments**

Respondents were given the opportunity to make any further comments that they felt would help the evaluation. Despite having covered so much ground so perceptively, some still had sufficient energy and commitment .left to make the following comments.

**8.** Please feel free to add any comments about the past and the future of the GCF which you feel would be appropriate to this evaluation.

> "GCF has **wonderful and dedicated leadership**, though **lean**. It has an opportunity to meet its objectives."

> "A final word is that **churches should be well-informed** about the process of the GCF; and in turn they (churches) should be ready to offer their common witness."

> "One of the fundamental challenges the GCF is facing and has not been able to live up to is **communication.**"

> "The future of the **GCF leadership** needs to be thought through carefully. The varied church structures represented on the continuation committee make it very fluid. **Highly institutionalized churches find it easy to keep representation and participation on track** while the **less institutionalized may lack constancy.**"

> "God bless and use GCF as an instrument for his glory."

> "I am a **true believer in the work of GCF**. I believe that it is moving an a very good direction. I will probably resist any attempt to move it off its current trajectory precisely because within my Pentecostal community it is making a huge difference."

*Conclusion*

Two additional points were stressed:

1. Relating to leadership. The past leadership of Huibert van Beek was recognized as 'wonderful and dedicated' and the lean style appreciated. It was also hinted that the future leadership might need to be somewhat different; that the style of an inspirational, idiosyncratic leadership required to get the GCF started, depending so much on existing contacts and relationships, might not be appropriate for the next stage of the GCF's development, especially when dealing with 'institutions' that are more used to dealing with other organizations in a structured and 'institutionalized way.'.

2. The issue of communication was again raised: how to get the vision and methodology of the GCF shared more widely when, of its very nature, so much depends on personal relationships.

# CHAPTER 5
# THE NAIROBI FORUM ATTENDEES RESPONSES, WHAT DO THEY THINK?

### Sources of data

Approximately 236 senior leaders of different churches and Christian organisations attended the Nairobi Forum, the culmination of the GCF's endeavours, in November 2007. It was sought to investigate the views of these key figures by a questionnaire. They were key people both because they were part of, and also the target of, the GCF. A questionnaire was developed which built on the views expressed by the members of the Continuation Committee, on the stated aims of the GCF literature and by the evaluation objectives. The questionnaire was largely quantitative in nature to get some 'hard' responses from the attendees. The questionnaire is included as Appendix Ad.

Of the 236 attendees on the Participants list, I did not include the 16 from Southern and Central America, as it was agreed that these should be surveyed separately. Approximately 19 of the listed participants were members of the Continuation Committee or members of the Conference Staff, who were not expected to respond, and 17 participants were 'unobtainable' by e-mail, leaving a total of 184 attendees who, hopefully, received the questionnaire and from whom one might have expected a response. In the event 57 questionnaires were returned, giving a response rate of 31%. Whilst one might have hoped for an even greater return, this can be considered a good return from the whole Forum attendees, and the views expressed are fairly representative of the whole.

### Analysis of Section 1: Personal and Professional Details

Respondents were asked to indicate which option 'most nearly fits your own situation.'

**1.i. Gender of Attendees**

| Male | Female |
|---|---|
| 44 | 13 |

77% of the attendees were male.

**1.ii. Age of Attendees**

| < 30 | 31-40 | 41-50 | 51-60 | 61-70 | > 71 |
|---|---|---|---|---|---|
| 0 | 4 | 18 | 26 | 5 | 2 |

77% of the attendees were between the age of 41 and 60. 12% were over 60.

On the whole the Africans were younger than the Europeans and the Americans.

**1.iii. Region of birth**

| Africa | America (North) | America (South or Central) | Asia | Austalasia | Europe | Middle East |
|---|---|---|---|---|---|---|
| 13 | 10 | 6 | 9 | 1 | 17 | 0 |
| 23% | 18% | 11% | 16% | 2% | 30% | |

**1.iv. Region in which you currently live and work**

| Africa | America (North) | America (South or Central) | Asia | Austalasia | Europe | Middle East |
|---|---|---|---|---|---|---|
| 15 | 9 | 4 | 5 | 1 | 22 | 0 |
| 27% | 16 | 7% | 9% | 2% | 40% | |

Though each region was represented, except the Middle East, there was a high proportion from Europe and the Americas.
It is interesting to note that though the total numbers in each of the categories for regions of birth and of working were similar, there were a significant number of attendees (16 or 28%) who had changed categories: Africans who were now living and working in Europe, Europeans who were now working and living in Africa etc. This represents an international and mobile populace.

**1.v. Church tradition/denomination in which you currently worship.**

| African (AIC) | Evangelical | Orthodox (Russian and Eastern) | Pentecostal | Protestant Traditional | Roman Catholic |
|---|---|---|---|---|---|
| 3 | 12 | 2 | 14 | 18 | 8 |
| 5% | 21% | 4% | 25% | 32% | 14% |

It will be seen that the Forum had a preponderance of traditional Protestants, Pentecostals and Evangelicals, the latter two groups being notable by their absence at earlier ecumenical initiatives. The Orthodox, the RICs and the Roman Catholic Churches were present but less well represented.

NB. An analysis of the Church tradition derived from the list of all the participant who attended the Nairobi Forum is as follow. This matches well the analysis of those who responded to this attendee's questionnaire, given above. This suggests that the sample responding to the questionnaire represents the whole very well.

| African (AIC) | Evangelical | Orthodox (Russian and Eastern) | Pentecostal | Protestant (Traditional) | Roman Catholic |
|---|---|---|---|---|---|
| 5% | 20% | 5% | 18% | 32% | 4% |

**1.vi. The type/sphere of work in which you are principally employed.**

| Academic | Church leader, Minister, Pastor, Priest | Denominational Administrator, Leader | Inter-church Organisational Administrator | Retired |
|---|---|---|---|---|
| 6 | 15 | 17 | 20 | 0 |
| 10% | 26% | 30% | 36% | |

The most common group represented were the administrators from the inter-church organizations. Leaders from the different denominations were also well represented. Only about one quarter might be said to be still church based, as leaders of their local churches. It was, indeed, a high-powered gathering as was intended. The participants included seven Archbishops, 25 Bishops, one Commissioner, two Metropolitans, and 36 Rev. Doctors! Though it was not always possible to analyze fully from the questionnaire the role played by the respondents in the inter-church organizations it was noted that there were at least four Presidents, one General Secretary, two General Superintendents and one Executive Director. Clearly the GCF had been successful in attracting representatives from the Churches and the organizations from the highest level..

(It was encouraging to note that no one declared themselves 'retired' even though two were over 71! In the Christian world one never retires!!).

**1.vii. Source of funding for your attendance at Limuru, Nairobi.** (Who paid for your travel, accommodation and expenses?)

| Your employer | Grant from GCF | A mixture of GCF and employer | Paid for yourself. | A mixture of personal, GCF and employer |
|---|---|---|---|---|
| 29 | 15 | 6 | 2 | 5 |
| 51% | 26% | 10% | 3% | 9% |

Whilst 12% of the participants paid for all or some of the costs in attending the Nairobi Forum, the vast majority had their expenses paid either by their employer, or by the GCF or a mixture of both. Clearly the expenses incurred in attending such an international forum is beyond the reach of most people's personal funding, and necessitates the commitment of the sending organizations.

**1.viii. Previous involvement with GCF** (have you been to a GCF meeting/consultation before?)

| Not been to GCF before | Been to one GCF before | Been to two GCFs before | Been to three or more GCFs before |
|---|---|---|---|
| 37 | 11 | 4 | 4 |
| 65% | 19% | 7% | 7% |

Nearly two thirds of the participants at the Nairobi Forum had not previously attended any GCF meetings. A third had been to one or more GCF meetings before. The advantage of attending more than one meeting is that there is a chance of building up relationships over a period of years, the advantage of having new people at each meeting is that the vision can then be spread to a wider audience.

*Conclusion*

The GCF had been successful in attracting church leaders from a wide area of the world and from a wide and diverse range of Church traditions. It was still heavily represented by the 'old world' with Asia, the Middle East and, considering it was located in Nairobi, Africa under-represented. Of the Church traditions, the Pentecostals, the Evangelicals and the 'traditional' Protestants were most heavily represented, with the Orthodox, Roman Catholic and AIC churches under-represented.

Those attending were predominantly elderly males, which probably represented well the church leadership for whom it was aimed. Church leaders at a high level, largely from the denominational and inter-church organizations, and senior administrators formed the majority of the Forum, with a smattering of academics These were the people whom the GCF was targeting, people who would be able to influence their organizations in the future.

About two thirds of the Forum had not been to a GCF event before. Most of the attendees had their expenses paid either by their own organizations or came on the GCF funds.

## Analysis of Section 2: Your personal vision for the GCF

In seeking to find what the attendees thought the GCF should be about, they were asked to consider a list of different objectives for the GCF. This list was derived from the comments of the Continuation Committees and the literature. In each objective one or two words were highlighted to emphasize the particular theme of that objective. It was found that eight distinct objectives could be discerned emphasizing service, mission, witness, theological unity, political theology, mutual respect, developing relationships and common challenges. These objectives are listed in the table below.

Attendees were asked to rate each of them on a four point scale (4 = Most important, 3 = Very Important, 2 = Important, 1= Not Important). They were asked first how they think the GCF has been working so far, and then how they would *like* theGCF to be working. In each case an average score was derived from the responses to ascertain a rough score of perceived importance.

**2.i.** Please consider the following objectives for the GCF and rate each 4, 3, 2 or 1, as to how you think the GCF has been working so far.

The table below lists the given objectives and also the average rating that the Nairobi attendees gave to each.

| **Objective** | **Average Rating** |
|---|---|
| a. To unite the Body of Jesus Christ, for more effective **service** to the world | 2.74 |
| b. To bring the global Christian community into fellowship, to strengthen **mission** | 3.02 |
| c. To provide a space where all Christian traditions come together, to promote visible unity and common **witness** to non-Christians | 2.98 |
| d. To create a space where people of different denominational affiliations can talk together and find a greater sense of **theological unity** | 2.77 |
| e. To have a point of witness to our nations and develop a common **political theology** anchored in Christian orthodoxy which will speak to the nations | 1.81 |
| f. To create an open space where Christians from different churches can gather to foster **mutual respect,** and understanding. | 3.53 |
| g. To bring Christians from different traditions together to **develop relationships** which will yield greater unity between all Christians | 3.60 |
| h. To bring Christians together to explore and address together **common challenges.** | 2.98 |

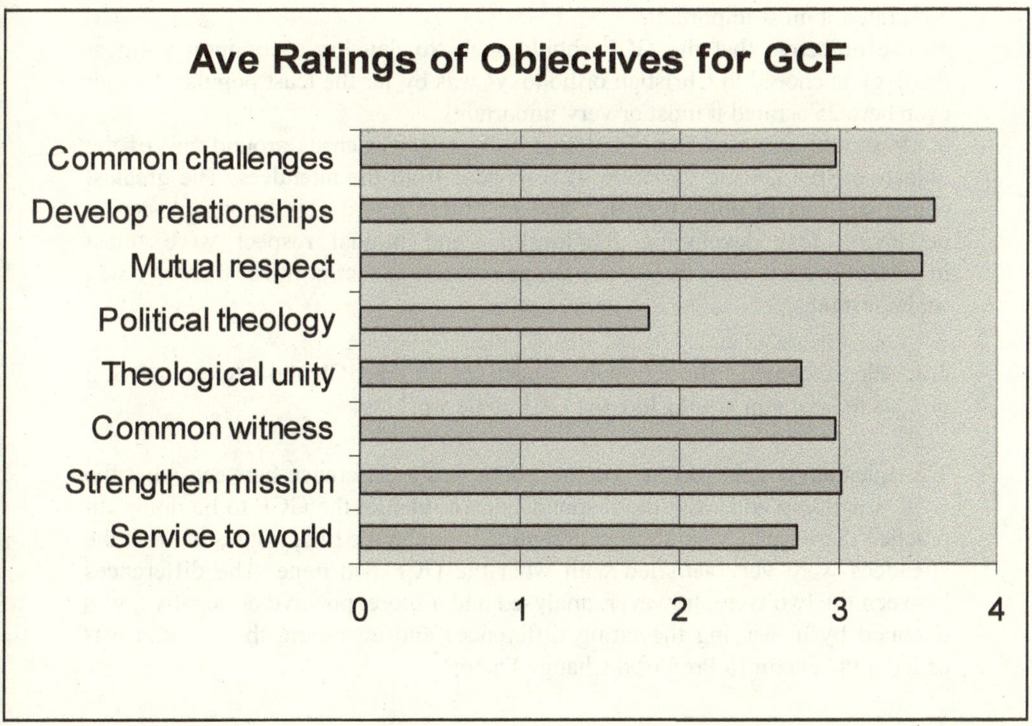

*Conclusion*

It will be seen that all of the objectives were perceived as having some importance, with the following points of particular significance:

1. The two objectives that respondents perceived the GCF held as most important were g and f, 'bringing Christians together from different traditions to develop relationships', and 'creating an open space where Christians from different churches can gather to foster mutual respect and understanding.' These themes of bringing Christians together to develop relationships, mutual respect and understanding are central to the GCF's vision.
2. Other themes, of 'strengthening mission', and 'promoting witness', were also seen as very important. These objectives suggest that the GCF should be doing something for the benefit of the 'outside world' rather than just bringing together different parts of the church itself.
3. A third theme, and one that is stated in the GCF's stated vision, the objective 'to bring Christians together to explore and address together to address common challenges', was also considered very important.
4. Though the first objective, a, to make the Church 'more effective in service to the world' was rated on average fairly low, it should be reported that a significant proportion, 54% rated it most important or very important, indeed 33% rated it most important.
5. The objective that the GCF should seek 'to develop a common political theology anchored in Christian orthodoxy' was by far the least popular, though even here 25% rated it most or very important!
6. It should be noted that there was no strong consensus around any of the objectives, but a wide variation of responses from the attendees. The greatest consensus was in objectives g, f and e – there was a very strong clustering perceiving that developing relationships and mutual respect were 'most important', and a very strong clustering perceiving that political theology was 'unimportant.'

**2.ii.** . Please consider the following objectives for the GCF and rate each, 4, 3, 2 or 1, as to how **you would like** the GCF to be working.

This question sought to find whether there was a difference between what the GCF was doing and what the respondents **would like** the GCF to be doing. In practice there was a very strong agreement between the two, suggesting that the attendees were very satisfied with what the GCF had done. The differences between the two were, however, analysed and a score, positive or negative, was obtained by measuring the rating differences and averaging them – this was called a PC Factor (a Preferred Change Factor)

| Objective | PC Factor |
|---|---|
| a. To unite the Body of Jesus Christ, for more effective **service** to the world | +0.35 |
| b. To bring the global Christian community into fellowship, to strengthen **mission** | +0.12 |
| c. To provide a space where all Christian traditions come together, to promote visible unity and common **witness** to non-Christians | +0.15 |
| d. To create an open space where people of different denominational affiliations can talk together and create a greater sense of **theological unity** | +0.05 |
| e. To have a point of witness to our nations and develop a common **political theology** anchored in Christian orthodoxy which will speak to the nations | +0.33 |
| f. To create a space where Christians from different churches can gather to foster **mutual respect,** and understanding. | +0.05 |
| g. To bring Christians from different traditions together to **develop relationships** which will yield greater unity between all Christians | -0.10 |
| h. To bring Christians together to explore and address together **common challenges.** | +0.31 |

*Conclusion*

It will be seen that there was no strong preference for change, with a small plea that more emphasis be put on offeriong more service to the world (a), developing a political theology (e), and exploring and expressing together common challenges (h).

## Analysis of Section 3: The Nairobi Forum, Nov 2007

**3.i** Please rate your impressions of the Nairobi Forum, as a whole and on the different aspects, on a four point scale (4 = excellent, 3 = very good, 2 = good, 1 = not very good)

This was a very pragmatic question to evaluate how the attendees at the Nairobii Forum rated the different components. The table below records the Average Rating for each:

| Aspect of Nairobi Forum | Average Rating |
|---|---|
| a. Overall impression of Nairobi Forum | 3.25 |
| b. Bible studies | 2.69 |
| c. Morning and evening prayers | 2.69 |
| d. Plenary talks | 2.88 |
| e. Plenary discussions | 2.56 |
| f. Sharing of personal journeys | 3.45 |
| g. Group discussions | 2.58 |
| h. Meetings per region | 2.43 |
| i. Meetings per tradition | 2.74 |
| j. Closing celebrations | 2.81 |
| k. Informal meetings and conversations | 3.37 |
| l. Quality of accommodation | 2.73 |
| m. Quality of meals | 3.23 |
| n. Quality of organisation | 3.40 |

*Conclusion*

The overall rating for all aspects of the conference was very good, which should give quiet satisfaction and pleasure to the Forum organisers.

1. The most appreciated parts of the Forum was i) the time spent 'Sharing of personal journeys'. This innovative part of the GCF methodology is clearly highly successful in building up mutual respect and understanding and developing positive relationships. And ii) the time spent on 'Informal meetings and conversations.' As in all such conferences and gatherings these informal meetings, outside the official programme, are invaluable in building up contacts and personal relationships.
2. As to the components of the formal programme, the inputs and the discussion, there was more divergence of opinion though the vast majority found them good or very good.
3. Perhaps the most lack of enthusiasm related to the meetings, by region or by tradition, and group discussions, though these would have varied depending on which group the respondent was in.

**3.ii.** Please consider the following objectives **for the Nairobi Forum** and rate each 4, 3, 2 or 1 according to how important each had been to you personally (4= Most important, 3= Very important, 2= Important, 1= Not important)

Different people would have come to the Forum with different hopes and expectations.

The table below rates the Average Rating for the respondent's personal objectives.

| Objective | Average Rating |
|---|---|
| a. To deepen ones own personal, spiritual journey | 2.60 |
| b. To meet, and get to know, Christians from other traditions | 3.41 |
| c. To increase understanding of similarities and differences between tradition | 3.25 |
| d. To make a public witness of Christian unity | 2.95 |
| e. To move the Church towards more structural unity between traditions | 1.86 |
| f. To move the Church towards common Christian action for the poor and justice | 2.62 |
| g. To move the Church towards common Christian action in mission | 2.54 |
| h. To clarify the future structure and purpose of the GCF | 2.85 |

*Conclusion*

The strongest reason that attendees had for coming to the Nairobi Forum agrees with their overall vision for the GCF:

1. They wanted to meet and get to know Christians from other traditions and to increase their understanding of similarities and differences between traditions.
2. The lowest rating was that aiming to move the 'Church towards a more structural unity between traditions.' This was rated far lower than that 'the

Church should move towards common Christian action for the poor and justice' and 'towards action in mission.'

**3.iii.** One of the problems that the GCF faces is communicating its message to the wider world. Many people, many Christians still do not know of the GCF. Please note below approximately how many people you were able to tell about the Nairobi Forum on your return. Please also note whether you were able to communicate to others through writing an article or in broadcasting (on radio, on T.V. or on the web)

This question sought to get a feel for the scale of the communication problem, sharing the vision and news about the GCF with the wider Christian world. Clearly the people who had been to the GCF would be the best advocates, speaking, writing and broadcasting to their contacts in their contexts.To this end the attendees were asked to give an estimate of the number of people they had spoken to about the GCF, the largest figure is recorded, and whether they had had the opportunity to write or to broadcast about the GCF.

| Means of communicating about Nairobi Forum | Number | Percentage |
|---|---|---|
| a. Spoke to less than 10 people. | 3 | 5% |
| b. Spoke to between 10 and 100 people. | 28 | 47% |
| c. Spoke to more than 100 people. | 29 | 48% |
| d. Wrote article on Nairobi Forum | 40 | 71% |
| e. Broadcasted about Nairobi on radio, TV or web | 18 | 32% |

*Conclusion*

Whilst it is impossible to know exactly how many people one has spoken to about the GCF, whether individually or to meetings, about half of the attendees estimated that they had spoken to less than 100 people whilst they other half had spoken to more than 100. Most, 71%, had written about GCF, either as an article or in a newsletter, and about a third, 32%, had broadcast about it either on radio, T.V. or the web – where the audience, and the effect on the audience is not easily determined.

Letting others know about the GCF is an intractable issue. Whereas the best way of communicating, especially when the message is about building relationships, is done in a personal, one to one, face to face manner. But when only 200 or so people are directly involved and each speaks to, say 100 people that will still only reach 20,000 people. And that, in a world of about 2,000,000,000 is a pretty small proportion.

**3.iv.** What was the most important outcome of the Nairobi Forum for you?
**3.v.** What aspect was most disappointing for you about the Nairobi Forum?

These two questions provided an opportunity for respondents to express in their own words how they had felt about the Nairobi Forum. Most responded very positively.

**3.iv.** What was the most important outcome of the Nairobi Forum for you?

1. The most common, and the most enthusiastic response, spoke of the fact that the Forum had happened. That Christians from so many different traditions had met together, sat together, prayed and discussed together, got to know each other, had shared fellowship, build trust, respect, and relationships in an atmosphere of fraternal love. 65% of respondents described some aspect of this, often in a tone of amazement that long standing prejudices, walls, had been broken down. The inclusion of the Pentecostals and evangelicals alongside the orthodox traditions was especially mentioned. In the words of one respondent this was the 'most important ecumenical meting I ever attended (and I have been to 100s!)'

2. The second most common response (11%) spoke of the commitment to continue the work, the process, of GCF, and the new sense of optimism and hope in the future for a new type of ecumenism, of churches sitting and working together, (another 8%).

3. Others spoke of specific parts of the programme. The time spent sharing personal journeys of faith together was mentioned (8%) as were the 'wonderful' bible studies (6%). One person mentioned the time when groups confessed their sins to each other.

4. Two people spoke of the importance of public witness, and the endorsement of the joint statement.

**3.v.** What aspect was most disappointing for you about the Nairobi Forum?

1. The most common response to this question was nothing, many left the question blank, others (21%) quite explicitly wrote in 'nothing' and often expanded on this positively.

2. Some (11%) spoke of the lack of opportunity to discuss matters of differences between the traditions in greater depth, others (7%) regretted the opportunity to discuss social issues of justice and equality, poverty and mission.

3. Some (12%) mentioned the lack of clear indication about the ways forward, for GCF, especially in some regions.

4. Certain organization issues were raised, the accommodation, and that it was separated from the Forum meeting place, lack of time, too many in discussion groups, plenaries not focused sufficiently, Bible-studies too much of a lecture and not discursive, but these were all individual reactions and often counteracted by others expressing opposite opinions! The absence of local press and TV was regretted.

5. Issues of the imbalance were mentioned in different forms, lack of women and young people, lack of Greek Orthodox, predominance of Pentecostals, absence of certain important Church leaders.

6. There was some indication of hurt feelings and judgmental attitudes, that the ecumenical efforts of the past were being disregarded, that the AICs were viewed with suspicion, that some appeared better than others, that some were trying to high-jack the meeting with their own agenda, but again this seemed minority feeling and should be seen I the much more positive attitudes felt by the vast majority.

*Conclusion*

1. The overwhelming response to the Forum was positive. The significance that it had happened, that church leaders from so many different traditions had met actually together amicably, in genuine harmony and respect, and had delighted in each other's company and faith journeys, cannot be over-emphasized.
2. The programme itself was well received, especially the informal sharing of journeys of faith and informal relationships and friendship opportunities. Though there was a certain criticism of particular events, these were personal and often mutually contradictory. The need to leave unstructured time and space for informal conversations is strong, and that will have implications for questions of accommodation and social space and time.
3. Different, contradictory, views were expressed about two issues. Should attempts be made to engage with past theological differences at a deep level? Should the Forum include discussion about 'social issues and mission', poverty and injustice etc? These differences are, I suspect, incompatible and could lead to a detrimental effect on the atmosphere of the Forum, concentrating as it does on what folk have in common.
4. There was a perceived imbalance in the Forum. Whilst folk were delighted to see the Pentecostals and Evangelicals at the Forum, there was a feeling that they were now predominant. The Orthodox churches were under-represented, as were the new African churches. Women were under-represented, as were the younger generation - though whether such a Forum designed for leaders in the church is the appropriate place for young people, or whether indeed GCF's focus should be on youth, is a matter for debate.

**Analysis of Section 4: The Future for the GCF**

The Nairobi Global Forum was the goal of nine years work for the GCF. So now the question was, and is, 'where do we go from here?' The Continuation Committee members provided some suggestions, and other possibilities suggest themselves. In this section the Nairobi attendees were asked to rate each of 21 possible ways that the GCF could seek to develop. Their responses are averaged and recorded, along with the possible future directions, below.

**Please consider the following possible actions for the GCF to pursue in the coming years, and rate how important you consider each to be. (4= Most important, 3= Very important, 2= Important, 1= Not important)**

| Possible future action for Global Christian Forum | Average Rating |
|---|---|
| a. To promote, through publications and the media, the GCF vision. | 3.17 |
| b. To appoint a leader, an 'ambassador', who will network and inspire leaders of the different traditions about the GCF vision. | 2.77 |
| c. To establish a well resourced secretariat for GCF. | 2.83 |
| d. To organise a series of global and regional Forum, like the Nairobi one. | 3.15 |
| e. To support/promote regional organisations to prosper GCF type activities in their own regions. | 3.21 |
| f. To continue the open-ended journey in the open space to see how God will bring His Church together. | 3.28 |
| h. To continue to build relationships between Christians of different traditions at the organisational level. | 3.17 |
| i. To hold regular encounters with the leaders of the different Christian traditions, perhaps every 2/3 years.. | 3.01 |
| j. To set up a series of joint workshop groups to consider and develop united responses to common Christian issues. | 2.75 |
| k. To organise a grand Global, all-tradition, Celebration of Christian Unity in a decades time. | 2.79 |
| l. To maintain the GCF process of working, a relational process of working, avoiding any large, bureaucratic structures. | 3.31 |
| m. To increase the number and variety of GCF Forum around the world. | 2.76 |
| n. To focus on certain issues common to all Christian traditions, and experiment with ways of dealing with these. | 2.02 |
| o. To use GCF to encourage the Churches to become more involved in political issues, eg fighting injustice and supporting the poor. | 2.56 |
| p. To revisit each of the regions which have had forum and focus on one (or more) issue of particular relevance to that region. | 2.38 |
| q. To organise a series of forum on a smaller regional, possibly national, level to bring together the traditions at a more local level. | 2.95 |
| r. To develop a series of guidelines which would be available to others in different regions so that they might benefit from GCF's experience | 2.87 |
| s. To infiltrate each Christian tradition at the highest level to engender through personal persuasion the GCF vision of relational unity | 2.73 |
| t. To engender a spirit of organic unity where Christians of different traditions work together in the service of their local communities. | 2.84 |
| u. To work towards terminating the existence of GCF, having successfully completed its task of acting as a model to stimulate unity in others. | 1.80 |
| v. To elicit a formal commitment from each of the main traditions and denominations to support GCF in terms of statements and resources. | 2.78 |

*Conclusion*

Perhaps unsurprisingly, each of the suggestions got strong support from most of the respondents but not entirely helpful in view of the limited resources likely to be available to the GCF in the future as in the past. The Continuation Committee will inevitably have to prioritize. The responses could be grouped as those who favoured continuing along the same path that had been trodden so far and those who favoured new initiatives.

1. As before, there was wide divergence between different attendees of the Nairobi Forum, with no strong consensus for a single course of action. The strongest consensus was around suggestion u, which suggested the possibility of moving towards terminating the existence of the GCF, having successfully completed its task as stimulating and catalyzing a new approach to unity – this suggestion was strongly rejected. This, and the very positive responses to all the other suggestions, suggests that everyone is very optimistic about a future for the GCF and wants, even assumes that, the GCF will continue strongly into the future.

2. The suggestions most strongly supported objectives, l and f, both supported the GCF approach 'to maintain the GCF process of relational working' and 'to continue the open-ended journey in the open space to see how God will bring His Church together.'

3. The next most popular suggestions group around the activities that the GCF should promote, d, e, a, and h., followed by k and l. 'To organise a series of global and regional Forum, like the Nairobi one' and 'To support/promote regional organisations to prosper GCF type activities in their own regions.' 'To organises a grand global, all-tradition, Celebration of Christian Unity in a decades time' and To increase the number and variety of GCF Forum around the world.' 'To continue to build relationships between Christians of different traditions at the organisational level' has practical ramifications for the type of staffing GCF should seek, as does the communication role inferred 'To promote, through publications and the media, the GCF vision.'

4. The development of regional GCFs was further supported in q, r, as well as d and e above. 'To organize a series of forum on a smaller regional, possibly national, level to bring together the traditions at a more local level' suggests an even more local level than at the regional levels and this might be supported by the 'development of a series of guidelines which would be available to others in different regions so that they might benefit from the GCF's experience.

5. Suggestions about the resourcing of the GCF in the future formed the next group, c and b. 'To establish a well resourced secretariat' and 'To appoint a leader, an 'ambassador', who will network and inspire leaders of the different traditions about the GCF vision.'

# CHAPTER 6
# THE MANAGEMENT STRUCTURE OF THE GCF

One of the most remarkable aspects of the GCF is, what might be euphemistically called, its management 'structure.' This section addresses the questions of how the GCF is run, how it is managed, what personnel is employed, what facilities it has, and how it is financed. The answer is quite remarkable, because there appears to be no management 'structure' in the accepted sense of the word, certainly not one that would be recognised in any organisational sense. But then the GCF is not an organisation rather more of a concept, a vision, driven by a group of like-minded Christians, lead by one individual Huibert van Beek. The GCF has, deliberately, a very light structure. (In this it follows the example of Jesus and his disciples, who also had no organizational structure – and look what they delivered!!).

The data on which this evaluation is based was supplied by Huibert van Beek in response to a series of specific requests, and supplemented by financial statements and other records. The questions, and this analysis, were based on aspects of Personnel, Structures and Office Arrangements, and Financial. (See Appendix Ae). All the accounts provided appeared to be in good order, (though they appeared not to have been audited externally and the evaluator is not a financial expert!)

## 6.1. Personnel, who runs the GCF?

*The GCF Secretariat*

Since 2004 there has been only one person employed at the GCF Secretariat, Huibert van Beek. Though officially a half-time appointment, in practice it is a full-time job. There is no secretarial support at the Secretariat, neither paid personnel nor volunteers. Prior to 2004 Huibert did this work as part of his portfolio as the WCC Programme Executive in the Office on Church and Ecumenical Relations of the WCC where he had administrative support.

*The regional meetings*

The main planning, organisation and management of the regional consultations have been performed by the Secretariat.

There has been a varying degree of organisational support by local people, often provided freely by a local supporting organisation, with some supportive help from local volunteers. The degree that the local organisations, the CCA, the CCZ, the CLAI and the WCC freely provided the time, expertise and support of members of their staff is a measure of their commitment to the GCF.

| Regional Meeting | Voluntary Support | Estimated time |
|---|---|---|
| Pasadena, 2002 | One person | 5 person-days |
| Asia, 2004 | One executive staff member of Christian Conference of Asia, plus administrative help | 10 person-days |
| Africa, 2005 | Three staff members of the Council of Churches, Zambia. | 30 person-days |
| Europe, 2006 | All done by GCF Secretariat. | |
| Latin America, 2007 | One executive staff member of Latin American Council of Churches, plus administrative assistance | 40 person-days |
| Nairobi, 2007 | Four WCC staff. | 30 person-days. |
| | Local committee of ten for year. | ? |
| | Moderator and Secretary of local committee | 60 person-days |

*Committee Meetings*

The Consultative Committee has met 13 times since 1998, with an average of 2 meeting days each. This took approximately 4 days per year, for each member over each of the nine years, in time freely allowed by the members' employing organisations. In total, reckoning on average ten persons attending each committee meeting, that is 360 person-days in total.

All of this time, and expertise, was given freely and constitutes a vast input of personnel at no cost to the GCF.

The GCF has always maintained that it wished to have a 'light' structure, avoiding becoming an organisation with large staffing commitments. The research shows that the Committee members and the Nairobi Forum attendees all wish it to remain working in such a way. However, there are questions about whether quite such a light organisational structure can work effectively as the GCF seeks to develop and expand in the future.

### 6.2 What does the Secretariat do, and where?

The Secretariat works out of a room in a private apartment in Geneva.

The main tasks of the Secretariat, as estimated by the present incumbent, are as follows:

| Tasks | % time spent |
|---|---|
| Organising the GCF committee meetings; convening, practicalities, agenda, papers, note-taking, report-writing, follow-up etc | 10% |
| Maintaining regular contact with committee members by email; updates, requests for advice, feedback etc | 10% |
| Organising meetings and consultation; invitations, practical arrangements, programme, report-writing, follow-up etc | 30% |
| Financial management; budgets for GCF activities and administration, fundraising, monitoring income and expenditure, keeping detailed accounts, financial reporting on consultations and annual reports | 15% |

| | |
|---|---|
| Communication; GCF website, written material on GCF, news bulletins, speaking assignments | 10% |
| Official correspondence on behalf of committee, with churches and organisations participating in GCF, responding to inquiries | 5% |
| Maintaining database of all churches, organisations and individuals involved with the GCF | 5% |
| Keeping the archives of GCF | 5% |
| Policy making; oversight of GCF process, maintaining the vision and the momentum, providing direction, formulating proposals, interaction with the main actors, drafting of policy documents | 10% |

*The Office*

The working space is a single room in a private apartment with a computer, laptop, telephone, fax, scanner, ADFSL and two printers - all of which (except one printer) is the personal property of the secretary.

The WCC occasionally provides administrative support, such as photocopying documents, as well as providing financial management for the GCF.

*The Status of the GCF*

The GCF is not a registered charity. It has no legal status and no trustees. It is not incorporated. It has no formal links with any other organisation. It has no formal status and is responsible only to itself, its Secretariat and its Committee members. It is a free spirit within a free body! The GCF is currently (2008) in negotiation with the WCC and the World Evangelical Alliance to take responsibility for the institutional and legal aspects of the GCF Secretariat around a Memorandum of Understanding.

## 6.3 Finances,

*a) Where does the money come from?*

Money has been required to run the activities: to pay for the Secretariat, the administration, the cost of travel and accommodation for the Committee meetings and for support and subsidies for attendees at the consultations and the Forum. Up to and including 2005, the WCC paid the salary of the secretary and related administrative costs and the costs of the Committee meetings. The WCC still supported the office of the Forum, covering the cost of the GCF Secretariat on a consultancy basis. Since 2006 several Christian World Communions have begun to contribute to the cost of the Secretariat.

| Organisations financing the Secretariat | 2005 | 2006 | 2007 |
|---|---|---|---|
| World Council of Churches | * | * | * |
| Anglican Consultative Council | | | * |
| Baptist World Alliance | | | * |
| Catholic Church | | | * |

| | | | |
|---|---|---|---|
| Disciples Ecumenical Cons, Council | | * | * |
| Lutheran World Federation | | * | * |
| Mennonite World Conference | | | * |
| Seventh Day Adventist | | * | * |
| The Salvation Army | | * | * |
| World Alliance of Reformed Churches | | * | * |
| World Evangelical Alliance | | | * |
| World Methodist Council | | * | * |
| **Approx Totals given** | **$25k** | **$30k** | **$33k** |

Donors have been asked to give support for specific meetings. Most of the money for the meetings has been obtained by requests from the Secretariat, and has come from a wide range of churches and ecumenical organisations. The table below indicates who supported the different consultations with the total given for each given in US dollars (n.b. the figures have been approximated into US$ from Swiss Francs, Euros, and UK£s. They are approximate as exchange rates have varied over the years.)

| Organisation financing for Meetings | 2000 | 2002 | 2004 | 2005 | 2006 | 2007 | Nairobi |
|---|---|---|---|---|---|---|---|
| Reformed Church in America | * | | | * | ** | | * |
| Church of Sweden | * | | | | | * | * |
| Council for World Mission | | * | | | | | * |
| World Vision International | | | * | * | * | | * |
| Salvation Army International | | | * | * | | | |
| Church of Norway | | | * | * | | | * |
| World Council of Churches | | | * | | | | |
| Protestant Church in Netherlands | | | | | * | | * |
| United Methodist Church | | | | * | * | | ** |
| World Vision Germany | | | | | * | | |
| Union that nothing be lost | | | | | | * | |
| Presbyterian Church (USA) | | | | | | * | * |
| United Church of Canada | | | | | | * | * |
| EMW Germany | | | | | | * | |
| Methodist Church UK | | | | | | * | * |
| Evangelical Lutheran Church in USA | | | | | | | * |
| Aeropagos (Norway) | | | | | | | * |
| Episcopal Church USA | | | | | | | * |
| Mennonite Central Committee | | | | | | | * |
| Mission Covenant Church of Sweden | | | | | | | * |
| FAP (France) | | | | | | | * |
| Pontifical Council for PCU | | | | | | | * |
| Evangelical Lutheran Church Finland | | | | | | | ** |
| APCM (Germany) | | | | | | | * |
| Stichting Rotterdam | | | | | | | * |
| Christian Aid UK/Ireland | | | | | | | * |
| Kerk in Actie (Netherlands) | | | | | | | * |
| International Church of the Foursquare Gospel | | | | | | | * |
| **Approximate Totals given** | **$20k** | **$40k** | **$26k** | **$43k** | **$31k** | **$42k** | **$240k** |

It will be seen that a total of $442 has been donated by 28 churches and Christian organisations to support the meetings, the consultations and the final Nairobi Forum, that have been held by the GCF. The vast majority of the financial support for the meetings has come from the traditional Protestant churches (56%) and the inter-denominational, ecumenical, organisations (42%). A very small amount (2%) has come from Roman Catholic organisations, even less (0.5%) from the Pentecostal church. It will be seen that no financial support has been provided by the Orthodox churches, Greek or Eastern, by the Evangelical organisations or churches (though there will be evangelicals within the traditional Protestant churches), or by the African churches.

Protestant churches in Scandinavia and America, and World Vision have been particularly supportive. Unsurprisingly all of the donations have come from the rich countries of the North.

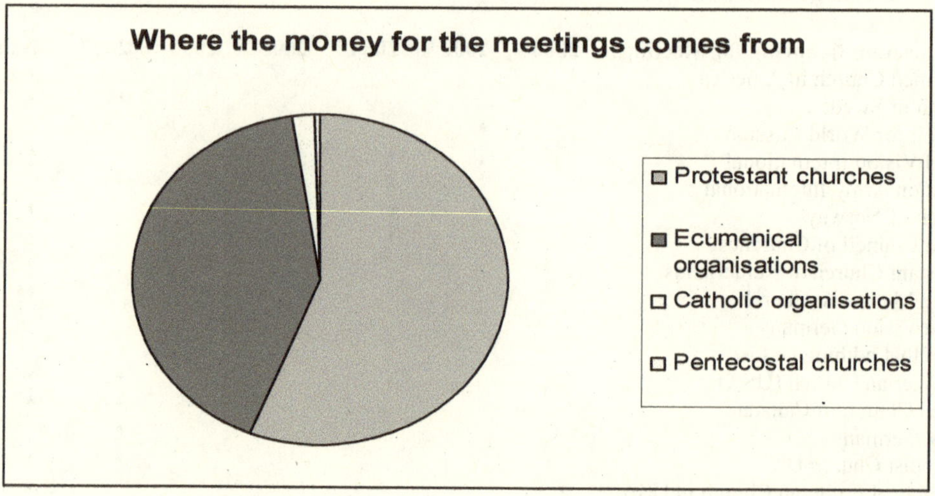


*b) Where does the money go to?*

The annual budget of the GCF Secretariat is approximately $30,000 and this covers the salary of the secretary and the running cost of the Secretariat.

The main costs arise around the meetings, especially certain subsidised travel and accommodation expenses for attendance at the consultations and Committee meetings: a Committee meeting is always held at the same time and place as a consultation to save travel costs. Some of the Committee members and delegates attending the consultations have all of part of their expenses paid by their employers. The expense report of the Warburg, Germany, consultation of 2006, will indicate typical travel and accommodation costs, (accounting for $11,500 of the total £31,000 budget);

| | |
|---|---|
| Travel for 10 delegates | 56% |
| Travel for 4 committee | 32% |
| Accommodation for 3 delegates | 4% |
| Accommodation for 3 committee | 8% |

There have been some small 'hidden costs' in holding meetings when the host organisation has made no charge for some accommodation, services and meals.

Similarly the GCF was designed and is now supported by the Evangelical Fellowship of India, with support from the Secretariat.

The Evangelical Fellowship of India who also produced the book on *The Global Christian Forum*, under the leadership of a GCF committee member, Richard Howell at no cost to the GCF. The GCF pamphlet was produced by the Evangelical Fellowship of India, whereas the Syrian Orthodox Church produced the second print.

To date, none of the activities that the GCF would have liked has been prevented through lack of money.

It appears that the financing of the GCF is very much a 'hand to mouth affair.' Money has been requested specifically for specific events. The words of the secretary in his *'Story of GCF'* is illuminating and worrying; *"In 2003 the Continuation Committee drew up a comprehensive budget including the cost of meetings, of the secretariat etc for the period 2004-2007. Until now it has not been possible to raise the funds for such an overall budget. The financial situation for the Forum is fragile and vulnerable."*

# CHAPTER 7
# CONCLUSIONS

These conclusions have been based on an analysis of the data received in the evaluation.

## Conclusion 1

The Global Christian Forum (GCF) has been a very remarkable and worthwhile initiative which has sought to introduce a new sort of ecumenism. It has sought to bring together leaders of all the main Christian traditions, from the South and the North, so that they might meet together, have fellowship together, learn more about each other, and thus build up trust and relationships in a non-threatening environment. In this aim GCF has succeeded. This in itself is a remarkable achievement and well worth pursuing further.

## Conclusion 2

GCF has brought together leaders from the traditional Anglican and Protestant churches, the Orthodox Churches and the Roman Catholic Church (who had traditionally been involved with ecumenical activities) with leaders from the Pentecostal, the Evangelical and the newer African churches (who had been cautious about ecumenical endeavours in the past). It had been particularly successful in getting Pentecostals and Evangelicals involved. Though the Orthodox churches were less well represented at the Nairobi Forum, they played a constructive and active part there, and fully endorsed the final affirmative Guiding Purpose Statement of the Forum.

## Conclusion 3

The GCF deliberately aimed to build up relationships and trust, and was not concerned with any form of structural unity or discussion of doctrine. It saw itself as a *process*, even a methodology, and not as an organisation. It aimed to 'journey together' rather than to achieve an end-point. This approach, in line with the current postmodernism in society, has been effective in keeping Christians from quite different traditions, and beliefs, in harmony. This has been effective in avoiding dissension through into the Nairobi Forum. Whilst some believed that the GCF should 'have gone deeper' in theological discussion this would have put such harmony under strain.

### Conclusion 4

This 'process' approach meant that an evaluation of what was actually achieved was not possible. Meeting together at the GCF meetings to develop relationships became an end in itself where the question of 'what are we meeting for?' was not asked. There were some, both within the Committee and at the Forum, who would have liked the GCF to have addressed issues relating to strengthening mission and being of more effective service to the world.

### Conclusion 5.

The Purpose Statement stated that the GCF should *'create an open space wherein representatives from a broad range of churches and inter-church organisations, which confess the triune God and Jesus Christ as perfect in His divinity and humanity, can gather together to foster mutual respect, to explore and address together common challenges.'* The GCF has been successful for over 250 Christians from over 24 different churches and 18 different inter-church organisations in fulfilling the first part of this purpose, *to gather together to foster mutual respect.* It has not been successful in the final phrase, *to explore and address together common challenges.*

### Conclusion 6

Though one of the aims of the GCF was to be more global, universal in its geographical coverage, and more representative of the South where the Christian Church is most active and growing the fastest, the leadership of the GCF still appears to be rather Eurocentric, still very much lead by the 'old world.' This may be partly due to the Secretariat being based in Geneva and the global leadership of many of the churches being based in the 'West'. The growing, thriving churches in Asia, South America and Africa are under-represented on the Continuation Committee. S.E. Asia and China, especially, are under-represented.

### Conclusion 7

The original aim of the GCF was to hold a global Forum within two years whereas in reality it took nine years since the programme was conceived in Bossey, 1998. However, the setting up in sequence of preparatory regional meetings for Asia, Africa, Europe and South America and the Caribbean, and then the main global Forum in Nairobi, took much longer than anticipated – partly because of the tiny size of the secretariat, one person working largely without secretarial assistance. In retrospect, the Committee believe that the longer time span was beneficial in developing a 'way of working' and building up relationships. Nine years is a short time in church history. Nevertheless our judgement is that given more organisational resources, a shorter time span would have been preferable for building up and maintaining momentum.

### Conclusion 8

There has been one consultation meeting in each of the four regions. It would be hoped that such consultation would lead to further self-motivated networking in each region, to carry forward the GCF vision without further input from the Secretariat. It seems that this has happened to some extent in Asia and in South America. The development of such self-sustaining Forum in each region will be a test of the success of the GCF.

### Conclusion 9

The GCF has been taken forward by a tiny Secretariat, one remarkable man working part-time out of his 'office' in Geneva, supported by a Consultative Committee. This Committee has consisted of about ten men and women representing the different Church traditions, regions and gender. All are volunteers and are working full time in responsible and demanding jobs for their employing body. This volunteer nature of the Committee has been helpful in that they have been fully in touch with other Christian leaders in their tradition and are thus influential there, but it has the problem that they do not have the time to help significantly with the running of the GCF. Though the Committee have very different perceptions in many ways, they all share the GCF vision both in their personal and professional lives. They form a network which has wide contacts in the ecumenical fields. The commitment and consistency of the core members of the Committee over the nine years of GCF has been impressive. There is, however, a predominance of people from the 'old world' traditions in Christianity. There will be a need of replenishing the Committee with more representation from the newer churches in the South if it is truly to engage with the churches in the developing world.

### Conclusion 10

The organisation, maintenance and existence of the GCF has depended almost exclusively on one man, Huibert van Beek. He has been the GCF. The dependence of the GCF on this one, remarkable man can not be over-emphasised. His retirement from the GCF in 2009 will indeed be a watershed. Both the role and the resourcing of the Secretariat and leadership of the GCF will determine how, and whether the GCF continues.

### Conclusion 11

The GCF is indeed at a watershed. Having become established and delivered its first main objective in the Nairobi Forum, and with the staffing of the founding Secretariat about to change, the question of whether the GCF wants to 'continue as before' or to consolidate into a more secure 'structure' will need to be faced. This is the challenge for the Continuation Committee.

### Conclusion 12

The members of the Continuation Committee and those attending the Nairobi Forum are the people, the leaders of the Churches, who constitute and who are the targets of the GCF. Their views as revealed by the research questionnaire are thus absolutely vital in considering the future for the GCF, the way that the GCF should develop. They strongly assert that the GCF had been successful and should continue.

Of the 21 possible ways forward, six were rated as most, as very, important. Primarily, they wished to maintain the GCF process, a relational process of working, avoiding any large bureaucratic structures and they wished to continue the open-ended journey in the open space to see how God will bring His Church together – to continue working as before. They wished to support/promote regional organisations to prosper GCF type activities in their own regions – to develop regionally. They wished to promote, through publications and the media, the GCF vision and to continue to build relationships between Christians of different traditions at the organisational level –to promote, advocate the GCF to church organisations. And they wished to organise a series of global and regional Forum, like the Nairobi one – to hold meetings.

### Conclusion 13

The organisation and management of the GCF has been deliberately 'light'. Every one involved has resolved that it shall not become 'an organisation.' It has no legal structure, nor any board of governors to whom it is accountable. It is based on competence, good judgement and personal integrity of all those involved. It has been supported financially by donors from 28 churches and inter-church organisations, on a day-to day, 'begging' basis. All the donors are from the North, the vast majority from the 'old world' protestant, ecumenical organisations and churches. Whilst recognising the wisdom of not wanting to become too organisational, our judgement is that the current structure is too light and that if the GCF is to survive, even to develop, then it needs more staff, more accountable management and sounder financing.

### Conclusion 14

The climax of the GCF process has been the Nairobi Forum, which was reckoned to be a great success by those who attended it. In the two main objectives of the Forum, to develop relationships and to foster mutual respect, there was a very strong feeling among the attendees that it had succeeded. It attracted 226 leaders, from each of the main Christian traditions and, judging by the number of Archbishops, Bishops, and General Secretaries present, it achieved its aim of attracting influential leaders at the very highest level. It consciously aims at influencing the leaders of the churches and inter-church organisations, it is up to them to disseminate the GCF vision to its lay members. This group is the appropriate target, but it necessarily limits the public influence of the GCF - it is a top-down strategy.

### Conclusion 15

One of the great successes of each of the consultations and the Forum has been the time spent when each person shares the story of 'their personal journey' with God. These times, though time consuming, have been unanimously found to be humbling and inspirational, and of enormous value in helping to realise the important commonality and reality of each others Christian experience. This, above all, has been most important in developing mutual respect and trust, and to build up relationships.

### Conclusion 16

Perhaps the greatest weakness in the GCF has been the limited communication of their vision to the wider Christian world. They have communicated through personal contact, through periodic newsletters and press releases, through the distribution of a pamphlet flier, through the distribution of a book about the Global Christian Forum, and through a website. Though this evaluation did not seek to find how far the work of GCF has penetrated the Christian world, or has been an act of witness to the outside world, personal enquiries to a random sample of church leaders suggest that this communication has not been effective and that the GCF is unknown among the church as a whole. However, in so far as the GCF is not aiming to communicate directly with the Christian world as a whole, but to the leadership of the different Christian traditions, this awareness of the GCF by the church as a whole is not unsurprising, or inappropriate. If a greater direct influence was hoped for among the church as a whole, then a less top-down approach would be needed.

## Conclusion 17

Early approaches to ecumenism have sought to bring Christians together in some form of doctrinal and ecclesiastical unity. The GCF have developed a different and distinctive approach where Christians from different traditions have been brought together in a non-threatening context, to develop personal relationships and trust through sharing their own personal spiritual journeys. This has been effective. But should it be an end in itself? There is another, a third, approach to ecumenism in which Christians from different traditions come together to work together on common tasks in service to the needs and the needy in God's world. The GCF will need to consider whether they are satisfied with the second approach or whether they would want to move into the third, an organic, approach to ecumenism, where the churches are encouraged to work together in the Lord's service.

## Conclusion 18

The number of those directly interacting with the GCF process has inevitably been small, less than 500 people, and the task that it has set itself, bringing together the whole of Christendom across the whole world, is enormous. The team so far working for this vision is tiny, as indeed is the resourcing. The differing historical traditions and the mistrust between the different branches of Christendom remain tremendous problems. The aim of the GCF might be seen as quixotic! However, where there are such men and women as the GCF Committee seeking to answer Jesus' prayer that 'they may be one as we are one' then the work of the GCF must be encouraged and supported.

# CHAPTER 8
# RECOMMENDATIONS TO THE GCF.

On reflection and consideration of the data and the conclusions above the following recommendations are made to the GCF and its Continuation Committee. The recommendations have deliberately been written in strong terms, so that they may sharpen the debate on the underlying issues that the Committee will need to confront. It is hoped that, in this way, they will provoke further constructive debate within the GCF and be helpful to them in reaching the most appropriate action as the GCF moves into the future.

### Recommendation 1

The Secretariat and the members of the Continuation Committee should quietly and humbly congratulate themselves on what they have achieved through the GCF in the past decade, and give thanks to the Lord whom they have served and in whose strength they have achieved such positive achievements.

### Recommendation 2

The committee should seek to review, to re-establish, to sharpen and re-focus, its aim and vision, and modify where appropriate. In particular, should it be aiming at the churches' leadership only or to the Christian world as a whole? Should it be aiming to develop relationships and trust only or seek to take the church leaders onto more corporate acts of witness, of service, of mission and of tackling the world's problems? Our recommendation, in view of the limited resources likely for the work of the GCF, is that the GCF should focus exclusively on the leadership of the churches, and that its prime aim should be about building relationships and trust there. Any secondary aims, such as presenting a common Christian witness to the world or seeking to tackle the spiritual and physical needs of God's world, good and important though they are, should be left to other agencies within the churches.

### Recommendation 3

Underlying the aim of the GCF should be an organic view of ecumenism, in which the churches witness to, and work together in God's service for the good of His needy and suffering world. It should not concern itself with a structural form of doctrinal and ecclesiastical unity. It should accept and welcome differences among those who recognise and worship the triune God and Jesus as their Saviour and Lord, and should readily work and worship together.

**Recommendation 4.**

The GCF should seek to build constructive relationships between the leaders of the different church traditions in three ways: by holding a Global Forum once a decade, by holding regional or national forums more regularly, and by personal networking at both the global and the regional levels.

**Recommendation 5.**

The GCF vision should also be pursued among church leaders at the Regional level. The original GCF pattern of working, with a volunteer co-ordinator and supporting committee representing the main church traditions in the region, should be encouraged there. Its aim would be to develop good working relationships between the regional and local leaders and to hold a periodic regional, high profile forum.

**Recommendation 6**

Whilst the Continuation Committee has been effective in the past it should be modified in three ways. 1. Its role should be explicitly as a Steering Committee, and should be renamed as such. 2. Its membership should be as representatives of the different Church traditions, who should be approached specifically to make appointments as their representatives, though *ad hominem* suggestions could be made from the Secretariat. 3. Its membership should seek to be more geographically representative, especially from the South and from S.E.Asia. It would be the Committee to which the GCF staff would be accountable.

**Recommendation 7**

The main, global direction should remain under the guidance of a steering / continuation Committee. The actual physical location of the central Committee is less important in these days of electronic communication, than the appointment of the 'right person', whereever in the world they live and work. It should be located where the principal member of staff is living, with consideration given to where the key church leaders and 'gatekeepers' are to be found. It should communicate electronically and meet as a Committee at the same time and place as one of the regional meetings. Any office should be a 'virtual', electronic office.

**Recommendation 8**

Whilst it *is* possible that the 'genius' of the GCF could continue unstructured and uninhibited by formal organisational structures, and the GCF Continuation Committee should seriously consider that possibility, it is our judgement that it will be better served by moving into a consolidation phase with a more secure organisational structure, though keeping that as light, apolitical and sensitive as possible.

**Recommendation 9**

As the GCF is moving from its conception and implementation phase to its consolidation phase, the staffing, and the role of the staff, should be reconsidered appropriately. A minimum of two full-time equivalent, paid staff are required. The role of the staffing should be a) as an 'ambassador' to further the GCF vision and b) as a supporting Secretariat.

**Recommendation 10**

The CEO of the GCF should have the ambassadorial role, with the prime brief of promoting the GCF vision to Church leaders and 'gatekeepers' through networking and personal contact. This should be a full-time, paid appointment, though it would be possible, perhaps even desirable, to have a job share with two GCF ambassadors working part-time, alongside another part-time job, in different regions of the world.

**Recommendation 11**

A paid Secretariat alongside the CEO should be appointed, probably at the same location as the CEO. Again, this might be a spilt appointment if the ambassadorial post was split.

**Recommendation 12**

Regional committees should be set up in each of the regions to prosper the GCF vision and arrange regional forum. These should be voluntary, focussed on a volunteer co-ordinator, containing at least one person from each of the main church traditions who would represent and be supported by their employing church organisation. Other members might represent inter-church organisations.

**Recommendation 13**

A programme of Global and Regional Forums should be planned, possibly about once every five years.

**Recommendation 14**

The GCF should produce a regular Newsletter, both electronically and in hard copy, aimed at the leadership within the main church traditions and inter-church organisations. This would necessitate the appointment of a Director of Communication, probably available on a voluntary basis. Such a Director of Communication would be a member of the Continuation Committee and have responsibility for the GCF website. The existing book, *Global Christian Forum: Transforming Ecumenism,* and the brochure *One Face, Many Voices,* should remain as an excellent basis for informing folk about the GCF, and should be promoted more.

**Recommendation 15**

Any organisational structures should be kept 'light', a Steering Committee (evolving from the old Continuation Committee) representing each of the main Church traditions and some inter-church and ecumenical organisations should suffice. Such a Committee would not only guide and support the GCF in its policy but would ensure that their parent bodies took some responsibility for its affairs, both legally and financially. The accounts of the GCF should be audited regularly.

**Recommendation 16**

Though the finances of the GCF should remain modest, a budget should be set up for the next five years, to pay for the staffing (one full-time Ambassador post, one full-time Administrative support), and the expenses necessary to run the Secretariat, the travel and accommodation. Separate budgets should be set up for the regional and global Forums. A Director of Finances should be appointed, and be a member of the Continuation Committee. This post should be honorary, with expenses paid.

**Recommendation 17**

When the budget has been developed, probably in the order of $250k per year, funding should be sought from the different Church traditions and denominations, and also from the inter-church organisations and Christian NGOs. Regional budgets should seek funding largely, but not exclusively, from their regional church organisations. Those supporting the Nairobi Forum should be the first to be approached. Donors should also be sought from Asia, especially, and the developing churches in the South, as financial commitment also produces support and involvement.

**Recommendation 18**

Whilst Huibert van Beek will, thankfully, remain in post until the end of 2009, his priorities should be in building up the Steering Committee representation from the different main Church traditions and inter-church organisations, and their financial commitment, and encouraging regional committees around selected Regional co-ordinators.

# THE GLOBAL CHRISTIAN FORUM 1998-2007, AND BEYOND

## AN EVALUATION REPORT BY CENTRE IIMO UTRECHT UNIVERSITY, THE NETHERLANDS

## INTRODUCTION

### Background

In early 2008, when Mr. Huibert van Beek, on behalf of the Committee of the GCF, approached Centre IIMO, the plan was to have a joint evaluation of both Centre IIMO and the Oxford Centre for Mission Studies (OCMS in the UK). However, it was not possible to conduct this evaluation for both organizations simultaneously, and the Committee of the GCF decided that each centre would each carry out its own evaluation. To avoid duplication, it was decided that each of centres would assume a particular focus in its evaluation. Centre IIMO would focus on the leadership of churches and organizations which were represented at the Limuru gathering, whether or not they personally attended any GCF-gathering, while OCMS would concentrate on the participants of the Limuru meeting. Huibert van Beek reported that a third evaluation would be conducted in Latin America, the implication being that Centre IIMO did not have to approach Latin American churches and organizations. Occasionally, the IIMO researchers experienced misunderstandings because of this complicated situation.

### About this report

We begin by offering an account of our working method. In subsequent chapters, we describe the opinions we encountered through our interviews and through responses to our questionnaire. Most of these chapters end with a few concluding remarks. The last chapter summarizes the conclusions of the preceding chapters and calls attention to a number of points as well.

We have not included in this evaluation our own description of the history of the Global Christian Forum. Instead, we refer to the description of the GCF written by its secretary, Huibert van Beek, and available on the website at www.globalchristianforum.net. Readers who are not well informed of the aims, work and structure of the GCF, are advised to read that document first. We have also included it with this report as Appendix 4.

**Methodology**

The process of the evaluation was structured as follows:

1. To begin the evaluation, Mr. Huibert van Beek, secretary of the Continuation Committee of the GCF, was asked to provide the researchers with all the documentation available on the GCF. This included reports, notes of committee meetings, participants lists of meetings, financial documents, letters of invitation to meetings, as well as other documents. The researchers themselves complemented this material with documents from the World Council of Churches and from other organizations and churches.

2. After studying the documentation, a work plan was formulated.

3. Dutch ecumenical experts from different denominational backgrounds were asked to function as an advisory board for the researchers. This board discussed and amended the work plan. Members of this board included Dr. Martien Brinkman (Reformed, Professor of Ecumenical/Intercultural Theology at the Vrije Universiteit), Dr. Anton Houtepen (Roman Catholic, former Professor of Ecumenics and former Director of Centre IIMO) and Dr. Leo Koffeman (Reformed, Professor of Church Law and Ecumenism at the Protestant Theological University). As it was not possible to add Ref. Peter Sleebos, Pentecostal Church leader, to this board we conducted a long interview with him.

4. The next step was to have interviews with representatives of the leadership of churches in the Netherlands, with people active in different church bodies (Roman Catholic, Protestant, Old Catholic, Pentecostal) and ecumenical experts. We held a total of 12 interviews in the Netherlands.

5. In the meantime, the researchers planned a week's visit to Geneva to conduct interviews with staff members of organizations in and around the Ecumenical Centre. From May 26 to 30, both researchers visited Geneva. During one full day they interviewed the secretary of the GCF. The other days were filled with interviews with 17 representatives of the World Council of Churches (WCC), Lutheran World Federation (LWF), World Alliance of Reformed Churches (WARC), Moscow Patriarchate, Conference of European Churches (CEC), Young Women Christian Association (YWCA) and World Student Christian Federation (WSCF), totalling 16 interviews. Topics besides the GCF were discussed in these interviews too, in particular, the future of the relations between churches and church families. In chapter 6, 'Ecumenical Perspectives', we have included important remarks made during the interviews with regard to this issue.

6. After returning from Geneva, the researchers designed a questionnaire which took into account the issues indicated by the Committee as important criteria for the evaluation (see *Terms of Reference* of 07-01-2008, Appendix 1). The questionnaire is divided into seven sections: the initiative of the GCF, the appraisal of the purposes of the GCF, the importance of the GCF, the appreciation of the Limuru meeting, the future of the GCF, ecumenical

perspectives and additional comments. In the questionnaire, ample space was given for respondents to share their views on the issues at stake. The evaluators realized that method might yield an overwhelming number of opinions, however, they chose this method so they could get a full picture of the respondents' rationale for their opinions.

7. A list was compiled that included a selection of churches from all church families which attended the Limuru meeting and all organizations present in Limuru.

8. The questionnaires were sent to churches and organizations on this list, for which official addresses were available to the researchers. In cases where no addresses could be found, the questionnaire was sent to the representative of the church or organization who had attended the Limuru meeting and included a request to forward the mail to a suitable person in the leadership. A *Letter of Introduction*, written by the secretary of the GCF on the request of Centre IIMO, explaining the background of the evaluation, was attached to the questionnaire. New e-mail addresses were chosen to replace those which were repeatedly returned as undeliverable.

9. Of these 72 questionnaires, 8 were returned by the 1st of August, the date stated deadline for returning the questionnaire.

10. As this number was regarded as too small to reflect the scope of opinions of the participants of the GCF, and because it appeared that not all church families were adequately represented in the replies, the deadline was extended to September 1st and people at the non-responding addresses were reminded of the request for their co-operation. In some cases new addresses were used. Twelve new contacts were added for the same reason. Some contacts responded that they had already sent in their reply; it appeared they had mixed up the OCMS-questionnaire with the one of Centre IIMO. As a result, a total of 16 questionnaires were returned by the leadership of churches and organizations or church staff members assigned to the task of ecumenical relations, and three responses - one short and two elaborate - laid out why the respondent had not completed the questionnaire.

11. As mentioned, the Centre IIMO primarily focussed on the leadership of churches and organizations. After some time, the researchers realized that they would not succeed in getting as much responses from this group as they had hoped. At the same time, they began to feel the need to consult with more people involved in ecumenical debates and in theological study centres of all denominations. As there were no financial resources to support travel to interview people in other countries, we chose to send letters to several people engaged in ecumenical research in different countries around the world, with special emphasis on experts from denominations not sufficiently represented at that point. These contacts were given the option of completing the questionnaire or writing their views on the present and future of the GCF in their own words. Thus, in July and August, 38 experts were contacted. Eight responses were received. The researchers were surprised to learn that several

ecumenical experts knew little of the GCF; sometimes so little that they declared themselves incapable of completing the questionnaire. The fact that so many of them did not react at all - even though in several cases they were acquainted with one of the evaluators and their advisors and had promised they would complete the questionnaire or express their views by letter - could also indicate they were not well enough informed on the subject to participate. We will return to this observation in our conclusions.

12. The returned questionnaires and answers as well as the reports of the interviews were then used as the source for the report. *In total 156 people were addressed and 59 of them participated in this evaluation in one way or another.* Where deemed important in reporting responses, we distinguish between answers given by leaders of churches and organizations and answers given by ecumenical experts. Sometimes, answers given in the questionnaires were placed in one section, when, in the eyes of the evaluators, they belonged in a different section with the result that remarks made under 'Further Comments' were dispersed over several other sections.

## Anonymity

The respondents were guaranteed that their names would not be attached to their quotes; if the researchers decided a name should be attached, permission would be sought. This did not become necessary.

## The division of the respondents

We decided that, after the division of the respondents into church leaders and ecumenical experts, the next most important division among respondents was their denomination and the type of organization they represent. Since the questionnaire had been send to individuals at 'top levels' within their church or organization, we did not consider their role within their church or organization an important division. Where necessary and possible, then, these groupings are indicated in the reproduction of the answers. Below we give a snapshot description of the participants. In Appendix 3 a more detailed differentiation of the respondents is given.

### *a. Interviews*

A total of 31 people were interviewed. Without including Huibert van Beek these included 16 people working in different ecumenical organizations, 6 ecumenical experts, 6 church leaders and 2 representatives of youth organizations. These 30 people represent Anglican, Lutheran, Reformed, Old Catholic, Orthodox, Pentecostal and Roman Catholic backgrounds. Of course, often leaders of churches and ecumenical organizations or networks are ecumenical experts too, but it seemed appropriate to mention their formal function as this was the reason why they were consulted.

*b. Questionnaires to churches and organizations*

The division between churches and organizations made by the GCF itself in its list of participants of meetings was used for the questionnaire. With the exception of Latin America, wherever churches were situated in different countries, a geographical variety was assured. In some cases, more than one address was used for the same church or organization. Seventy-four questionnaires were sent out in June, and another twelve in August. In some cases the researchers had already interviewed staff members of these churches and organizations; these were deducted from the number of addressees. Nineteen, or 22 per cent, of these 86 yielded responses.

*c. Questionnaires to ecumenical experts*

Several ecumenical experts from diverse church backgrounds were interviewed (see previous paragraph). Forty other experts were asked to give their views by completing the questionnaire or responding in their own way. Nine of these, or 23 per cent, responded.

In the final chapter we share our conclusions regarding the responses to the questionnaire, but here we would like to point out that of the five main traditions - Orthodox, Roman Catholic, Protestant, Evangelical and Pentecostal - we received no responses from anyone representing the Orthodox Church. The only input in this evaluation from the Orthodox tradition were the four interviews held in Geneva. Of the less dominant traditions, we only received responses from the African Instituted Churches, Old Catholics and the Seventh-day Adventists.

## Abbreviations used

As much as possible, no abbreviations are used to describe the respondents, except where they facilitate legibility of the text. In these cases the respondents are indicated in the following ways, for reasons of anonymity and convenience: African Instituted Churches: Afr.Inst.Ch.; Anglican: Angl.; Ecumenical Organizations: EcO; Evangelical: Evan.; Migrant Churches Together: Migr.; Pentecostal: Pent.; Protestant: Prot.; Reformed: Ref.; Roman Catholic: RC; Seventh-day Adventist: Adv. Staff members of ecumenical organizations who were interviewed are indicated as: 'Orth/Ref. etc. in EcO'. Ecumenical experts are indicated as 'RC/Ref. etc ecumenical expert'.

## To conclude

The evaluators are aware that the working method they applied does not guarantee that a representative picture of all different opinions is given in the report. However, they know that the future of the GCF is not decided upon by democratic voting, but by carefully weighing views and opinions and by exploring new ways in ecumenical encounter. That is why we think it is more important that we gathered as many opinions as possible from those who play a role in the reflection and the decision-making processes of churches and church-related and ecumenical organizations. We are not likely to provide *the* answer to the future of the GCF with this report, but we do think it can offer important building blocks for reflecting on the GCF's future.

## 1. On the Initiative of the GCF

**Did you consider the initiative of the GCF in 1998 to be a necessary step?**

Space was given for elaboration in answering to this first question. Two respondents critiqued the word '*necessary*': an Evangelical church leader said it was '*a very desirable step*', and an Anglican ecumenical expert preferred to speak of it as a '*timely, appropriate, prophetic*' step.

The respondents gave several motives for the founding of the GCF. Most of them mentioned the need to engage Evangelicals and Pentecostals in the ecumenical debate. Additional motives were also given: the crisis of the traditional ecumenical movement, the changing times which make a different approach to ecumenical encounters necessary, and the position of the Orthodox in the WCC.

### To meet Evangelicals and Pentecostals

All other respondents answered that in their view, the establishment of the GCF was necessary. The ecumenical movement in its present form cannot do what the GCF does at this time. As a Reformed church leader said in words confirmed by a Reformed ecumenical expert:

> I believe the WCC in its current form could not find a way to engage the Evangelical and Pentecostal communities, nor could it find an organizational place for the Catholic Church.

Almost all respondents referred to the position of the Evangelical and Pentecostal churches (although some, especially Roman Catholic respondents, speak only of '*communities*') being outside the multilateral ecumenical encounters despite their growing numbers and influence. Evangelicals stressed that, until now, no other forum or organization had had the inviting capacity of the GCF to bring together leadership from various Christian traditions. A forum like the GCF was needed because almost all of the respondents felt embarrassed that until the GCF started, Pentecostals and Evangelicals were not included in ecumenical encounters as a matter of course. Several respondents mentioned the fact that many Pentecostals and Evangelicals have strong reservations about the traditional ecumenical movement which made a new initiative necessary. An Orthodox church leader noticed the same reservations in his church. We will come back to this issue in chapter 6.

### Change is needed in the traditional ecumenical movement

A Reformed church leader shared a sentiment that was echoed by an Evangelical church leader. He noted that the WCC has learned to see that change is needed and that the traditional churches might benefit from the presence of the Evangelicals and the Pentecostals in their midst. He added that this change would continue even after the creation of the GCF. He also said:

> While I am grateful to the WCC for its role in helping the GCF get started, the WCC itself has run into walls and barriers it cannot seem to overcome. I compare it to some national experiences (USA, UK) where councils of churches are either replaced or supplemented by more flexible alliances that include all traditions.

A Pentecostal leader was glad that the GCF was able to convince Evangelicals and Pentecostals that the whole church would benefit of their participation in certain ecumenical arenas, and he continued:

> The GCF offers a means by which they can get their feet wet without being compromised. Once they have learned to trust other ecumenical partners, they might be more open to engaging them in a more substantive way. I think the GCF is playing a critical role in that agenda.

At the same time, an Orthodox staff member of an ecumenical organization cautioned that the attention given to Pentecostals and Evangelical could take the attention away from 'traditional' ecumenical partners for each other.

### Other motives: different times

Other motives for the formation of the GCF were also mentioned.

A Roman Catholic ecumenical expert remarked that, compared to the oikoumene that developed in the 20th century, a new situation has arisen: a new constellation of Christianity for which the instruments that were developed in the past are no longer suited. New instruments and new methods of discussion are needed. That is perhaps what an Anglican church leader meant when she wrote that the GCF was necessary for '*breaking away from the sort of ecumenism that begins (and often ends) with too narrow a focus on divisive faith/order questions*'. Something similar was said by an Evangelical church leader:

> GCF has made it possible to incorporate the broader 'Evangelical' movement and Roman Catholicism in ecumenical conversations on a non-dogmatic level. This is certainly a gain for ecumenism.

An Orthodox expert thinks that the way membership, membership fees and structures are no longer attractive is '*in the air*'; nowadays we must talk of new ecumenical spaces and not about ecumenical structures. That makes the GCF more interesting. The WCC has to learn to cope with this development.

A Reformed ecumenical expert stated that the GCF is born out of despair, because there are so many disappointing developments which ask for change, like the growing number of ecumenical organizations, and, in relation to that, the existence of an ecumenical caste with its own language. In addition, he deplored the fact that, as a reaction to globalisation, churches nowadays focus more and more singly on their own identity at the cost of reflecting on their international engagement. Furthermore, in his view, 'conciliarity' was not successfully developed within the WCC, but was discarded due to impatience and instrumental thinking.

Another, a Roman Catholic expert, denied that the Evangelical or Pentecostal challenge is the main problem in the official ecumenical bodies. For him, the main problem is the unwillingness of most Orthodox churches to agree on the working methods of the WCC and other institutions. He recalled that Metropolitan Kirill of the Russian Orthodox Church already proposed something similar: a forum for church families. Therefore, he considered the GCF to be a helpful institution, although in his view its relationship to the other ecumenical bodies is still somewhat unclear.

An expert from the Seventh-day Adventists stated:

> Although it may seem counter-intuitive, a variety of 'ecumenisms' and of global ways of encounter between churches do not contradict one another but may help to provide space for movements and churches which cannot easily or full-heartedly relate to some 'traditional' forms of ecumenism.

Some ecumenical experts place the GCF in a broader ecumenical history and context. One refers to the meetings of the Christian World Communions. Because they were never intended to come to decisions or agreements together, it was possible that the representatives of the different traditions to get to know, trust and appreciate each other. For this interviewee, the CWCs came to the GCF in Limuru with their constituencies, in order to have that same experience. And it turned out, he added, the method worked in Limuru as well.

## The history of the GCF

Representatives of different ecumenical organizations and networks such as student organizations said that they see themselves as a kind of GCF - some of which have been established since the 19th century! - in which people from different background come together in their meetings and are able to discuss issues. They have already learned how *'to manage differences and to celebrate communalities'*. Organizations that until recently only brought together members of 'traditional churches' experienced that people with an Evangelical and Pentecostal background join their activities, including the discussion on faith issues. *'If you take the time for these discussions, nobody leaves unchanged.'*

Another ecumenical expert with a long history in ecumenical encounters recalled the origin of the GCF. In the eighties, there was concern within the WCC about the future of the ecumenical movement. In the WCC the movement had been institutionalised and many hoped the WCC would be able to recapture again something of the creativity and élan of the World Student Christian Movement which was at the root of the ecumenical movement and which brought forth 90% of the great ecumenical leaders of the 20th century. In his view, the idea of the Forum was to invite whoever was willing to come, to discuss this issue. The format would be that of a Forum, where discussions and reflection would take place and ideas would be launched, without decisions being made, and people would see where the Holy Spirit would lead. But later on, this idea, too, became institutionalised: it was institutionalised into a Forum with the intention of broadening the membership of the institutionalised ecumenical movement.

### Preliminary conclusion

The GCF was needed and came at the right time: that can be concluded from the answers given in the questionnaire and in the interviews. At the same time, different perceptions about why the GCF was needed are likely to result in different expectations for the future and content of the GCF, as we will see in the following chapters.

## 2. Appraisal of the Purposes of the GCF

In 2002 the GCF formulated a Guiding Purpose Statement with six purposes.

To create an open space wherein representatives from a broad range of Christian churches and interchurch organizations, which confess the triune God and Jesus Christ as perfect in His divinity and humanity, can gather to foster mutual respect, to explore and address together common challenges.

In the spirit of John 17:21 'that all of them may be one … so that the world may believe that you have sent me' and because of our faith in a reconciling God (2 Cor.5: 18-21) a forum could pursue the following:

- Deepen our commitment to God's Word and mission in the world;
- Enhance our understanding of contemporary expressions of Christian mission;
- Pursue principles and practices that enable us to deal freely, responsibly and peaceably with our Christian differences and distinctive qualities;
- Engage in theological reflection in areas of mutual concern;
- Strengthen the wholeness of the church by encouraging communication and cooperation; and
- Foster relationships that may lead to common witness.

### Introduction

In the second question, the respondents were asked to rank the importance of the six purposes by ranking each on a scale from 1 to 5, 1 being the lowest priority and 5 the highest. The respondents were also asked to reflect the extent to which they think these purposes have already been realised. The majority of the respondents (indicated by the abbreviations explained on page 7) ranked most of the six purposes with a 4 or 5 (see the surveys below). We conclude from this that the six purposes are wholeheartedly supported by representatives of all the Christian traditions, from leaders of churches and ecumenical organizations to ecumenical experts.

Some interested ecumenical experts who have never been involved in meetings of the GCF remarked that it was almost impossible to evaluate the six purposes adequately. A Roman Catholic ecumenical expert expressed his concern by saying that all six purposes should of course be taken to heart, but could not say how far they have been realized. *'Looking around I would say: I fear in fact less than we pretend in our declarations.'*

In the interviews, the evaluators presented no explicit purposes, but asked the interviewees to formulate the purpose of the GCF themselves. It is noteworthy that in many cases interviewees chose wording that was less theological and more strategic than that used by the GCF itself. This explains, at least partly, the difference that can be seen between the results of the questionnaire and the interviews. Of course, this does not necessarily imply that people do not support the official GCF purposes, but apparently the wording of the official six purposes of the GCF are not the only ones many Christians use in discussing ecumenical activities.

In their answers, most respondents refer to the Limuru meeting.

**Purpose I. Deepen our commitment to God's Word and mission in the world.**

The poll below shows the results of 16 respondents:

| Digit awarded | Number of times | Division by denomination |
|---|---|---|
| 1 | 1 | RC |
| 2 | 0 | |
| 3 | 0 | |
| 4 | 5 | Evan. - EcO - Angl.- Pent. - Evan. |
| 5 | 10 | Ref. - Pent. - Evan. - EcO - Prot. - Pent. - EcO – Adv. - Afr.Inst.Ch. - Angl. |

The phrases 'commitment to God's Word' and 'mission' are widely supported by every respondent. We share statements below that further this observation. Of course, this is not stunning news: mission belongs to the heart of Christian faith. Mission is the only notion mentioned twice in the six purposes. A Protestant and Adventist respondent wrote that at the GCF meetings the discussion about mission itself does not yet seem to be explored.

There was one deviant voice from a Roman Catholic ecumenical expert affirming that for many churches, this purpose can be reached as efficiently without the GCF. For him mission is not a high priority goal for the GCF. The subject of mission will come up again under urgent topics for the forthcoming agenda of the GCF (see question V, 3).

The following are comments of leaders of churches and ecumenical bodies:

> In today's globalised world, if we are committed to this purpose, we HAVE to do it TOGETHER; how otherwise can other faiths, and people of no faith at all, be expected to take Christianity and its values seriously? This is only put into practice at grassroots level. We have learned that when people of different

nationalities and church traditions meet together with a spirit of acceptance of one another as equal before God, we ARE ONE. (Prot.)

In the sense that some Evangelicals and Pentecostals are beginning to take seriously an ecumenical agenda, I think it is a useful purpose statement. So far, I think it has been highly successful. (Pent.)

I find it quite interesting that these two are put together in the same sentence. Although I agree that both are important, and that the one needs the other, still it is striking. I think that the GCF can especially be helpful for deepening our commitment to mission and to seek for ways in which we can work together in this regard. (Evan.)

For me the GCF (i.e. the discussion with other Christians) is important to strengthen the mission of the churches worldwide. (Pent.)

*The realisation of the purpose*

We note two remarks about how far this purpose has already been realised:

Partially - because we are still in a pilgrimage as we strive to preach the gospel to all nations and make people Christ's disciples. There is so much along the way that derail our efforts that we are far from fully realizing this goal. (Angl.)

As a non-participant but very interested observer, I have the impression that this purpose is a long-range purpose and has not been dealt with much. Regarding 'commitment to God's Word': Since testimony, spirituality, and interaction was in the forefront, the more classical disciplines of Bible study and discussion of theology went into the background. Regarding 'mission in the world': Certainly the particular approach of the Forum meetings have helped to advance commitment in this area. (Seventh-day Adventist ecumenical expert)

**Purpose II. Enhance our understanding of contemporary expressions of Christian mission.**

| Digit awarded | Number of times | Division by denomination |
|---|---|---|
| 1 | 0 | |
| 2 | 2 | RC - EcO |
| 3 | 2 | Adv. - Angl. |
| 4 | 6 | Ref. - Pent. - Pent. - Angl. - Pent. - Afr. Inst.Ch. |
| 5 | 6 | Evan. - Prot. - Evan. - EcO - EcO - Evan. |

Compared to the ranking for the first purpose, the ranking for the second is more varied, but again by far the majority ranked it a 4 or 5 as the survey shows.

A Pentecostal church leader explained his position as follows:

> As churches we should not all stay on our own islands, but encourage each other to be missionary, present in the world. That is not the same as 'recycling of the saints': I am not interested in luring away people from other churches. It is the non-believing person I am concerned about. And for that purpose we need each other.

*The realisation of the purpose*

The respondents made several remarks about the extent this purpose has been realized. A Lutheran expert said that it is hard to say if there is any improvement and the Roman Catholic expert repeated that for many churches this purpose can be achieved without the GCF; therefore, he does not regard it as a goal of high priority. An Evangelical expert who gave this a 5, explained that a major step forward has certainly been made on this issue. For him the very fact that Christians ranging from Orthodox to Evangelical and from Roman Catholic to Pentecostal listened to one another for an extended period and spoke about religion in the first person (rather than the third) definitely helped to enhance this understanding. Here again, we share comments of leaders of churches and ecumenical bodies, and of ecumenical experts:

> A small beginning, but it will require outcomes such as partnerships growing from the Forum experience to measure realization. (Ref.)

> It is ongoing. More time would be required. (Pent.)

> People are still making efforts to achieve this goal. The problem is that we are all culture bound and many people tend to think about their cultures as superior to others. Consequently, little effort is made to understand different expressions of Christianity on the basis of peoples' social location. (Angl.)

An Anglican ecumenical expert added:

> My hunch is that while the 'understanding' of one another's practice of Christian mission has advanced quite a long way, it is still rather far from having been adequately shared among the rank and file of our very different churches and fellowships, so that it is hardly yet at a stage when we can presume it is good enough to lead to distinctively fresh, let alone united practice. (Angl.)

**Purpose III. Pursue principles and practices that enable us to deal freely, responsibly and peaceably with our Christian differences and distinctive qualities.**

| Digit awarded | Number of times | Division by denomination |
|---|---|---|
| 1 | 0 | |
| 2 | 0 | |
| 3 | 1 | Evan. |
| 4 | 3 | Pent. - Evan. - Adv. |
| 5 | 12 | Ref. - Evan. - RC - EcO - EcO - Prot. - Pent. - Angl. - Pent. - EcO - Afr.Inst.Ch. - Angl. |

As the survey shows, all respondents were very much in favour of this purpose. Nevertheless everybody realized that the purpose will require a thorough follow up. Ecumenical experts strongly supported this goal, too, but they also had their reservations concerning the degree of realisation. The words 'beginning', 'some progress' and 'slowly' in the answers underscored this. A Roman Catholic ecumenical expert underlined that the meetings in the GCF are a learning process for all parties concerned, in particular about issues on which we differ, like ecclesiology, pneumatology, etc. One dissenting but confident Lutheran expert expressed that on this topic *'considerable progress has been made already'*. For two experts this purpose was a crucial or most important one.

The following are comments from a church leader and a staff member of an ecumenical organization:

> This has been a critical purpose statement. I think it has been profoundly important to the process and it has been quite effective in bringing the various groups together. (Pent.)

> The most important purpose is to discover the uniqueness of each others traditions and to build an environment in which that uniqueness becomes common property of the church. This is a parallel to the story of the Pentecost. This is a purpose of the GCF I experienced when I attended the Limuru meeting. I also discovered that being
>
> Lutheran means being ecumenical. To me, it was once again a confirmation of the obligation to be ecumenical. That is not an option: it is an obligation. The search for Christian unity, which is worldwide, is senseless if it does not also include the transformation of humankind into human family. (Lutheran in EcO)

*The realisation of the purpose*

Some comments on the realisation of this purpose so far:

> Some progress. The first meeting was important for 'ecumenists' to see the open piety and concern in the 'others', while the Evangelical and Pentecostal leaders had to respect the Ecumenists passion and respect for the more traditional ecumenical instruments. (Ref.)
>
> A beginning is made. (Evan.)
>
> We are slowly becoming aware of the need of this approach. Many people are still very intolerant of the views of others. Others are retrogressing by adopting fundamentalist mentality on religious matters which is not conducive to peaceful co-existence with other people. (Angl.)

Two comments from ecumenical experts:

> It is clearly one of the crucial goals of the GCF, and one that will need to be kept closely among the priorities of all future meetings. Yet, again, I cannot believe that it has grown so far and been spread so fast in all the Christian fellowships involved, as to be already something we can presume to be 'realised' at all widely. (Angl.)
>
> I do not have the impression that this theme has been worked on much. Perhaps the most important thing would be to continue gathering people in the testimonial plus spirituality setting manner and then slowly proceed to more touchy themes such as the 'differences' mentioned here. (Seventh-day Adventist)

**Purpose IV. Engage in theological reflection in areas of mutual concern.**

| Digit awarded | Number of times | Division by denomination |
|---|---|---|
| 1 | 0 | |
| 2 | 4 | Ref. - EcO - Adv. - Evan. |
| 3 | 3 | Pent. - Angl. - Pent. |
| 4 | 4 | Evan. - Prot. - Pent. - EcO |
| 5 | 5 | Evan.- RC - EcO - Afr.Inst.Ch. - Angl. |

Purpose IV is more contested than the other purposes. The survey shows that theological reflection in a multilateral setting like the GCF is not a high priority for all participants. The explanations given make clear that theological reflection in this context is still at an early stage. The considerable divergence among Evangelical voices is remarkable. Obviously, expectations regarding this purpose vary. Although the purpose is strongly supported, some respondents indicated that the GCF is not the appropriate platform for theological reflection. Roman Catholic voices asserted the necessity of ecclesiological discussions and, therefore, affirmed that until now the GCF is not a real alternative to the bilateral dialogues between the Vatican and the other Christian traditions. A European Roman Catholic church leader was disappointed that in Limuru: *'No ecclesiological or theological issue was tabled: this is clearly impossible and problems would have been enormous'*. An Orthodox respondent commented that while there may be assent with Pentecostals and Evangelicals on moral issues, there still is a huge disparity on ecclesiology among the Orthodox and the Evangelical and the Pentecostal traditions. One Lutheran and one ecumenical expert said that very little has been done in this respect and that it has not been a priority for the GCF so far. A Seventh-day Adventist ecumenical expert said he has the impression that, after decades of theological dialogues, the major task that a forum like the GCF can handle is not more dialogues, not even multilateral ones, but support to foster experience that can ultimately become part of dialogues and other forms of theological encounter and work. A Reformed voice declared that this discussion has just started and that theological convergence is a tough agenda:

> Christian World Communions have been at this for decades, and they have a better chance of working on this than in the GCF context.

A representative of an ecumenical organization expressed that more trust is needed than one global meeting can generate before such a theological discussion could take place, but '*The first meeting in Limuru was a step in the development of such trust.*' The following are comments of church leaders and heads of organizations:

> There is not enough time during the GCF's for this. Other methods of engagement i.e. Newsletters should be included. (Pent.)

> A long way still to go. (Evan.)

> This was not one of my primary concerns. My primary concern was that of introduction and the building of trust. To the extent that engaging in theological reflection in Bible study on the question of unity has been useful, I want to affirm it wholeheartedly. Occasionally, however, there are those who wish to inject issues of theology that separate various participants from one another without taking the time to build relationships first. At this point, theological reflection short circuits what I see as a primary goal of the GCF. (Pent.)

> Although I think this is very important, I do not think that the GCF will be the right platform for this kind of dialogue. Rather, it is very possible that contacts that have been laid at the GCF platform may result in local or international theological dialogues. (Evan.)

Two Roman Catholic ecumenical experts included the following:

I have the impression this is not of high priority to the GCF itself, although it would be necessary.

*The realisation of the purpose*

How far has the GCF come with this purpose?

I hope: further than I could have expected. But if I put this a little lower in priority than the others, it is because I see the all round 'personal' awareness and respect for each other as fellow-Christians as the most important of the break-throughs for which the GCF will be thanked and hymned in years to come. (Anglican ecumenical expert)

In general, the Purpose I and V must happen first, to provide a context in which the other areas can be pursued. I think we have made considerable progress in the Purpose I and V, and the effect of these are gradually being felt in the other areas. But cooperation in mission and theology can happen outside of GCF-run initiatives, i.e. we facilitate and catalyse the building of new relationships, which (we hope) can then take on a life of their own. (Angl.)

**Purpose V. Strengthen the wholeness of the church by encouraging communication and co-operation.**

| Digit awarded | Number of times | Division by denomination |
|---|---|---|
| 1 | 0 | |
| 2 | 0 | |
| 3 | 1 | EcO |
| 4 | 6 | Pent. - RC – Pent. – Adv. - Afr.Inst.Ch. - Evan. |
| 5 | 9 | Ref. - Evan. - EcO - Evan. - Prot. - Angl. - Pent. - EcO - Angl. |

Again the ranking is high. It reflects the longing of the respondents for better communication and co-operation within the whole Christian family. Ecumenical experts support this goal too (twice a ranking of 4 and once of 5). Once more it was affirmed that the process for this purpose is in the beginning stages. To put it in the wording of a Lutheran voice: '*Remarkable initial progress, but much left to do*'. One deviant comment added that the purpose has largely been realized. Altogether, few clarifications on the purpose were given. Again, we share here some comments of church leaders and heads of ecumenical bodies:

> I view this as an extremely important purpose, and for the most part I would give our work here, very high marks. I think that we have not only encouraged communication and cooperation, in a sense we have facilitated it. And it seems to be working quite well. (Pent.)

> We need to do more in this area. (Afr.Inst.Ch.)

> This is being done at different levels in the area of missionary work, education, health, socio-economic development and others. There is a need to continue working together in a number of fronts by reaching out people of other faiths especially those who look totally different from ours. (Angl.)

*The realisation of the purpose*

Two church leaders and two ecumenical experts commented on the realisation of this purpose:

> A reasonable start. Because of the GCF experience, there are some leaders who will at least pay attention to communication from others. (Ref.)

> Communications have begun. (Evan.)

> Cooperation must become tangible, and I am not sure in which ways the GCF could help to initiate new forms of cooperation. However, it surely has encouraged communication by actually creating a space for communication of church leaders who would otherwise hardly communicate (and if they did, perhaps they did not always do so in a constructive manner) (Seventh-day Adventist ecumenical expert)

> Certainly nowhere near as far as we all must hope it can grow to in the next 20 or 25 years. But as one of the key purposes of the GCF it deserves to be central in every meeting from now on. As soon as the members can all witness gladly to the fact that all other members are among God's gifts to his Church for effective mission and ministry, then it is vital that this be shared throughout the churches in ways that can reinforce that mutual trust and respect, all the more so because the 'modern media', in Europe and N. America (and possibly in other areas as well) will do their damnedest to drive wedges between what so many outside 'powers' will see as a most dangerous new alliance among the Christians! And this sharing of communication and cooperation will by no means prove easily accepted by all members of the presently divided churches! (Anglican ecumenical expert)

**Purpose VI. Foster relationships that may lead to common witness.**

| Digit awarded | Number of times | Division by denomination |
|---|---|---|
| 1 | 0 | |
| 2 | 1 | EcO |
| 3 | 4 | Pent. - RC - EcO - Adv. |
| 4 | 2 | Ref. - Angl. |
| 5 | 9 | Evan. - EcO - Evan. - Prot. - Pent. - Pent. - Afr.Inst.Ch. - Evan. - Angl. |

As shown in the survey above, the majority ranked this purpose as a 5, however, other opinions are also evident. By all appearances, Purpose VI is strongly supported by all respondents, particularly Evangelicals. One Evangelical reaction: '*I think this is the best purpose that GCF can really work for*' and a Lutheran added: '*Again, a good start.*' However, the respondent that offered a ranking of 2 revealed that according to him/her there has been '*Not much done yet*' in respect to fostering relationships for common witness.

> Witness to each other is an invaluable beginning of being able to witness together to people outside the meeting, and in the long run to shared and mutually trusted witness in many different and difficult situations that we have long faced only in separation, let alone in repudiation of the other(s). (Anglican ecumenical expert)
>
> Depending on what 'common witness' means, this may be very helpful or it may lead to curtailing one or another church's way of being a witness. In this sense, the purpose is open for interpretation - and may be interpreted differently by different people. (Seventh-day Adventist ecumenical expert)

An Anglican working in an ecumenical organization pointed to the fact that we are living in a post-secular era, where the common witness is badly needed:

> There have been terrorist attacks by people who feel very much attached to their faith. Faith in important, and that is why the Christian presence in the world is important. We have to be effective in the public sphere.

*The realisation of the purpose*

Some comments from leaders of churches and ecumenical bodies:

> It is hard to build relationships on one meeting. We can only gauge this when there are follow-up meetings. I know I have had almost no contact with people I met for the first time last November. (Ref.)

> Like the previous purpose, this one is critical. We have brought people together who would never have believed that such a thing was possible. We have placed them on an even platform. We have given them a minimum of guidelines, and we have turned them loose to develop relationships. It has been a wonder to watch. (Pent.)

> The Limuru meeting was a major step in this direction. We need to give life to the Limuru statement by operationalising it at the local level. This will help strengthen our common witness. (Afr.Inst.Ch.).

> This is very vital but in most cases people have made one step forward and two steps backwards. As a result, there are no tangible ways in which we can truly say that people have managed to foster relationships that can lead to common witness. There is much suspicion and mistrust to the point that we prefer to work alone in our ministries for the sake of safeguarding our own flock! (Angl.)

> The Forum should grow to become a space for public witness. (Protestant in EcO)

### More goals of the Global Christian Forum

Here we offer a short overview of other goals of the GCF which were mentioned in the interviews As stated in our introduction many interviewees (experts and leadership of churches and ecumenical organizations) expressed their own vision of the GCF and formulated their own purposes for the GCF. We frequently heard variations of the idea of bringing together the world of the ecumenicals with the world of Pentecostals and Evangelicals:

> To create a wider and different space than the ecumenical movement has created until now. (Luth.)

> To create a space for different traditions to come together; less important is to discern what we will do together: for that purpose we are not far enough yet. (Prot. in EcO)

> To give a global Christian response to the problems of today, to show the face of a unite Christianity in certain issues. (Orth.)

> The GCF is a provisional assisting instrument through which people will learn to take each other seriously and can meet without falling into discussions on dogmas. We need that because at the moment the walls between Christians are high. I experienced that in my own country too: we have to meet first. And more can grow out of that. (Old Catholic church leader)

> There are many different goals: healing of memories, opening doors, creating understanding. We should not begin to discuss institutional matters too early,

because there is a lot of mistrust and fear of by approaching the one losing the other. (Anglican in EcO)

But I am convinced that the Forum can already be a useful and stimulating meeting place between Christian bodies that do not meet in other contexts and so to become acquainted with one another personally beyond the existing boundaries, prejudices and commonplaces as institutions. (Roman Catholic ecumenical expert)

**Some preliminary conclusions drawn from the rating in this overview**

1. The Purposes I (Deepen our commitment to God's Word and mission in the world) and III (Pursue principles and practices that enable us to deal freely, responsibly and peaceably with our Christian differences and distinctive qualities) received the strongest support. They are supported by all and have the highest scores of all the purposes, even from respondents that give all others purposes a lower score.
2. Purpose IV (*Engage in theological reflection in areas of mutual concern*) had the lowest score as well as the widest range of scores.
3. Purpose VI (*Foster relationships that may lead to common witness*) received the second lowest score. Public witness is not seen by all as an important common goal.
4. There is no clear division between the different denominations in the pattern of answers. All respondents, with two exceptions, are positive on all purposes. One representative of an ecumenical body is mainly positive on the purposes I and III; and the RC respondent on the purposes III, IV and V.

**Some preliminary conclusions drawn from the evaluation of the purposes of the GCF**

1. In general there is strong support for all six purposes.
2. There is still a long way to go in the realisation of the purposes. We often heard the sentiment: *'We are at the beginning stage'*.
3. It is also obvious that many respondents regard the position of the GCF as rather fragile but do not consider speeding up the process as the appropriate way to achieve the six purposes.
4. There is a clear disparity regarding theological reflection. In particular Roman Catholic and Orthodox respondents would like to do more in this field. One of the issues mentioned most by various ecumenical experts is that of the Ecclesiology. A Roman Catholic ecumenical expert said in an interview that especially Pentecostals and Evangelicals have to learn a lot in this respect. For more about this, go

to A.3. in Chapter 5 under 'urgent topics for the future agenda'. As we noted earlier, it is obvious that different partners in the GCF have different expectations of the outcome of the GCF.

5. Many respondents are very positive about the encounters they have in GCF meetings, but the question remains whether something is being done with these experiences. The Reformed voice quoted above in Purpose VI regarding the follow up of fostering relationships leads us to wonder. What will the participants present in Limuru do with the 'momentum' of Limuru? Is Limuru more than an event on its own? Does Limuru really generate fresh relationships?

## 3. The Importance of the GCF

**Please, describe in your own words what in your view the importance of the GCF is**

This was the third question, which was followed by several quotes, of which some were a bit provocative, to stimulate the thinking of the respondents.

a. The GCF is an open and safe space where all the Christian traditions can meet on an equal base.
b. It should have a low profile structure without competing with other ecumenical bodies.
c. A promising enterprise broadening inter-Christian fellowships.
d. A necessary step in reshaping the ecumenical movement in the 21st century, in which Pentecostal and Evangelical churches are involved.
e. A new vitality for the institutionalised ecumenism as well as the established churches.
f. A substitute for the present World Council of Churches.
g. An unnecessary enterprise wasting time and money if it does not contribute to the struggle of the churches for a better world.
h. Nothing new.
i. An additional layer to ecumenical cooperation.
j. Encounters without further mutual commitment.

Several respondents related their answers to these statements.

### The essence of the answers

> The GCF is a space where Christians can come together in fellowship as brothers and sisters in an environment where there are no power or hierarchical structures.

These words from a representative of the African Instituted Churches are a good summary of the essence of the answers of most respondents. A Reformed church leader stated:

> The forming of personal relationships among leaders across Christian traditions is a very influential and necessary element of the search for Christian unity. It may take years to see concrete results, but such relationship are powerful in the breaking down of barriers between Christian communities.

A representative of a Pentecostal church added that, therefore, it '*should be nurtured very carefully*'. An Evangelical church leader regards the GCF as '*the most suitable way to get Evangelicals and Pentecostals enthusiastic about ecumenism.'* A Roman Catholic ecumenical expert regarded it as a condition for success:

> It must first of all be a meeting-place for 'persons' and not for 'institutions'. The persons participating should be loyal towards their own church-body and as such representative but at the same time they should be 'free' and 'ready to listen, to speak out in a real and genuine dialogue'.

Many respondents mentioned that the GCF offers possibilities for a new kind of dialogue, referring to the very personal character of the encounters of the GCF. Two examples:

> The GCF implies a new ecumenical paradigm, moving the attention to spirituality, listening, and fellowship, supplementing other spaces for inter-church encounter and expressing the unity of the church in a fresh manner. (Adv.)

> The GCF has a dynamic that traditional dialogue meetings lack. Less theological, more personal. People were willing to commit themselves, to be open. And so the feeling was: we are all Christians, and inspired by the Spirit we are all looking for what binds us. There was mutual respect. (Roman Catholic ecumenical expert)

### Additional layer in ecumenical relations or substitute?

Some statements in the question were provocative, and this resulted in several remarks on the issue of a possible addition of the GCF to the WCC or the substitution of the WCC by the GCF. Nobody, however, regards the GCF as a substitute for the WCC, although in the long run, it could change relations because of its special character:

> GCF is not a substitute but a facilitating body. (Evangelical church leader)

> Initially it is probably advisable to be independent of WCC/CEC/CCEE (World Council of Churches/Conference of European Churches/European Catholic Bishops Conference) etc, but cooperating with the same; but as it builds, it could surely substitute for them, providing a more honest and cohesive body, reshaping the ecumenical movement of the 21st century. (EcO)

> We must be careful not to copy or usurp the role of existing councils, but they will be inevitably renewed by the life of the GCF and similar organizations. (EcO)

> It should have a low profile structure without competing with other ecumenical bodies. (Adv.)

> It should however not be seen as a replacement of other ecumenical models/methods, nor as a 'low level' ecumenism. (Evan.)

As this is part of the broader issue of ecumenical relations in the future, we will come back to that in chapter 6 on Ecumenical Perspectives.

### What has been achieved?

An ecumenical expert from the Anglican Church is happy with what has already been done:

> The GCF has achieved, in the years since the Harare Assembly of the WCC, even more than any of us could have foreseen then. It has enabled a few persons from virtually the entire range of different, and all too often sadly divided churches, to meet, listen to, come to respect and at best recognise as valuable common disciples of God, as known in the same Christ and made present among us all by the same Holy Spirit. If this 'progress' can be kept up over many years and involving many more people in and representing all these churches and any other sorts of Christian Church that may spring up, it will immensely contribute to a quite new universality and depth of truth in the witness of all Christians and thus to the building of a 'new world' much closer to the 'Kingdom of God' that Jesus has told us to look out for than today's world can be considered to be.
>
> In Asia GCF has enabled the Christian Conference of Asia and the Catholic Bishops Conference to relate with the Evangelical Fellowship of Asia in an ongoing relationship. (Evan.)

A Reformed church leader from Europe indicates that there is much to learn within the GCF:

> European ecumenical meetings are not very attractive, they are drudging, we do not come to conclusions. There is much more vitality in e.g. Africa, and in migrant churches as well. We need them, we need their spirituality. That was what I learned from Limuru. World Christianity outside Europe has a different spirituality.
>
> The GCF offers us the opportunity to learn from one another without prejudice. It is important to become 'listener with the hearth', to listen to learn where the other enriches my approach to the common good. (representative of a youth organization)

Others see the GCF as a promise or a necessity for the future:

> GCF can be a means to bring a missionary sentiment to all churches. (Pentecostal church leader).
>
> I believe the GCF does have the potential to renew both the churches (especially those in Europe and North America) and ecumenical institutions as well. (EcO)

> The relation with Evangelicals is an important issue for all churches, because we find Evangelicals in all traditions, with all the disputes that come with that (like on homosexuality). (Anglican in EcO)

## Cautions

Cautions were also given. We should not be satisfied too quickly. An Orthodox respondent working in an ecumenical organization stated:

> The GCF is in the beginning of the beginning. The wish to be together is neither something bad in itself, nor by definition something good or useful. If it does not lead to a contribution in the overcoming of differences it is of no use. To listen to one another and to respect one another are a proof of progress, but are no goals in itself.
>
> My concern is that for the sake of unity, we will have to give up our public witness for a long time, and I do not agree with that. We cannot afford that, there is too much injustice in the world. In the WCC unity has always been at the service of the struggle for Justice, Peace and Integrity of Creation. (Protestant in EcO)

A Roman Catholic ecumenical expert is afraid that the advantages of the GCF can also be a risk:

> The advantage that there is no accent on doctrine is also the weakness of the GCF: the degree of commitment is unclear.

## Change

We end this chapter with a quote from an Orthodox respondent working in an ecumenical organization, who shows how much has already changed because of the existence of the GCF:

> Personally, I have learned from what I heard people say about the GCF:
> - a Pentecostal saying: it is because of the WCC that the GCF has come this far;
> - a Roman Catholic saying: we are interested, but we want to maintain what we already have (so: no substitution of WCC with GCF)
> - an Evangelical saying: first we were only interested in life after this life, but now we also engage in social issues;
> - an Orthodox saying: we are interested, but don't want to loose what we gained in the WCC, the ecumenical ethos.
>
> This means the GCF is a challenge for all of us; we should continue with it.

**Preliminary conclusion**

We can summarise all the statements in the following way: the GCF is important, but still in its beginning phase. Some respondents are hesitant, because they want to discuss issues they value highly such as theology and justice issues, while the majority of the respondents are afraid of risking the trust that has grown by putting contested issues on the agenda of the GCF too early.

## 4. The Appreciation of the Limuru Meeting

**How was the Limuru meeting (November 2007) appreciated?**

The fact that the questionnaire focussed on the leadership of churches and organizations, does not imply that all respondents were present at the Limuru meeting. For that reason, the first part of the question was different for those who did attend and for those who did not. Before we consider the answers, we offer a more general reaction of someone who did not attend the Limuru meeting, but did attend the European Forum in Warburg. This answer reflects many of the elements of the answers of the Limuru participants:

> I attended the European Global Forum in Warburg, and I was very moved of what happened there. Of course, it was because of the participants themselves. They were one by one, Christians, who were humble and very much open to criticism from others, yet also open for encouragement in the faith from others. Things, which are, although often denied, very rare. That was the difference with other conferences, which were held mostly on institutional base. Their presence here was not as representatives of (church)institutions, but as vulnerable Christians. So, it was clear that Warburg was felt to be successful because of its concept (faith paths) and because of the mindset of the participants. (Migrant churches)

**A. If you attended the meeting in Limuru, what is your feeling about this meeting? Please, give in max. 50 words per time your personal impression.**

*Did you appreciate the methodology of sharing personal journeys of faith?*

In the questionnaires as well as in the interviews, there was great enthusiasm for this methodology. (One person returning the questionnaire - without filling it in - rejected wholeheartedly the word 'methodology'. That is understandable since it is, of course, more than a method). To give an impression of how this method was appreciated, we offer a few quotes:

> The method worked very well: it created a spiritual fellowship, because we recognised each others stories and we learned that we all have gifts we can share with others. This made it possible to discuss - later on, in smaller groups - issues we were afraid to discuss earlier. It is a useful way of dealing with problems. (Lutheran in EcO)

> They went well. One has to trust the Spirit of God at work through the process. Some people came a little fearful and reticent, but we readily found we could open up to one another. Most people were excited by this new way of getting to know one another's faith journeys. (Anglican ecumenical expert)

For several of the participants the methodology was not something new:

> For us as Pentecostals this was a familiar methodology. In Limuru it helped to recognise others as Christians, to see who Christ is to them.

We can conclude from the answers received, that the method of sharing 'journeys of faith' is appreciated. The evaluators noticed, however, especially during the interviews, that these words of appreciation were often followed by different words of caution, hesitation or reservation:

> I appreciated the method very much, although I had no experience with it, and it is not my favourite thing to do. But I experienced the presence of Christ in the stories of those present in my group. There was recognition of each other as Christians, although not always in their church function as e.g. bishop (this kind of problems was not yet discussed, and were present 'only at the edges of the room') (Lutheran in EcO)

> The method of working with personal stories has also been used in the Women's movement, and in the WCC Assembly of Porto Alegre the method of faith journeys was applied as well. But we cannot stop there, we also have to discuss what divides us, in terms of commitment, theology, society. The GCF has to work towards these kind of questions, because there are great differences between the participants. Like on the issue of conversion: for many witness and conversion are not the same thing, but for others they are! (Protestant in EcO)

> For Pentecostals and Evangelicals it is a more attractive working method than for us, Orthodox. I felt myself a bit uneasy with it. For us, but I think for Roman Catholics too, faith is a matter between God and myself in the first place. We do not use personal confessions. The only reason why I cooperated, was to find out whether it would help us reaching our goals; you could see it as a compromise, and not as a way to please myself. And it was a good experience to listen to each other, hear each other's experiences and to be together as brothers and sisters. But the sharing of personal stories is only the beginning, a first step. We have to find ways for a dialogue on really important issues. (Orthodox church leader)

This is confirmed by a Roman Catholic ecumenical expert:

> The method offers the opportunity of overcoming prejudices. But theological reflection remains important! This method resembles the initial method used by the Roman Catholics and Orthodox in their so-called Dialogue of Love (tomos agapis) which made it possible to overcome an isolation of centuries and to get to know each other better. But such an encounter should be followed by a more formal dialogue.

Representatives of youth and student organizations showed appreciation for the method, expressed the concern that life stories and faith stories become disconnected; they are inter-woven, and it would not be appropriate to make a separation between the two. They also stressed the role of culture, which penetrates all aspects of life, including faith. There are great differences even within one tradition, as a result of a difference in culture. This should be taken into account. Besides, not every person is likewise suited for these kind of discussions; some say: 'So what? Lets get to business' (business being the political/social/ethical issues we are concerned about), and that should be respected and valued as well. Student organizations experienced that students from different backgrounds (including Pentecostals and Evangelicals) share the preference of discussing issues over discussing faith. Organizations engaged in concrete social work, see their members from different church backgrounds working together in projects without any problem and with great openness to one another.

Several times respondents indicated they will apply, or have already applied, the method themselves:

> I used the method in a bilateral dialogue meeting on international level and it worked out well; I would not want to do without it now, because it helps to deepen the discussions. (Lutheran church leader)

*Did you appreciate the Bible studies?*

Most respondents appreciated the Bible studies: the introductions and chairmanship were very skilful (only one respondent had a different experience with a less skilled chairperson) and two of them (coming from Protestant churches) noticed an openness to discussing hermeneutics. For a staff member of an ecumenical organization, the strength of Limuru was in the focus on Bible texts. He expressed the hope this will be continued by asking the question how this relates to what is happening in the world.

Representatives of youth and student organizations are cautious in one respect: not all religious families have a tradition of Bible studies, so prudence is needed. But on the whole, they have very good experiences with Bible studies (even better than with the 'faith journeys') in their own work.

> Because the Bible is a gift we all share, hermeneutic and exegetic differences are expressed and can be discussed.

This is confirmed by a Reformed church leader:

> I think testimonies and Bible studies are key to establishing our Christian bona fides with each other. The topics were good, but they could have been almost anything that did not begin with the classical differences among us.

*Do you have any other reactions?*

The first part of the question also included information on the discussions in small groups and the general atmosphere in Limuru. As many more general remarks in the groups were made under question 2, we combine the answers under this heading.

All respondents gave positive reactions in relation to the atmosphere in the Limuru meeting, and found that very helpful:

> A very positive atmosphere was generated. This brought down the walls of prejudice and promoted request for forgiveness. (Roman Catholic church leader)

> I noticed that the goodness of the atmosphere faded away temporarily when the person who spoke tended to emphasize his/her denomination identity. (Protestant church leader)

Compliments are given, like:

> The composition of the groups was organised very well, even so after the split of the group: all different traditions were and stayed present. (Lutheran in EcO)

> I was rather proud of the message. This was the only document we worked on together, and I felt it was better than the average ecumenical message document. (Reformed church leader)

That being said, there are also individual remarks with criticism about special topics, things that were missed and worries for the future. Some of these are easy to avoid a next time, like:

> We needed more time in the plenary to discuss the issues which were coming from the small groups and to engage with the papers which were presented. (Afr.Inst.Ch.)

> The worships were too short: if you really want to come into the 'rhythm', feel the spirituality, you need more time, to prevent you from staying in your own world. (Protestant in EcO).

> The publicity before and during the meeting was not organised well, because of the fear of the Committee that publicity would harm the growing confidence. For the same reason the location of the meeting was also not very attractive for press people: in a remote place. Afterwards this proved to be an unnecessary precaution. More people would have heard of the meeting taking place if this had been organised differently. But one has to admit that probably because of the lack of 'high level' participants, the press would not have had an overwhelming interest in the meeting after all. (Lutheran in EcO)

Other critical remarks touch on the differences between the groups present:

> After the first days of telling each other your journey of faith and getting to know each other, on the third day people also began to make critical remarks: from churches in South India on 'sheep-stealing' and from the Netherlands on rebaptism. At that moment the discussions became more complicated, but that is not a bad thing in itself. (Reformed church leader)

> The GCF is a work of the Holy Spirit, and Limuru was a unique event, a milestone (as a part of a journey) and a watershed moment. Like a waterfall: it can still go in any direction. But mutual accountability and fellowship are lacking, and these are very important characteristics of the ecumenical movement; churches that engage in the ecumenical movement have the experience how important these two things are, and they also felt it as missing in Limuru. (Reformed in EcO).

A Reformed church leader seemed to be glad that at the Limuru meeting he did not have to worry about questions he encounters in 'traditional' ecumenical gatherings (as mentioned by the previous respondent):

> The beautiful thing about the GCF is that for a moment we do not have to worry about issues like organizational structures and all kind of problems we have in the traditional ecumenical movement. It is an uncomplicated way of being together, and to celebrate that we are together. Get to know each other. To see the vision again, to discuss world problems without becoming too detailed. Limuru was more inspiring than the recent ecumenical events of Sibiu and Porto Alegre.

Some respondents asked themselves the question whether Limuru will contribute to a change in the traditional ecumenical thinking and acting. Their answers diverge:

> The general impression is that a new door has been opened which may also bring a new way of thinking into the ecumenical movement and ecumenical bodies. (Roman Catholic church leader)

> I am sceptical on the question whether Limuru will be able to create a new ecumenical élan, but definitely Limuru showed it is possible to break through borders. Evangelical organizations signing a declaration as in Limuru happened, is a new development. (Reformed ecumenical expert)

> I know that the Limuru meeting was very successful in bringing much greater interest to ecumenical possibilities among the Pentecostals. (Pentecostal church leader)

*Preliminary conclusion*

From the many positive testimonies of the working method and atmosphere in the Limuru meeting (and the GCF meetings in general) one may conclude that the GCF succeeded in finding a method of reflecting and discussing difficult issues. This is appreciated by many and makes it possible to cross borders and remove barriers. For churches and communions in the Pentecostal and Evangelical traditions, this more personal way of discussing is not new. This method could serve the traditional ecumenical movement as well. Some say this has to be done with caution, as it does not suit all cultures and faith traditions in the same way. Others point out that the success of this method in GCF meetings will not automatically be duplicated in other meetings, as the participants of the GCF meetings are likely to be selected because of their willingness to engage in these kind of encounters.

*What was your feedback to your church/organization?*

Most respondents indicate that they gave feedback to their church or organization by writing a report or an article or by giving an account in a meeting. Two of them added, that they did not get the impression that there was great interest, nor that something would be done with their information:

> I reported on the Limuru meeting in my church, and everybody listened politely; but there was no real interest. (Old Catholic church leader)

One Pentecostal church leader answered:

> I reported in my church, also in other continents, and told them that I missed them.

More positive answers came from others who related the reflection processes in their church or organization which were inspired by their reports. In the WCC a thorough discussion took place as well as an attempt to interpret all what was said and done in order to draw conclusions for the reflection on Ecumenism in the 21st Century. The Anglican Church made great efforts in discussing the results of Limuru:

> There has been a variety of feedback, through the Inter Anglican Standing Commission on Ecumenical Relations which issued a resolution in support of the GCF; other Anglican participants made reports to the Archbishop of Canterbury and to their own Provinces. There was a session on the GCF at the just-finished Lambeth Conference, and the work of the GCF is affirmed in the Reflections produced at the end of the Conference
> (p22, *http://www.lambethconference.org/vault/Reflections_Document_(final).pdf)*

But, we must add, another representative of the same church, writes he has not heard it mentioned in any church meeting nor read about it in church magazines.

**B. If you did not attend the meeting in Limuru: what feedback or impressions did you or your church/organization receive from the event?**

The answers diverge on this question. There are some who say things like:

> Our representative reported it was a fruitful and important event and that our involvement should be continued as this is an important development for our church/organization.

Other respondents report that there has not been much or even any feedback.

> The information did not filter through to the grassroots level.

*Preliminary conclusion*

This is also a statement used by several respondents. One must conclude (and this is confirmed by other experiences of the evaluators) that much more could have been done to offer feedback and communication. This is clearly an area that needs attention.

**C. In Limuru about 50% of the representatives were from a Pentecostal or Evangelical background. *How do you value these numbers?***

Practically nobody has a problem with this 'over-representation' of Evangelicals and Pentecostals. Their arguments:

> Pentecostals and Evangelicals are catching up, so that is no problem. Beside, in the groups discussions always all denominations were represented. (Reformed church leader)

> That is o.k.: if you want to invite people in a meaningful way, you will have to adjust the numbers. I would not mind if it stayed like that. But I did notice that the mainline churches did not feel represented in the lectures given at the Limuru meeting, although personally I did not mind. (two Protestant ecumenical experts)

Or, as a Roman Catholic ecumenical expert wrote:

> This 50%/50% division was important because it stimulated the participation of the Pentecostals and Evangelicals, because it anticipated on their fear that they would be overruled (and made invisible) by a majority of Catholics, Orthodox and other churches already engaged in the ecumenical movement.

A representative of an ecumenical network regards these numbers as a good sign:

> Significant in the sense that Pentecostals and Evangelicals are willing to come together to start dialogue with other confessions.

For an Anglican church leader this high number of Pentecostals and Evangelicals is

> very encouraging but we need the participation of the Roman Catholic Church to complete the picture.

Only two voices are a bit cautious about these numbers:

> These numbers should be a bit lower, like thirty or forty percent. (Roman Catholic ecumenical expert)

A representative of one of the 'over-represented' churches surprisingly writes:

> This is, in my opinion, good but maybe a bit too much. Roman Catholics and Orthodox should be well represented as well. (Evangelical church leader)

While the numbers for general attendance are not a problem, the planning (e.g. of lectures) must take into consideration that everyone who comes must hear their own tradition represented.

Many respondents of the mainline churches articulated their appreciation for the possibility of getting to know Pentecostals and Evangelicals better:

> In Limuru I got to know Pentecostals and Evangelicals better, and their differences as well. (Reformed church leader)

> Having had very bad experiences with Pentecostals and Evangelicals in the past, I am happy that Limuru helped me to become a new person: less prejudiced, although I am still suspicious and careful. (Reformed in EcO)

> My feeling was that interesting developments are taking place within Pentecostal and Evangelical groups. There is a growing sense of awareness of identity, away from American influences, and there is a growing attention for local and regional problems like HIV/Aids, poverty, bad governance etc. This implies that the frontiers between groups are changing, that similarities with others arise and different forms of cooperation are possible (and often necessary: in many situations you cannot afford to live with borderlines set by foreigners). (Protestant in EcO)

> Some people within the traditional churches feel attracted by an Evangelical and Pentecostal approach. So there is much to learn for the traditional churches. I do hope it will not lead to just another extra denomination. (Roman Catholic church leader)

Several statements also reflect on the possibility for a mutual learning process:

> The sensitiveness with Pentecostals in many mainstream churches is related to the fact that these churches often lack a clear vision of their own identity. In that sense, it is a challenge for these churches to develop ways of speaking with inspiration in the world. (two representatives of Protestant churches).

> The encounters will change all of us. I hope the Pentecostals will discover that church cannot live without a structure. I have the feeling they are already developing an ecclesiology. We have learned that the charismatic and the structural side of the church do not contradict each other. The are both instruments of Gods Spirit. (Roman Catholic ecumenical expert)

One Orthodox respondent feared the great number of representatives of churches that are not members of the WCC will have a negative effect:

> Sometimes, there is too much attention for Pentecostals and Evangelicals, at the cost of the attention of the member churches of the WCC for each other. That is caused by the newness of this relation, and will change in the future, once relations are built up.

*Preliminary conclusion*

Overall, we conclude that all participants of the Limuru meeting are very positive about the possibilities for getting to know people from other church traditions. They are willing to accept special arrangements (like over-representation) to serve that purpose.

**D. Did the event in Limuru influence your church/organization? (e.g. articles, information on your website, agenda items, etc.).**

There seems to be some reluctance to answering this question. Influence is hard to measure. And the GCF is not known by that many people because of a lack of publicity in most countries. As a Roman Catholic ecumenical expert said:

> At the time of the meeting in Limuru, I did not follow the event, so I cannot answer the question. But my lack of interest is due also to the fact that the event was not particularly highlighted in the ecumenical literature I follow. I would like to add that the interest for the ecumenical movement (and especially the WCC) is very low indeed in our press, and so also among the ordinary faithful, and even clergy.

There are two – important - exceptions to this tendency:

> On the surface, it seems there was not much influence - except the fact that it seems that our church will soon send a representative to the Continuation Committee, which, in itself, is quite remarkable given the long history of ecumenical scepticism in our denomination. It appears that the kind of inter-

church relations that the Forum represents is exactly what Adventists are interested in. (Adventist church leader)

It had a significant influence upon the Pentecostal world. The Pentecostal World Fellowship has come aboard as supporting the initiative. The General Superintendents of the Assemblies of God and the various Bishops of the Church of God who attended, wanted to go on record as supporting the initiative. (Some churches have given donations.) The General Superintendents of the Assemblies of God who participated were vocal about it at the recent meeting of the World Assemblies of God Fellowship meeting in Portugal, and they wanted to make a strong statement to the Assemblies of God leadership in the US who did not participate, that they had missed out on something very important. (Pentecostal church leader)

**E. What concrete actions did your church/organization already develop as a continuation of or in line with Limuru 2007? (e.g. articles, webpage information, meetings in the spirit of GCF, policy making, agenda items, new encounters with other denominations/organizations, methodology of sharing faith journeys etc.)**

Answers to this question yielded a similar reluctance. One respondent was very pessimistic:

My church did not do much. Pastors lack ecumenical feeling and knowledge, and the church does not stimulate that (contrary to what I experienced in the past, e.g. with Uppsala, 1968). Churches and theological education have become provincial. Church leaders do not give a follow up to ecumenical meetings. They only complain about the costs. (Reformed ecumenical expert)

Neither can others mention any concrete action taken so far. At the same time, no one shows an unwillingness to co-operate with future requests for action. That is good news. As Colin Williams (General Secretary of the Conference of European Churches) wrote in *CEC-Monitor* (April 2008):

In Europe we seek in a more determined way to engage with what in most of Europe are known as the Free Churches, commonly Pentecostal in character, traditionally allergic to anything that smacks of ecumenism, but now increasingly actively courted by the more traditional churches, not least through the WCC's Global Forum. In this context we must be aware of the good work which is already being carried out in parts of Europe to engage with this developing ecumenical agenda. In Norway, to take just one example, Pentecostal churches play an active part in the ecumenical structures. Before we ourselves at CEC go too much further on this issue we need to carefully map the good work which is already being done by our member churches, so that we can feed to other member churches stories of good practice and try at a regional level to build on the important work which is being carried out nationally.

There are other examples of actions like the one in Norway. Representatives from two different churches said they already successfully applied the method of the GCF themselves. Other developments in the same field are:

> In the organization of the next Assembly the WCC is discussing to offer a shared space to a wider group than only the member churches. (Orthodox in EcO)

> Independent from the GCF, in the Netherlands an initiative like GCF was taken, to have a yearly encounter of the Dutch Council of Churches with non-member churches like Pentecostals and Evangelicals. The method of one of these meetings was inspired by the GCF, the story telling on the personal journey of faith. It worked well. These encounters follow no concrete pre-designed path; the agenda and method are chosen for each new meeting. A concrete result after five years is that we now know each other and know how to find one another in cases of emergency and to prevent working against each other. It is a platform, not a structure. As for social engagement: in that platform the ecumenical churches have to step back, but I am convinced that in the coming generation this will be different. (Reformed ecumenical expert)

The evaluators received some articles on the GCF and found some on the Internet themselves. Some websites of churches and ecumenical organizations give information on the GCF, but very often that information is absent or obscure.

*Preliminary conclusion*

A conclusion could be drawn that much more could be done to communicate the work and results of the GCF. At the same time, one wonders why the participants of the Limuru meeting and other meetings of the GCF, do not communicate more of the experiences they themselves value so highly. Is it a matter of individualism? Fear of criticism? Lack of time? Is the experience hard to communicate? Or did the positive feelings fade away quickly?

If communication is only seen as a task for the Secretariat, it is likely to fail due to lack of time, knowledge and money. Those of each church family present in a GCF meeting are in the best position to give a trustworthy and convincing report to their fellow church members of the GCF. This task cannot and should not be fulfilled by a Secretariat on a global level.

## 5. THE FUTURE OF THE GCF

### General remarks

One of the key issues for the Global Christian Forum is its future. This part of the evaluation deals with its content, forthcoming agenda, format, participation, structure, Secretariat and finances.

During the period of our assessment, we were confronted with a mixture of opinions - positive as well as hesitant - about the future of the GCF. We noticed appeals for patience to decide on its future because it is 'too early' to draw conclusions concerning its outlook. Words of caution were also given with statements like *'it cannot continue as it does at the moment'* and *'we first need some kind of formalisation'*. After Limuru in November 2007 and 10 years after its beginning, the future of the GCF is at a crossroads. On the one hand, the Forum is considered a success because it overcame huge difficulties before it could start. But it is also described as a possible threat to the achievements of the ecumenical movement so far, like commitment and fellowship. Quite a few observers regard it as too early to say something useful of the agenda and structure of the GCF because it is still growing. One Reformed ecumenical expert even said: '*It is too early to decide about structures, etc. Perhaps we should first have another world Forum again*'.

Below we add some comments reflecting the field mentioned above:

> The GCF needs time, we should not make the mistake of the past to hurry into conclusions. (Reformed ecumenical expert)

> You get to know others best by working with them. Low-profile actions, like evangelisation together. And perhaps have a celebration together. I hope it will continue. We do not want to join existing structures, like the WCC and national councils of churches. Unless many things change. But we do want to discuss with others the possibilities of something new, like the GCF. (Pent. church leader)

> We see the work of the Holy Spirit in the fruits, so we will have to wait to see whether Limuru bears fruit. (Orthodox in EcO)

> It might be wise to consult a sociologist who is acquainted with the churches and ask him or her to assist in the process of thinking about the future of the GCF. (Roman Catholic ecumenical expert ).

> It is important that there is some kind of formalisation of the GCF. At the moment attending the meetings depends much upon the personal willingness and enthusiasm of some. That is not enough for the future and a danger for its future prospects. (Roman Catholic ecumenical expert)

One voice is more negative:

> It is too early to draw conclusions concerning the future of the GCF. I heard too many negative signpost (like: 'no structure', 'we do not want ...'). Looking at it from the outside, I cannot become enthusiastic: no hot topics, a declaration with little content. It is all very preliminary. It is a necessary step, perhaps, but what will it change, for whom? What does it mean for ordinary church members? (Reformed in EcO)

**What future steps do you see?**
**A. in terms of content:**
**1. The continuation of the methodology of sharing personal faith stories.**

In general this methodology was strongly supported by the leadership of churches and ecumenical organizations. It was seen as a inclusive means for further co-operation and deeper reflection, a foundation preparing common soil for any further conversation and discussion. Some also indicated that other methods could be explored. In particular, this was confirmed by interviewees of student and youth organizations:

> It was good, but can take a long time. It should be well regulated. (Pent.)

> This is the basis of realising our oneness. (Evan.)

> It should be enlarged by sharing communitarian faith stories, and common theological reflection on them. (RC)

> In designing this methodology, we were looking at something that did not privilege ecumenical insiders over ecumenical outsiders. Thus, we decided not to begin with sophisticated theological papers, but rather, with personal experience. In our earlier discussions, some of the ecumenical insiders feared this approach. That made me pursue it all the more because the ecumenical outsiders were already disadvantaged by being invited to an overtly ecumenical meeting, which they feared. With fears on both sides, the question remained, how best to get the conversation started. We suggested two possibilities. Each person could talk about how he or she had come to faith. No one would be left out. And since we were targeting Christian leaders, we believed that each person could bear witness to the path that brought them into ministry. I think that some have taken that to me that we were asking for 'personal faith stories', but these were the two questions we suggested, and in my introductory remarks, these are the two subjects I have told the groups to pursue. I am convinced that those who are ecumenical outsiders have never heard ecumenical insiders speak personally about their entry into the church or their calls into ministry. Evangelicals and Pentecostals hear in these stories something of their own story, and as a result, their defences come down very quickly. I know that some of the ecumenical insiders feel that it is a waste of time. I believe that without it, there would be not meeting at all. (Pent.)

The ecumenical experts agree with this (sometimes wholeheartedly), however, some indicated this method has its limits too, in particular in the long run. One voice reveals restlessness and wants to go further. On the other hand, the need to take time to expand relationships is clearly indicated:

> This method is excellent. It helps to focus on something that often (not always, but more often than not) connects Christians rather than divides them. And even where experiences differ, we must learn to respect experiences that others made. Therefore, I consider this element as almost indispensable. (Adv.)

> Building trust takes time, so yes this method will be necessary, especially in the coming decades. (Ref.)

> 'Will on the long run not be sufficient for people from the 'institutional' churches. (RC).

> This is fine for establishing trust, but GCF will need to move beyond it to more sustained reflection. (Luth.)

**2. More space to discuss themes more profoundly.**

This position is strongly supported by church leaders and persons in charge of ecumenical bodies. There is clearly a strong need for additional space and extra time for discussion.

> To start discussing in depth issues that the global church is facing. (Evan.)

> There should definitely be more space to discuss themes more profoundly and genuinely. (RC)

> Yes and more on the concern of doing mission together rather than on issues of church doctrines and practices. (Prot.)

> One area where I see particular potential for development is to bring together those in the breadth of Christian families who are dealing with particular themes / issues - e.g. mission or social justice or healing/health or children's work or …- and so helping them establish global networks of practitioners in these fields. (Angl.)

Ecumenical experts strongly supported this position - quite often they used the words '*of course*' - and regarded it as very significant with - again - the reservation that one should not move forward too quickly:

> Yes, but we have to take care because it could be that the relations are not yet solid enough to talk about issues that divide us. (Orth.)

Yes, personally I would like to discuss theological issues, but I fear the GCF is not yet that far: first trust has to be built through the personal faith stories. Perhaps a second issue to discuss could be the history of our churches. And after that the concrete problems of our modern societies. But that is much more difficult than it is in the WCC, because there is no basic commitment, no fellowship, on which you can built these discussion. (Reformed in EcO)

Will be desired once more churches and people participate and once the charm of encounter etc. is over. (RC)

Of course, the challenge of the GCF is in which direction to move - whether to devote more time to Bible study, to theological discussion, or the like. Certainly at some point this will be a necessity. Of importance will be, in my view, the spirit in which these discussions are conducted: if they aim at excluding some group, they will lead nowhere. (Adv.)

Of course, this process must be more than sharing personal faith stories, so gradually more profound discussions on common concerns, but also on divisive issues should get a place. (Ref.)

Always helpful, especially if it allows GCF to face divisive and controversial topics, which has not really happened yet. (Luth.)

**3. Urgent topics for the forthcoming agenda. (e.g. theological, social or moral issues). Give five suggestions for prospective topics in order of preference.**

Following is a list of the 82 suggestions for the future. We put topics with the highest scores at the top.

Theology 13
Mission 11
Social Justice 11
Interfaith dialogue 6
Cooperation of churches 4
Ecology/creation 4
Homosexuality 3
Images of God or the Divine 3
Unity 3
Worshipping together 2
Acceptance of each other as equals before God 2
Interpretation of Scriptures 2
HIV-AIDS 2

The following topics were suggested once: further dialogue with Pentecostals, faith-culture relationship, laity, leadership, division and differences, moral issues, Christian identity, Holy Spirit, Christ, decision making in church, reception of ecumenical agreements, dialogue, Eastern mysticism, persecution of Christians in Muslim countries, the relation of the GCF to the 'institutional' ecumenical movement and its goals and the level of institutionalization the GCF wants to (or will) reach. Three respondents declined to mention issues for various reasons (see below).

While there is a great variety of suggested topics for the future agenda, the issues 'theology', 'mission' and 'social justice' are decidedly seen as the most urgent topics. Among the category Theology, we include ecclesiology (6 times) and pneumatology (1). No additional specification was given except for the importance of the Catholicity of the church (2), with the warning of one voice that one cannot set an agenda from above. Where 'Mission' was suggested, quite often the notion proselytism (*'sheep-stealing'*) was referred to. In the category Social Justice topics like racism, peace, poverty etc. were mentioned. Below we give some comments made during interviews:

> We should not discuss issues like baptism etc. in the GCF, but only ethical issues. There are possibilities in that field, because the contexts of the participants differ much: there are no longer monolithic blocks. By doing so, we will learn other things too, like that you cannot do ' sheep-steeling', etc. (Reformed ecumenical expert)

> My concern is that the GCF will not be able to discuss concrete issues for quite some time to keep all participants happy. And only sitting together is something we cannot afford: we are concerned about the unity of the church to work for justice, peace and integrity of creation. We need a moral voice in the world, an alternative voice. (Protestant in EcO)

> All the moral issues that divide us in the WCC at the moment, and in which we as Orthodox find ourselves closer to Evangelicals and Pentecostals. At the same time we experience a great distance to these churches as it comes to theological issues. It is hard to say whether a discussion on these issues is possible, as we totally differ from each other. (Orthodox in EcO)

> A discussion in the GCF might help my (Orthodox) church to enter into a constructive dialogue with Pentecostals, which was not possible until now because of the bad experience with conversion activities in the nineties in Eastern Europe. (Orthodox in EcO)

> Each region has its own hot topics. In Europe the interfaith dialogue would be an important issue; in Zimbabwe peace. (Lutheran in EcO)

> On ecclesiology there is a difference between Evangelicals and Pentecostals in the way they relate to this issue. Evangelicals belong to different churches, so their interest is mainly in evangelism. But Pentecostals, although not structured like traditional churches and not interested in structures until recently, have more

> feeling for the discussion on ecclesiology because they think about the future, about the formation of the next generation. And in Latin America you find Pentecostals asking themselves how to read the Bible. These are questions you do not ask yourself if you don't consider yourself being a church. (Protestant in EcO)
>
> On homo-sexuality it is my experience that it is important to show that your views are related to your belief, that you want to follow Jesus with this view. Doing so, I noticed that you can make steps forward in that way. (Reformed in EcO)

We include here four denomination-specific agendas in response to our questionnaire:

Adventist:
1. Christian Mission in the 21st century
2. The role of experience in theology and faith
3. Mobilization of laity for Christian service
4. Spirituality in denominational and inter-church perspectives
5. Relations to adherents of non-Christian religions

Pentecostal:
1. Social
2. HIV/AIDS
3. Poverty
4. Moral - transparency as Christians
5. Theological, including gay marriages

Roman Catholic:
1. Theology of unity
2. Councils and decision-making in the church
3. Reception of ecumenical agreements and convergence
4. Interreligious dialogue
5. Ethics of dialogue

Evangelical:
1. Racism
2. Eastern mysticism in the Christian church
3. HIV/Aids
4. The environment
5. Person and work of Christ

The explanations given by three respondents as to why they did not suggest topics for the future agenda revealed their concern:

> Here I am clear that it will be quite wrong for people who have not been part of the mutual sharing and witnessing to one another to suggest, let alone choose, the forthcoming agenda. It is of the essence of the 'pilgrimage' or 'exploration' that the GCF is pursuing and experiencing that any 'next steps' should be those that commend themselves to groups of people who have already begun to follow the pathway God is setting before them. So a person like me should positively refuse to suggest topics for future agendas - those must arise from the groups who have been listening and sharing deeply with one another. (Anglican ecumenical expert)

> Topics should not be formulated at the international level: on the local level trust must be built and issues should be mentioned and discussed. And even then, the first thing is to learn to understand each other, not to convince each other. (Orthodox in EcO)

> I don't want to give you any such topics. I do not believe that this is the role of the GCF. The GCF is either an interim means of bringing new people to the larger ecumenical table; of introducing them to some of the ecumenical players, of encouraging them to build relationships that they choose to enter, of offering them ample opportunity to interact with one another, and of turning them loose. Perhaps the GCF should only exist for a decade and then disappear. I see it as the role of existing ecumenical organizations such as the WCC, to take on the topics that the churches which have membership in them wish to bring. In my opinion, it is premature for the GCF to do other than what it has been doing. (Pentecostal church leader)

*Preliminary conclusions*

With regard to future steps of the GCF, church leaders, representatives of ecumenical bodies and ecumenical experts all strongly support the methodology of sharing personal faith journeys and the creation of additional space to explore themes more intensively. There is no dearth of topics that could be discussed at the GCF.

**B. in terms of format:**

**1. Should there be more frequent gatherings in the spirit of GCF? Yes/No. Explain.**

Although the overall responses from the leadership of churches and ecumenical organizations as well ecumenical experts were positive and encouraging, there was also some confusion with the question e.g. the word 'frequent' was debated. Some respondents already anticipated the next question about the level of future meetings:

> Yes. To the extent that funding is available, I think that an annual global event would be good, though it might not be possible except every other year or every

third year. In such a situation, I would hope that encouragement can be given to earlier participants to hold regional or local meetings in the interim. (Pent.)

This is the only way that we can come up with concrete ideas and strategies for the way forward. (EcO)

We should agree on the frequency of major gatherings - like Limuru. Having gathering like that every four years would be a good idea. (Afr.Inst.Ch.).

Yes. Because the more people meet the more come to know one another. (Ang.)

No globally. Yes, locally. (Prot.)

The GCF should not become another institution. We should be thinking now of how we make it part of WCC and WEA (and possibly others). (Evan.)

What is more frequent? The problem is that the Evangelical and Pentecostal churches have not yet representative bodies with a broadly accepted mandate within their denominations. For this reason, I would prefer fostering regional and local initiatives. A bottom up approach might yield the best results. (Reformed ecumenical expert)

**2. What should the level of future meetings be (global, continental, regional, national or local)?**

Varying from local to global and including some combination, all levels for future meetings were recommended by the respondents. There was no majority in favour of a particular level. While no conclusions can be drawn from the answers of this question, we share some of the comments:

Before Limuru I thought the regional would feed the global, but now I think both are necessary and will support each other. But we have to realise, that the local level often lacks the skills to lead discussions. Besides, it is problematic that many Evangelicals are not organised at a national and international level. (Lutheran in EcO)

It is also a task of the regional Councils of Churches to create spaces like the GCF does, especially as churches are no longer very much interested in structures and programs (like in the WCC). Churches are looking for places where they can discuss the questions they are confronted with. (Protestant in EcO)

It is not a task of the traditional ecumenical organizations to take the lead in GCF-like processes: if, e.g., the AACC would do so in Africa, Evangelicals and Pentecostals would withdraw. We should learn to become small, to create space for others (see John). The others must really experience it as something we are doing together. (Reformed in EcO)

We have to have more national and regional meetings; no events, but processes, and by doing so we will work towards a global meeting. We should be careful not to repeat the global event over and over again. (Reformed in EcO)

The local level is the best: there the contexts are the same, and the urgency of unity is more clear on that level (e.g. where churches are in a minority position or have difficulties with their governments). Besides, on the global level there is always the danger the discussion will be dominated by institutional interests. Beware of a discussion between institutes! It should be a Dialogue of Life! The GCF can stimulate that on the local level. (Protestant in EcO)

In Limuru we decided to go back to the regions and to the local level. That is important because e.g. Pentecostals are regionally very different. (Lutheran in EcO)

A global level is desirable, regional and local depend on the special region - somewhere it might be appropriate, somewhere less. (Roman Catholic ecumenical expert)

I still believe that various global meetings are necessary - perhaps every 3 years, for up to 15 years. I would strongly encourage those who have participated in a GCF meeting, to take a leadership role within their continent, region, nation, or city to engage others in a similar experience. I don't believe that it can be done by existing councils of churches, but I do believe that new relationships are being established, and from these relationships, the circle of influence could easily be expanded in these other areas. (Pent.)

In one way or another they will need to be within say 20 years at all these levels - and several more. (Anglican ecumenical expert)

### 3. What should the level of representation be? (consider church leaders, lay people, theologians, youth and gender balances etc.)

Most of the respondents favoured a good mix. Thus no conclusions could be drawn from the answers. Some indicated support for lay people, others gave priority to church leaders. Two noticeable responses took notice of the balances for representation (see below). Here we share some comments:

I would prefer a mix of these groups. (Reformed ecumenical expert)

It depends of the character of the GCF. The higher the commitment is, the more important is balanced representation. (Roman Catholic ecumenical expert)

The GCF should gather mostly lay people, including youth and theologians; gender balances should be naturally, but not artificially kept. (RC)

> Participants should be people who are in positions to influence others. (Reformed ecumenical expert)
>
> Priority should be given to clergy and church leaders because the problem of church unity does not seem to come from lay people. (Prot.)
>
> It would be refreshing if the majority was from the bottom up - with minimal hierarchical representation, so that the mainstream Christians might have their voices heard. (EcO)
>
> Our representation should be different: more young people, more lay people. Not the predictable batch of senior officials. (Evan.)
>
> All of these are important, but church leaders are the most important to begin with. (EcO)
>
> I am 40 years old and in Limuru I was one of the youngest. (Reformed in EcO)

The two deviant voices, however, from a different angle were:

> In the Seventies the WCC decided to work with quota for participation in meetings etc. (like so many women, youth, lay persons, etc., but the result was that inspired and inspiring individuals who were the hearth of the ecumenical movement were prevented from attending any longer. But by doing so, it was forgotten that the ecumenical movement is a movement of persons. If you withdraw them, the institution is the only thing that remains. (Methodist ecumenical expert)
>
> I am really quite tired of hearing about the need for all these balances that seem to permeate ecumenical thinking, and especially I am especially tired of hearing about the need for bringing in youths. I can assure you that in the Assemblies of God, it isn't the youths who are going to be making the decisions about whether to enter the ecumenical movement or how far we should participate. It will be Administrators, Clergy, and Theologians - male and female. If we want it to happen, the level of representation must be kept at that level. It is also these people that pay the bills. I would not look for exact balances, but would simply invite the leaders involved to think outside the box. (Pent.)

*Preliminary conclusions*

The call for more frequent meetings in the spirit of the GCF is strongly advocated, but it is not clear whether these should be on the global, regional or local level. Some believe there should be a greater presence at the GCF meetings of people below the age of 40, though one Pentecostal respondent said he is tired of hearing about the need for bringing in youth. In terms of proportional denominational participation for forthcoming meetings, nothing particular is recommended. The Roman Catholic Church policy is to attend meetings such as the GCF and the WCC Assemblies with a small delegation.

**C. in terms of participation.**

**1. Should proportional denominational representation be a directive for the forthcoming meetings?**

The comments were half in favour of proportional representation and half in favour of other options. Some responses:

> Yes, that will be good for discussions and developing relationships. (Pent. and Evan.)
>
> It depends of the character of the GCF. The higher the commitment is, the more important is balanced representation. (Roman Catholic ecumenical expert).
>
> No, not at this stage. Proportional denominational representation is too formal at this early stage. (Reformed ecumenical expert)
>
> Not in terms of quotas. A general move in that direction would be good, though. Mainline Protestants seem underrepresented at present. (Lutheran ecumenical expert)
>
> The whole point of the GCF is the quality of mutual relationship its members discover they can gain. That experience is what alone can produce the 'guideline' for any future stages in what will remain for years yet the tentative and exploratory beginnings made possible by the GCF. (Anglican ecumenical expert)
>
> No. I understand the composition was to gather five major families of Christians, so 'denomination' seems inadequate here. But there should be a general balance between Protestant, Catholic, Orthodox, Evangelical and Pentecostal, so that in small groups there is sufficient variety for everyone to encounter the other families. (Ref.)
>
> No. Equal numbers would do away with dominance of any group. Ecumenical groups like ours would only expect to send maximum 2 representatives. (EcO)
>
> We should be looking at innovation. Bringing those who are bringing new things rather than just lots of people who are not adding new initiatives. (Evan.)
>
> There are still groupings who have not yet 'come to the table' and we want to keep the door very much open to them - in a way that gives them a feeling of being a full part from the beginning, rather than being invited to join somebody else's party. And some traditions are still feeling their way in (i.e. among Pentecostals). Looking at the balance of denominations can be an important tool in this process. (Angl.)

No. I don't think that I really understand this question. If it is referring to the 50% split, then yes. If it means Assemblies, versus Foursquare, versus Church of God in Christ, etc., we have worked very hard to get anyone involved that we can. We have run up against some pretty hard walls in the past, so I think it is unreasonable to demand some kind of proportional denominational representation. (Pent.)

This also depends on the 'level'. It should be always balanced with a corrective for minorities that show interest. (Evan.)

**2. Are there any additional churches/organizations you would like to be invited to the process?**

Many respondents answered they would not know which ones to invite. Others:

See Bodies in Association of CTBI/CTE (Churches Together in Britain and Ireland/Churches Together in England), etc. (EcO)

All who are still on the margins or beyond!' (Angl.)

Other para church organizations like the Scripture Union, Catholic Biblical Federation and Fellowship of Evangelical Students, Catholic Youth Associations, Orthodox Youth. (EcO)

Theological faculties maybe; supra-ecclesial structures as IFFEC (International Federation of Free Evangelical Churches). (Evan.)

**3. How does the participation of your church/organization in the Forum relate to your participation in other ecumenical encounters?**

We received the following comments:

The GCF is in continuity with Adventist participation the CWC (Christian World Communions) secretaries' consultations. It also corresponds to the way Adventists have been participating in Bible Societies, Refugee and Development services, Medical Ministry, and other practical Christian work, but at the same time goes beyond these by engaging representatives of my church in encounter on the spiritual level, which is in my view important. (Adv.)

Working with AEA (Association of Evangelicals in Africa), this has helped greatly. (Pent.)

We are not yet participants in the Global Forum, but would welcome the option. We participate in CEC/CCEE - Together for Europe (Conference of European Churches and the European Catholic Bishops Conference) and events connected with our networking ecumenical groups. (EcO)

The connection between the Global Christian Forum and our participation in the National Council of Churches has been made – it is harder to make a connection with Evangelical platforms of unity. (Evan.)

It has set a new standard for personal encounter and helped me see how 'institutional' so many of our agendas are. (EcO)

The Forum is a development of what my organization does with the ecumenical movement to which it is affiliated. (Prot.)

Anglicans already have a very broad range of ecumenical relationships. One of our commitments to the GCF is as bridge-builders between those who do not have existing relationships. Those in the Anglican Communion Secretariat who have been to GCF meetings have valued their experience, and do draw on it in their work. (Angl.)

It is about the same, we are already in this. (EcO)

Participating in the GCF does not in any way affect the OAIC's (Organisation of African Instituted Churches)participation in other ecumenical encounters. In fact GCF helps to bring on board other churches and organizations who do fit existing ecumenical bodies. (Afr.Inst.Ch.)

**D. in terms of structure:**

**1. The GCF opted for a light structure. Do you think this is a suitable option also for the future (in relation to your ideas on communication, publicity, frequency of meetings etc.)?**

At least 75% of the respondents, both the leaders of churches and organizations and the ecumenical experts, are very much in favour of a minimal structure for the GCF. Some admitted, however, that they do not know what that would really be nor what the present structure of the GCF looks like. Many referred to the World Council of Churches which seems to have lost momentum by becoming an institution. Even staff members of the WCC itself supported this:

The GCF should not copy the mistakes of the WCC, which means: the GCF should not work with a (larger) global secretariat and global meetings. The global has no existence apart from the (commitment of the) local. So: make roots, not mainly global, a small secretariat, shared ownership (also financially). E.g.: the Committee could ask the Norwegian churches to organise a GCF in Europe, together with CEC (Conference of European Churches). The Committee could discuss experiences from different local situation. (Protestant in EcO)

The essence of the GCF has been its thorough, lasting and unbreakable agreement not to impose any conditions or conclusions on those who are personally involved in the meetings. Let **them** decide on when and in what sort of way a somewhat different structure might be appropriate for a next meeting or meetings. It is the

> quality of relationships and of spiritual openness and honesty that is of the essence, not any particular structure or device. Make sure that this stays the case throughout at least a second stage that lasts at least as long as the first. We shall only harm the exploration if any one group within it jumps to the assumption that we can skip parts of the next round! (Anglican ecumenical expert)

Other reasons for not creating a complex structure include lack of finances, the distaste for structure in some churches (according to some, Pentecostals in particular are allergic to institutions and the power structures that accompany them), the existence of so many structured ecumenical organizations already.

Comparisons with other international bodies were given as examples of various working models:

> We should work like the UN: not a big staff, but using the embassies to prepare meetings etc. Churches are too much civil service oriented, too much focussed on budgets etc: we should make a better use of the existing structures. The solution to many problems is as close by as your own shadow. (Lutheran ecumenical expert)

> We have to learn from organizations like WEA and the Lausanne Committee to have a small staff, but to work with active commissions. The problems of the WCC have a lot to do with the western emphasis on structures. (Reformed in EcO)

A Reformed ecumenical expert gave the advice

> The GCF should try to formulate what it does not want to be. Over against each negative phrase a positive should then be formulated. That helps the reflection process. If you do not be concrete in this, if you do not come to an understanding, it will only be pious prattle.

> A secretariat located at one of the organizations could be the best option but we have to keep the structure light. (Afr.Inst.Ch.)

A quarter of the respondents did not want to use terms like 'a light structure'. They called it an illusion to think the GCF can work without a structure. They pointed to the Pentecostals, who do not like structures at all, but now recognize that they too need some kind of institutionalisation. As a Reformed ecumenical expert said:

> It is non-sense to be proud of your non-institutionalised character: everything that does not get institutionalised, won't get lasting support: in the format of noting more than a forum the GCF will come to nothing. We should ask ourselves: what format, what institution suites conciliarity? Without institution, the GCF will fizzle out, moreover, because some of the participants are not really interested in conciliarity. It needs some kind of organization, even if it is only in liturgy or some kind of diaconal action.

And a Roman Catholic ecumenical expert has very practical reasons for rejecting a light structure:

> I do not think that a light structure is a suitable option for the future of GCF. It is very little effective, even counter-productive in relation to communication, publicity and the frequency of meetings.

One Reformed church leader had a somewhat different approach. He agreed that the GCF should not be institutionalised. It is a dilemma, he said:

> As soon as the GCF becomes an institution, it will collapse.

At the same time, this does not prevent him from opting for a Secretariat of approximately 12 people, because the GCF is too vulnerable the way it is now. But, he added, this staff should not be staff of the GCF itself, but staff of other ecumenical and church bodies who are 'lent' to the GCF.

**2. The main planning, organization and management of the Forum activities is done by the Secretariat, on paper a half-time but in actual fact a full-time job.** The Secretary is a retired person with an office at home. Many call this a vulnerable construction. Do you opt for a change e.g. a larger Secretariat; a Secretariat located at one of the organizations or churches that participate in the Forum; a responsibility for the Secretariat shared by more organizations, and if so, which?

The answers to the previous question show that most respondents opt for a light structure with a small Secretariat, which means a staff of one or two persons (as '*Huibert van Beek is the two-persons office at the moment*,' as a Lutheran ecumenical expert said), supported by volunteers if necessary. Several cautioned that it will be very difficult to find a substitute for the present Secretary, as he is a very experienced and very able person *('A less able person than Huibert van Beek would have created a new organization, which would have been a problem, as it would have diminished the possibilities of becoming a success*,' according to a WCC staff member):

> I totally agree that Huibert van Beek cannot be expected to go on for ever, but it will be vital that a no less careful and sensitive person be found, gradually to assist him and eventually take over from him, without making any big fuss about the office as such. (Anglican ecumenical expert)

But others did think the place of the Secretariat is an important issue, although the opinions differ:

> I prefer a responsibility shared by more organizations. It might be a proof of the preparedness to investigate in GCF if the main partners in this initiative were

> prepared to start paying a secretariat with one paid full-timer and one or more part-time volunteers. (Reformed ecumenical expert)
>
> I opt for a change as far as a larger secretariat is concerned. This secretariat should neither be located at one of the organizations of churches that participate in the Forum; nor should the responsibility for the secretariat be shared by more organizations; rather its place should be together with other ecumenical organizations, preferable in Central Europe. (Roman Catholic ecumenical expert)
>
> I would not support a larger secretariat, nor would I be willing to support a secretariat located at one of the organizations or churches. Such things communicate different agendas that we do not wish to communicate. I even have mixed feelings about whether a shared secretariat might work – e.g. WEF/WCC (World Evangelical Fellowship and World Council of Churches). I think that is highly risky. I want to go very slowly in this regard, lest we lose the decade of work that we have already done. I think the lighter the secretariat the better. (Pentecostal church leader)

At the same time, several respondents, especially in the Ecumenical Centre in Geneva, who know the situation well, are aware that the GCF depends too much on one person, Huibert van Beek. According to them, this is not a healthy situation. In order to be able to function after the departure of van Beek, the GCF should become the responsibility of more people,.

Several respondents (Reformed, Evangelical, Pentecostal) also mention the need for responsibility for the GCF to be shared: all the stakeholders should be accountable and the costs should be shared widely:

> I think the office needs independence, but costs must be shared widely. In particular, I think the Evangelical and Pentecostal families need to take a greater share of the costs. (Reformed church leader)

**E. in terms of finances**

**1. Did your church/organization supply resources to the GCF in the past?**

**2. Is your church/organization willing and able to contribute financially to forthcoming meetings (from local to global) of the GCF?**

The general tendency of the answers to this question are:

- yes, we do, but we think that others should contribute more
- no, we don't, but we cannot afford to do so (budget constraints)
- a little, but we cannot afford to contribute more (budget constraints)
- I do not know whether my church contributed.

As can be seen in the financial reports of the GCF, the GCF is mostly financed by the WCC and WCC member churches and affiliated organizations. Of course, this is reflected in the answers to this question: Roman Catholics, Pentecostals and Evangelicals supplied little or no resources to the GCF, although there have been contributions through personal commitment to the

GCF. Some answered this is a subject of discussion in their church or organization.

**3. What are your ideas vis-à-vis the financing of the GCF (future possibilities, proportionality of contributions etc.)?**

That Pentecostals and Evangelicals should contribute more in the future is a remark that was made more than once.

A church leader from the Seventh-day Adventist wrote:

> Of course at least some small contributions should be made by all the major denominations and organizations that participate. If some organizations volunteer to continue supporting more significantly (as some did), that would be great!
>
> That just like the New Testament Disciples, each should contribute according to what they have, ideas, money and time. (Pentecostal church leader)

Some suggestions were given:

> Let the activities pay the budget - that is a good way to ensure that only activities that are wanted will be organised. (Evang.)
>
> The GCF should be more creative. It should not work with contributions, membership fees etc., but is should ask churches to finance parts of the work. The staff would then remain the staff of the churches coming together, and not the anonymous staff of a far away institution. The GCF should have a spiritual leader, and someone behind that person for organizational matters. This should not be one and the same person. The new secretary has as his of her task to keep the happy zoo together. (Reformed church leader)

A Pentecostal church leader stated:

> I am opposed to too many rules (e.g. proportionality) at this point in time. This is not an organization, per se. It is an idea that has functioned very successfully as a facilitating agency bringing together people who would normally never darken the doors of one another's offices. It has been paid for, thus far, by people who have caught that same vision. I think it is premature to talk about regular financing. I view this as a vision of faith, and thus, something to be funded in the short term, by those who are exercising a little faith on its behalf. Yeah, I know - it sounds simplistic and naïve, but it has worked so far, and if this is really the Lord's will, I have no doubt that the bills will be paid in the future.

Our last quote in this chapter is from a Reformed church leader, and includes a warning:

Be careful with subsidies for travel and lodging for meetings: churches should ask themselves: how do we value going to that meeting?

## Conclusions

*1. The Secretariat*

Through interviews in Geneva, contact with members of the Committee of the GCF, and responses to the questionnaire, the evaluators observe that the Committee of the GCF, and consequently, the whole GCF, is rather vulnerable. Each member of the Committee has a particular expertise (mainly knowledge of his or her own church family), but the Secretary, Huibert van Beek, is the only one who has a view of the whole; all lines converge in him. Moreover, the Secretary is also the sole person responsible, sometimes with assistance, for the organization of meetings and, with support from the WCC, for financial matters that include everything from participant travel subsidies to fundraising and budgeting. He works from his home office (sometimes using the facilities of the WCC for such things as photocopying), but there is no plan for passing the work in the event van Beek is no longer able or ends his involvement as Secretary to the GCF. The Committee would be in great trouble if he stopped unexpectedly. This is not a sustainable situation, and physically and mentally overburdens the Secretary. The Secretary works full-time but is employed part-time. He also carries the burden of knowing that without him the GCF would probably collapse. For the sake of clarity, we note that this is not what the Secretary told the evaluators, but comes through interviews and observations.

We conclude that the GCF is 'lean and mean' merely at the expense of the Secretary. From both a management and a moral perspective, this would seem to be an undesirable situation, which should be ended in order to avoid future problems.

*2. Financial situation*

The financial situation also needs to be considered. Many respondents state that it is important the GCF does not depend on just one organization. Several of the respondents do not think too positively of the WCC. Yet the WCC supports the work of the GCF more than any other organization, but does not get the credit for doing so. In fact, the WCC's support is largely hidden out of fear that those churches that do not favour the WCC, will no longer participate. Furthermore, there are churches that do want to participate, but do not want their financial contribution be channelled through the WCC. A separate account has been created for this purpose. The present situation is not transparent and one could wonder whether it gives a fair representation of the actual relations. Hence, a thorough reflection on the issue of finance seems to be an issue that needs some thorough attention.

*3. Other issues in relation to the future of the GCF*

Most respondents opted for a light structure, mainly for two reasons: fear of institutionalising an initiative that should stay flexible and should only exist because of the support of the participants, and the belief that finances needed for a larger Secretariat would not be provided. If we relate this issue to things we heard in previous chapters - such as the critical remarks on the traditional ecumenical movement, the fear of simply adding a new organisation or layer to that movement, the negative aspects of flexibility such as less commitment - one wonders what motives underlie the desire to keep the GCF structure light. It is important that this is discussed more thoroughly, especially if what some respondents say is true: that becoming a structure is a necessary if the GCF is to survive. In this respect, it is interesting to notice that even in circles such as Pentecostal churches, where institutionalisation traditionally been rejected, the usefulness of some kind of structure has been discovered.

## 6. Ecumenical Perspectives

**Can you briefly describe what you consider to be the present or future impact of the GCF on organizations like the World Council of Churches, the Christian World Communions and other ecumenical bodies? (as far as you have not done it yet in previous points of the questionnaire).**

As this is a broad question which evoked broad answers, we have clustered the responses in different paragraphs.

*The word 'ecumenism'*

For quite a few people, the word 'ecumenism' is emotionally charged. As seen in chapter I, two representatives of the Orthodox Church said in their interviews:

> Many people in my church (Orthodox) have negative connotations with the word 'ecumenism': we should look for a different word. At the same time, many Orthodox have little knowledge of the ecumenical movement and are not really interested in it too. They think ecumenism stands for the creation of one super church with a mix of traditions. 'Interchurch dialogue' would be a better word.

This would be very difficult for others to accept. A Reformed ecumenical expert reacted:

> For me, giving up the word 'ecumenism' is a bridge too far: I am proud of what we achieved in the ecumenical movement, how far we have come and I am grateful for what we learned. We can and should not renounce that.

However, the feelings of these members of the Orthodox churches are shared by representatives of Pentecostal and Evangelical churches as well. A leader of a Pentecostal church expressed his difficulties with the term during the Limuru meeting and was, to his own surprise, applauded by Orthodox participants. Several participants from other member churches of the WCC expressed that they felt hurt by or even abhorred statements in the Limuru meeting on this issue. As a Lutheran staff member of an ecumenical organization said:

> I was shocked by the criticism on ecumenism I heard in the GCF (words like 'the stench of death was hanging over the ecumenical movement'). The GCF itself is an expression of ecumenism in the 21st century!

A Pentecostal church leader added to his criticism, that his church does not want to '*jump on a moving train*' i.e. to become a member of an already existing ecumenical body: '*We prefer to start something new*'. Of course, this explains something of the attraction of the GCF.

On the other hand, it must be said that not all representatives of these three traditions share these difficulties, and that not all representatives of 'traditional ecumenical churches' are as attached to the word 'ecumenism', as long as the issue at stake is preserved. As one of them said:

> Being ecumenical is an obligation, but I can only explain that to others, I cannot convince them. They will have to learn to see the positive sides of ecumenism. That they do not see them right now is because of experiences in the past that need healing. The GCF can support this healing process.

A staff member of the WCC also learned through the years, that ecumenism alone will not do:

> Within the WCC we realize that we have to revalue 'traditioned environment': people need that to produce meaning. Ecumenism is too thin an environment and cannot replace traditioned environments. Stressing too much the goals of visible unity is asking too much of the capacity of people to produce meaning. The reactions to globalisation taught us that.

### *GCF and WCC*

As we saw in chapter 3, many gave their views on the relation between the GCF and WCC. Several respondents indicated they do not want to compare the two, or do not want to replace the WCC by the GCF. But, according to many, there is much for the WCC to learn; the GCF is more in line with modern ideas of coming together:

> I think it is in the air: ecumenical councils are important, but things like membership and membership fees, structures, etc., have become difficult nowadays. The WCC has to face that. That is why the GCF is interesting and exiting as one of the possibilities of future models. The creation of new ecumenical spaces, and not new ecumenical structures. The WCC should also create these new spaces, on different levels. (Orthodox in EcO)

> You should not compare WCC and GCF: they are so different. For me it is too early to discuss this relation. The GCF is until now only the experience of meeting each other, that is all and cannot replace the WCC. (Orthodox church leader)

> The GCF is a challenge for the WCC: at the GCF you notice the same enthusiasm as at the foundation of the WCC in 1948. (Orthodox in EcO)

> It will encourage such groups to move away from so much institutional focus to a more relational focus: instead of WCC doing ministries for churches, it will network churches so they can do ministry together. (EcO)

A Roman Catholic ecumenical expert, who had not attended GCF meetings himself but had read documents and heard others' reports of Limuru, expressed his impression that in the traditional ecumenical movement '*meeting each other is a means to a certain goal*' whereas in the GCF '*meeting each other is the goal*'. The question, of course, is whether both 'parties' recognise themselves in this picture.

A Pentecostal church leader with a long experience in ecumenical contacts wrote:

> I have met MANY ecumenical leaders that do not really wish to meet, greet, and embrace Pentecostals and Evangelicals. They don't want to admit that this is the direction that the church is moving on the global level. They don't really want to move down the social class level. They don't want to have to listen to criticisms that they don't have. They wish that these groups would go away. Thus, education needs to go on in more than one direction. These meetings of the GCF give that a chance.
>
> I personally have no permanent commitment to any current ecumenical institution. I will not participate in those things that seek their harm, but all of them may have a limited life. Who knows what God has in store for His Church? All I want to do is to facilitate the possibility that those who have previously criticized one another can forgive one another and learn to live together in peace before the world, to the glory of God - Father, Son, and Holy Spirit.

An Anglican ecumenical expert warned against forcing anything:

> I would refuse in principle to try and lay down anything here. It is of the essence of the total pilgrimage that those who already stand in responsible positions in church life come to new decisions and recommendations, in the light of the new relationships they have discovered as real and possible in their own experience, to come up with proposals for their own churches and for the GCF as a whole for 'next steps' that it can take at various moments in the future. I feel confident that if the Limuru message is followed through with real care, energy and devotion by those who agreed it, it will in the long run make a huge and altogether positive difference to both the WCC and the World Confessional Families (and not only to them !) but the last thing I would wish to try and spend time on now is the consideration about future structural possibilities! Stick to the genuinely new and promising relationships and let them guide us into a long-term future that doesn't force anything on anyone!

And one Lutheran ecumenical expert went a step further by writing:

> GCF provides opportunity for greater representation, inclusivity. Ecumenical future surely lies with Pentecostals and Evangelicals; WCC and CWC will likely remain niche phenomena; GCF may be opportunity to move outward.

From the Roman Catholic side, several respondents stressed that in their view the GCF will never replace the WCC. The GCF facilitates the discussion between the different groups and should continue this for some time, but in the end it is a temporary arrangement. That is also formulated by Msgr. John, former Secretary of the Pontifical Council for Promoting Christian Unity, on the website in the article on the GCF (*Ecumenismo, una sfida a diffidenze e incomprensioni. L'esperienza del Global Christian Forum),* where he states that the GCF is not and should not become an alternative for the only goal of the traditional ecumenical movement: the visible unity of all Christians. Nor is it an alternative for the ecumenical dialogue on theological differences. Nor should the GCF become a new, expensive ecumenical organization.

A Reformed ecumenical expert, who served as a pastor for many years, noticed a fear in his church of Evangelical influences. Although he himself is in many respects critical towards the Evangelical approach, he sees that there are also many valuable things in that tradition. So fear is not the right attitude.

All this is well understood by the WCC staff:

> We realised that our self-understanding as WCC worked: we were well represented by our member churches and in that sense we experienced that ecumenism works. Moreover, from Roman Catholic side the importance of the classical ecumenism was stressed. At the same time we will have to find new ways of revitalising the ecumenical movement, because the old way has led to bureaucratisation. There are three main tasks for the ecumenical movement: deepening the fellowship of the member churches, broadening the participation and making coherence in the ecumenical movement. The problem is that the broadening of the participation (where the GCF is part of) is in contradiction with the seeking of coherence. And on the other hand: the Orthodox fear negative effects of broadening the participation. Coherence is important, and we should be careful that the GCF does not contribute to fragmentation by just creating a new table of discussion.

*Cautions*

Some people expressed caution about what might occur in the future. The traditional ecumenical movement taught member churches important lessons, and these should not be lost.

First of all there is the question of commitment. The fact that the GCF is an open space with independence and no real structure could be a threat to very valuable ecumenical structures already in existence because it is attractive for individuals and churches that do not want to engage in ecumenical relations. As an Orthodox working in an ecumenical organization put it (also as a warning of what might happen in his own church):

> In that sense the GCF is an expression of post-modernity: expressing your opinions, views and insights without taking responsibilities, believing without belonging, like living together without marriage to have the opportunity to leave

> when you no longer like it. There is no real commitment for a follow-up, there is no membership or a fellowship with a financial contribution. So: take care!

This problem is also considered by an other Orthodox staff member of an ecumenical organization:

> There are different types of ecumenism: the conciliair model of the WCC, the confessional model of the CWCs and the model of ecumenism by action. But what model is represented by the GCF? Many fear: a non-committed non committal type of ecumenism: we come, we speak, we celebrate together, and go home and then it is business as usual.

According to a Lutheran ecumenical expert, individualism is a second threat:

> The GCF is no alternative for the 'old ecumenical movement'. It is centred round the question: do I see a Christian in the other? But the traditional ecumenism is on the question: do I see church in the other church? If we had only the GCF there would be the danger of 'corrosive individualism'. We need church, so we need more structures than the GCF.

And related to that:

> It is a challenging idea to work towards ecumenical bodies that include all churches. At the same time we should be aware not to loose the possibility of a prophetic task. (Protestant in EcO)

There is also the danger that by focussing too much on new partners in the ecumenical debate, one might neglect 'old' partners:

> The WCC should not feel responsible for all other ecumenical initiatives, but should at this moment focus on the relation with the Orthodox, as the WCC is the only place were they have joined. There is still much pain within these churches because of domination by the West in the past. (Protestant in EcO)

*Not in a hurry*

On several occasions, warnings were given not to hurry things, while others emphasize that churches cannot afford not to be in a hurry because of the needs of the world. A Reformed ecumenical expert put this into a broader framework:

> What happens now in the GCF, is not yet impressive. Sociologically speaking you must say: it needs time. And time has to be taken. Haste and too much emphasis on reaching goals is a threat in our present time. The ecumenical movement did not take enough time to elaborate conciliarity too: it tried it for seven years, and then stopped. That threatens the GCF too. With the GCF the Holy Spirit gives us a second opportunity to work on conciliarity. A lot of reflection work has been done on this issue already: we can use that. We have to ask ourselves: what kind of

> structure is needed for conciliarity? You have to do that, you need some kind of a structure, because without a structure, the whole thing will fall apart. Because many of the partners within the GCF do not like the idea of conciliarity, like the Orthodox and the Pentecostals.

*Other remarks*

Someone working with migrant churches in Europe expressed her reluctance in bringing these churches to the GCF, as they are still too vulnerable to be open to others:

> Although I was moved by what I experienced in the GCF (in the Warburg meeting in Europe, 2006), I still am of the opinion that it remains difficult to bring migrant communities into this Forum. As the common aim of this Forum is to gather people in the faith, migrants of course, add another aspect, that of migration. An aspect of instability.
> The concept therefore, will still only be eligible to 'white' stable church institutions. With that I mean more 'national', be it mainline (WCC) or new (outside WCC) (Catholic, Pentecostal, Evangelical, Orthodox, etc.). Out of my experience of working with migrants, I do feel that you have to be stable and secure first. Only then will you be able to look beyond your own borders on the one hand, and on the other hand, be able to put yourself in a humble, open and vulnerable position. A paradoxal situation!

We conclude this chapter with two remarks made in the evaluation process by respondents:

> I see as a possible development the fact that ecumenism more and more becomes a matter of the South. Many reformed churches in Africa might as well be called Evangelical: the division line shifts. In Africa structures are still flexible: more is possible there than in Europe. (Reformed in EcO)

> GCF is in a way a renewed start of the ecumenical movement in the beginning of the 21st century. In the beginning of the 20th century it also took many years before the conferences of Faith & Order and Life & Work were supported by a broader public. Only in the sixties they were supported by the historical churches. So the GCF too, needs the time to grow. A time will come when new structures for the discussion on faith and order and the social and moral commitment of the churches are needed. The historical churches should wait until the Pentecostals and Evangelicals put these issues and the structures that are needed themselves on the agenda, because one should not create the impression that the agenda of the historical churches is to force the Pentecostals and Evangelicals into their own agendas. (Reformed ecumenical expert)

**Preliminary conclusions**

Again we must conclude that a majority of the participants of the GCF are very much attached to their own traditional approach of dealing with issues in relation to faith and church. During the meetings in the GCF, however, they have met people from others churches and communions, and have learned to see them as Christian. That is the success of the GCF. But the differences remain. And each time, after and through the positive words on the GCF meetings, these differences come to the surface. They will have to be discussed at some point. Some are afraid to do so too early. Others, among them people who are very much involved in the GCF process, are convinced that these discussions are possible, even at this moment, provided that they take place in a proper way. One of the issues to be discussed is the ecumenical movement itself. What has been lost, what has been gained and learned and should be preserved?

## 7. Observations in Relation to the Questionnaire

As it was not possible for budgetary reasons to travel to different countries in order to interview leaders of churches and organizations and ecumenical experts, the circulation of a questionnaire was the second best option. However, during the interviews it was possible to inquire further and deeper, and by doing so, to overcome the level of merely friendly answers. This added new and relevant information to the evaluation and is why the evaluators were glad they had the opportunity to interview 31 people from different backgrounds. A lesson can be drawn from this experience: it might be fruitful to discuss the issues included in the questionnaire in the GCF meetings itself and in personal encounters in smaller groups, in order to move beyond mere friendliness.

In this chapter we want to reflect a bit on the responses to the questionnaire: the number of respondents and their denominational and geographical origins.

### The number of respondents to the questionnaire

As already indicated in the Chapter on the Working Method and in Appendix 3, the response of the leaders of churches and ecumenical organizations to the questionnaire was rather low. At the closing date, few responses were received, but even after the reminder, the number remained low. While a response rate of 22% may not be low in other research, in this case it should have been higher as churches and organizations that showed interest in the GCF by attending the Limuru meeting could be expected to co-operate more widely.

What can we conclude from this? Several suppositions can be made. Perhaps the small number of respondents was the result of a lack of knowledge. A considerable number of respondents indicated that they had little or no knowledge of the GCF. Some returned the questionnaire blank, while others found information on the GCF (apparently on the Internet) and did their best to respond. It is possible that more people receiving the questionnaire realized they were not able to answer the questions and did not respond for that reason. Lack of time or disagreement with the aim of the questionnaire, or overburdened with questionnaires (as two of the people interviewed said) could also be reasons for not participating. A Reformed ecumenical expert told the evaluators he never fills in any questionnaire: he does not have the time to do so, he often does not know the evaluators or does not agree with the purpose of a questionnaire and he doubts its usefulness.

However, the fact that even the letter by the Secretary of the Committee of the GCF in which he strongly recommended participation in the evaluation had so little effect leaves us wondering. The questionnaire was sent to churches and organizations that were present in Limuru. Why did they spend money, energy and time to go to a meeting to which they were invited by the Secretary, but did not do the same when invited by him to co-operate with an evaluation? Does what a Reformed church leader said apply here: that one should beware that participation in international meetings should not be made too easy financially? On the other hand, there are churches which were initially supported financially to attend GCF meetings and later took care of their own costs.

**The denominational division of the respondents**

As indicated in Appendix 3, of the five main faith traditions (Evangelical, Orthodox, Pentecostal, Protestant and Roman Catholic) the Orthodox Church was not represented in responses to the questionnaire. The only input in this evaluation from Orthodox side was in the four interviews held with Orthodox staff members of organizations in Geneva.

Of the smaller traditions, responses were received only from the African Instituted Churches, Old Catholics and the Seventh-day Adventists (two!).

Although no main traditions are lacking, more input would have been generated if it had been possible to pay visits to such places as Moscow, Constantinople and Rome. The budget of the evaluation, however, did not allow us to do so.

The evaluators have heard in their interviews that the idea of conducting an evaluation specially focussed on the Orthodox churches has been considered. This still could proof to be useful. At any rate, the Commission should reflect thoroughly on what the visions and wishes of the Orthodox for the future are.

**The geographical division of the respondents**

Apart from the staff members of organizations who were interviewed in Geneva, who came from different continents, 7 respondents originated from outside Europe and the USA and Canada: 5 from Africa and 2 from Asia. This is a low response from non-Western regions, even taking into account that Latin America was excluded from this evaluation. Here too, the same questions posed above could be asked here.

## 8. Conclusions and Points of Attention

### 1. A good initiative

According to most of the respondents of this evaluation, the founding of the Global Christian Forum was a right step at the right moment. The traditional ecumenical movement was not able to get the Pentecostal and Evangelical churches and communions 'on board', although these are a growing part of Christianity all over the world.

### 2. Attractive working method

Particularly for those who attended GCF meetings, the new and for many, attractive feature of the GCF is that it offers a more personal and spiritual form of encounter than the traditional ecumenical gatherings, giving participants the opportunity to get to know each other better. For some of the respondents, this is a goal in itself, while for others it is a first step toward addressing issues that are really important. Especially for representatives of the Roman Catholic and Orthodox churches, these issues include theological debates on questions like ecclesiology. For others, these issues include responsibility of churches in relation to justice and peace. To overcome the reluctance of some respondents, the method of sharing personal faith journeys could be complemented with the sharing of the stories of the participants' journeys in and with their churches and could be enlarged by sharing life stories. In Youth organizations several creative methods have already been developed for this purpose.

Two conclusions can be drawn from the success of the 'GCF method':

a. The GCF offers what is for many churches and ecumenical organizations a new way of meeting each other and discussing issues, which results in the decline of misunderstandings and prejudices. Churches should take advantage of this and apply this method – with suggested revisions – more often.

b. As this method is so successful, it might be possible to apply it to more contested theological issues, such as mission, as well as social/moral issues such as homosexuality. The GCF would render a service to the churches by trying to apply its methodology in that direction too.

### 3. GCF and the traditional ecumenical movement

Most respondents regard the GCF not as an alternative to the traditional ecumenical movement, but as a means for renewal of that movement. This leads to two considerations:

a. It is a good sign that an idea which originated in the bosom of the WCC with the aim of bringing new life to the oikoumene and which has developed into an independent platform is seen as a contribution to renewal. However, during the evaluation process, the researchers often encountered the perspective through articles and quotes by ecumenical experts that the GCF is still regarded as a WCC project. This misunderstanding needs clarification.

b. It cannot be denied that the existence of the GCF raises fear and anxiety among many who cherish the traditional ecumenical movement. Both partners, the GCF as well as the traditional ecumenical movement, have to deal with this. The GCF could do so by clarifying what it adds to standard ecumenism.

### 4. How far has the GCF come?

How far has the GCF come in reaching its goals? Most respondents speak of a promising beginning. It is a start, trust has grown, suspicion has been diminished. But to be a lasting success the GCF needs to continue for a longer period. At the same time, most respondents and interviewees are not very outspoken about the future of the GCF. The success of the GCF will only be sustainable if the GCF method is applied at the regional, national and grass-roots levels too. The Conference of European Churches, for example, has already indicated it intends to support this in Europe. This kind of process empowers the GCF. The GCF could, like other ecumenical bodies, play a role in the mapping and sharing of 'best practices'.

### 5. Scope of participation

The scope of participation is good. In the eyes of most respondents at least no important churches or ecumenical organizations have been left out of the process. Of course, not everyone within those churches whose participation in ecumenical gatherings began with the founding of the GCF is convinced of its importance, but here too, a beginning has been made. Several of the respondents see a task for themselves in convincing their brothers and sisters of the importance of the GCF. This seems to be an important task for the future and should be supported by the Committee of the GCF.

### 6. Support for the Purposes of the GCF

The six purposes of the GCF are generally well supported though people who were interviewed about the GCF seldom mentioned them and referred only to essential aspects of the GCF itself such as broadening the table of the ecumenical debate, getting to know each other, overcoming mistrust and distorted images, all of which are included in the general mission of the GCF. But this does not imply that they do not agree with the Purpose Statement as a whole, although purpose 4 (*'Engage in theological reflection in areas of mutual concern'*) is supported less than the other purposes. Almost all respondents share the opinion that there still is a long way to go in the realisation of the purposes.

### 7. Format of the GCF meetings

Everybody appreciates the methodology of the meetings, although some see it only as a means to another end. The use of both local and regional as well as global meetings is welcomed as very useful. The GCF is challenged to consider its position regarding these different levels.

### 8. Subjects to be discussed

All kind of issues, theological as well as ethical and social (see pages 39-41), are mentioned as possible items for the future agenda of the GCF. Most respondents fear it is too early to discuss issues that are in dispute, but those with a profound experience of the GCF believe the GCF is already strong enough to discuss all issues, provided that it is done in a proper way.

### 9. Communications

Communication is currently one of the weakest aspects of the GCF. Surprisingly, quite a number of the ecumenical experts who were consulted by the researchers were not acquainted with the GCF and its activities. Moreover, during the time of the evaluation, the researchers were confronted with a lack of knowledge of the GCF in their contacts in churches and church meetings. With some exceptions, the GCF is not written about in articles in church magazines. An inquiry carried out by the GCF Secretariat itself regarding the results of the Limuru meeting among the participants of that meeting received little response. This was also reflected in the responses to the questionnaire and indicates that the 'momentum' of Limuru did not last long enough to 'spread the news'. This should be of serious concern to the Committee and should be a point of attention on the agenda of GCF meetings.

### 10. The structure of the GCF

Most respondents asked for a light structure. We discussed this issue and raised questions about it at the end of chapter 5. The minimal structure of the GCF is both a strength and a weakness. The evaluators believe this issue has not been reflected upon sufficiently by either the Committee or the participants. More attention should be paid to hidden and conflicting motives as well as to those harmful effects mentioned by some respondents.

## 11. The financing of the GCF

Financing is another difficult issue for the GCF. Here again we refer to chapter 5. The fact that the GCF is financed mainly by members of the 'traditional ecumenical movement' is not congruent with the GCF participants' understanding of the GCF.

## 12. Level of participation

The evaluators were confronted with conflicting statements about the participation of the different faith traditions in the GCF in general and the Limuru meeting in particular. Some voiced disappointment about the level of participation in general: for publicity reasons, the GCF is only interesting if it brings together high level church officials. But on the whole, people are satisfied with the level of participation of Protestant, Pentecostal and Evangelical churches, especially because many members of Pentecostal and Evangelical churches are known to be critical towards ecumenical initiatives, including the GCF. About the Roman Catholic participation views differed, but several voices pointed out that the participation in Limuru was in accordance with the Roman Catholic standards. In earlier events of the GCF the Pontifical Council for Promoting Christian Unity decided on the Roman Catholic delegation, but for Limuru a different approach was chosen: the Regional Bishop's Councils appointed the delegates. As a result a regional balanced Roman Catholic participation of 20 delegates for Limuru was realized, as a Roman Catholic church leader pointed out. Orthodox participation was regarded as lacking. This is also true of their response to the questionnaire. As noted in previous chapters, Orthodox churches have ambivalent feelings towards the GCF and the WCC because of issues like flexibility, commitment and the possibility of theological debate. The GCF Committee should continue to pay attention to the Orthodox involvement in the GCF.

## 13. Cautions

The evaluators also heard many cautions.

In relation to consequences of the GCF efforts:

a. the loss of commitment of churches as developed within the traditional ecumenical movement;

b. the loss of attention to traditional partners;

c. the loss of possibilities for public witness.

It should be noted that these cautions are offered only by a minority of the respondents; most are very positive about the GCF and see more possibilities for the GCF than for the WCC in its present form. But as the GCF seeks to address all traditions, it is important to consider these cautions.

There are also cautions about the possibility of transferring the GCF methods elsewhere:

> We have to be aware that until now only the people that are the most open within all denominations will have been present in GCF meetings, people who were able to look critically at themselves too.

Given by two respondents, these words need to be taken into account, especially for meetings at regional, national and local levels, where it is more likely that participants do not have much experience with encounters of this kind. At the same time, this quote also contains a mission for all the participants of the GCF meetings: to talk and write more about their experiences in their own churches and communions and with more emphasis.

# THE GLOBAL CHRISTIAN FORUM 1998-2007, AND BEYOND

## AN EVALUATION REPORT BY INSTITUTO TEOLOGICO FIET

### Investigation

The Instituto Teológico FIET with the collaboration of the Chilean office of World Vision has carried out this investigation.

- The evaluation took into account two sources of opinion: a. of those who had taken part in the Forum on some occasion. b. of those who have not taken part in the Forum.
- In the first case, we tried to measure the perception of the Forum of those who have taken part in it and the impact they consider it has made in the life of churches.
- In the second group, we tried to measure the level of knowledge of the Forum in churches in general, the impact it has made and the availability to take part in the Forum process.

The research was carried out during May-September 2008.

### Methodology

- Two questionnaires were prepared with "closed" answers: one for participants and one for non-participants.
- We took note of the religious affiliation of the people interviewed. We used four categories: Evangelicals (including Pentecostals), Protestants, Catholics and Orthodox. This enabled us to know the opinion of each group on specific questions. We also collected gender and age information.
- Apart from the questionnaires with "closed" answers, there were open answer questions to enable people to express their opinions.
- Finally, we made written, personal and phone interviews to Latin American church leaders: presidents of national alliances, denomination presidents, ecumenical secretaries and key leaders. The results of these interviews are not arranged in tables but are expressed rather as opinions and suggestions.

### Participation

- We sent the same questionnaires four times to the 83 Latin American participants. The questionnaires were sent by e-mail together with a letter that expressed the purpose of the evaluation.

The estimated time for the reply was 7 minutes. There were 20 responses, which amounts to 24%. 65% were Evangelical, 20% Protestant, 10% Catholic and 5% Orthodox.

- We sent questionnaires to church leaders of all the countries in Latin America and Ecumenical Secretaries of the Catholic Church. We received 20 responses from 10 countries. 87% were Evangelical and 13% Protestant. We got no reply from Catholics.

**Questionnaire for 'Participants'**

***AGE:*** *31-40:* *10%*
*41-50:* *40%*
*51-60:* *35%*
*61-70:* *15%*

***Evangelicals:*** *65%*
***Protestants:*** *20%*
***Catholics:*** *10%*
***Orthodox:*** *5%*

**N** = NOTHING **L** = LITTLE **P** = PLENTY **M** = MUCH

| N | Inquiry | Answers | | | |
|---|---|---|---|---|---|
| | | N % | L % | P % | M % |
| 1 | To what extent has the initial vision of the GCF been understood? | 5 | 15 | 60 | 20 |
| 2 | Has the vision evolved? | 0 | 60 | 40 | 0 |
| 3 | Has the goal of the widest possible participation been achieved? | 0 | 10 | 75 | 15 |
| 4 | How open has it been? | 0 | 15 | 50 | 35 |
| 5 | How much use has the Purpose Statement of the GCF been? | 0 | 15 | 55 | 30 |

| N | Inquiry | Answers | | | |
|---|---|---|---|---|---|
| | | N | L | P | M |
| 6 | Have the regional and global events enabled the GCF to reach its goals? | 0 | 15 | 55 | 30 |
| 7 | Have the meeting programs responded to the purpose and the intention of the GCF? | 0 | 10 | 70 | 20 |
| 8 | Have obtained concrete results in terms of new relationships? | 5 | 47 | 38 | 10 |
| 9 | Has the GCF helped to raise fundamental and critical issues? | 5 | 45 | 40 | 10 |
| 10 | Have you experienced the GCF as an "excessively diplomatic" space? | 15 | 60 | 25 | 0 |
| 11 | The GCF structure has so far been simple, i.e. a secretariat and small committees. Has this option served the interest of the GCF? | 0 | 10 | 70 | 20 |

| N | Inquiry | Answers | | | |
|---|---|---|---|---|---|
| | | N | L | P | M |
| 12 | Have the subjects and concerns of the Forum become part of the agenda of your church or organization? | 0 | 75 | 20 | 5 |
| 13 | How do you evaluate the quality of the personal and institutional commitment of the GCF attendants? | 5 | 35 | 45 | 15 |

| N | Inquiry | Answers | | | |
|---|---|---|---|---|---|
| | | N | L | P | M |
| 14 | Is the GCF well known among the leadership of your church or organization? | 5 | 65 | 25 | 5 |
| 15 | How well known is the GCF in other churches or organizations? | 10 | 75 | 15 | 0 |
| 16 | Do you believe the GCF has contributed to Christian unity in your context or region? | 10 | 55 | 35 | 0 |

## Questionnaire for 'Non Participants'

***AGE:*** *41-50:* *46%*
*51-60:* *46%*
*61-70:* *8%*

***Evangelicals:*** *87%*
***Protestants:*** *13%*
***Catholics:*** *No one answered the questionnaire*

**N** = NOTHING **L** = LITTLE **P** = PLENTY **M** = MUCH

| N | Inquiry | Answers | | | |
|---|---|---|---|---|---|
| | | N % | L % | P % | M % |
| 1 | Are you aware of the Global Christian Forum as an "open space wherein representatives from a broad range of Christian churches and interchurch organizations, which confess the triune God and Jesus Christ as perfect in His divinity and humanity, can gather to foster mutual respect, to explore and address together common challenges"? | 25 | 25 | 8 | 42 |
| 2 | Do you think the Forum has been successful in creating an "open space…"? | 8 | 35 | 19 | 38 |
| 3 | Do you share in some way the need for a space such as this? | 0 | 4 | 29 | 67 |
| 4 | Do you think the existence of the Forum is necessary or important? | 0 | 0 | 13 | 87 |
| 5 | Do you have information on the achievements of the Forum? | 41 | 17 | 42 | 0 |
| 6 | How do you evaluate the influence of the Forum in your church? | 42 | 50 | 8 | 0 |
| 7 | To what extent, is the Forum perceived as important in "Christian Unity" matters? | 23 | 55 | 9 | 13 |

| N | Inquiry | Answers | | | |
|---|---|---|---|---|---|
| | | N | L | P | M |
| 8 | Would you like to or do you consider necessary to take part in the Forum? | 4 | 4 | 13 | 79 |
| 9 | If you were invited, would you take part in an activity such as this one? | 4 | 8 | 13 | 75 |

| N | Inquiry | Answers | | | |
|---|---|---|---|---|---|
| | | N | L | P | M |
| 10 | To what extent is the GCF well known among the leadership of churches and church-related organizations? | 29 | 67 | 4 | 0 |
| 11 | To what extent is the GCF well known locally? | 46 | 54 | 0 | 0 |

**Commentaries on the Answers of Participants**

According to the opinion of the Forum participants:

1. The original vision of the Forum has been understood by those who took part but they believe it has not evolved.
2. They consider that the events, and especially the characteristics of the programmes of these events, have contributed greatly to achieving the objectives of the Forum.
3. 85% believe the Forum has served to some extent in developing new relationships and to discussing certain critical issues.
4. 90% believe the current simple structure of the Forum is the best for its functioning.
5. The large majority has not seen that the subjects of the Forum have affected the agendas of their churches or institutions.
6. The Forum is not well known, even in the churches and institutions of participants.
7. The majority thinks that the Forum has not contributed to the unity of churches in their contexts or regions.

*Note:*

Points 1 to 3 reflect the personal experience of those who participated: a) they understood the vision; b) they believe that the events and especially the programmes helped to achieve the goals; c) the Forum helped them to develop new relationships.

Points 5 to 7 show that beyond the personal experiences of those who participated, this positive experience did not reach the churches. The Forum affected the participants but not their institutions.

Therefore:

a) it (the Forum) did not affect the agenda of the churches.

b) the Forum is not known in the churches of the participants
c) the Forum has had no impact on the unity of the churches.

In summary, what can be said is that the Forum has had an impact on the persons (and that is very important) but not on their institutions.

### Commentaries on the Answers of Non-Participants

According to the opinion of non-participants in the Forum:

1. 100% agree with the need and importance of a space such as the Forum.
2. 80% believe it is important for the unity of the church.
3. 40% has had no information on the Forum and 60% only some information on its achievements.
4. 90% would accept being invited.
5. 100% believe the Forum is not well known in churches and organizations or in their context.

### Evaluation of Answers

We see that the people who have taken part in the Forum agree with the vision. They see it as a space for the development of new relationships and the discussion of critical issues, and they are very much in favour of a simple structure. There is a fatigue regarding institutions and dynamic and functional structures are preferred.

The large majority of non-participants agrees with the vision of the Forum and would agree to participate.

However, we see that the Forum has not been able to transcend the impact on those attending it. Even the churches of participants remain detached from this process and do not see that the intention of unity has translated into concrete actions.

It is interesting to note the low or lack of response from the Catholic Church to questionnaires and interviews.

### Recommendations

1. The Forum should maintain a simple functioning structure.
2. The Forum should work on a communication strategy to make its existence and vision known.
3. The Forum should focus on how to extend its vision in a practical and concrete way.

## Interviews

These are the opinions and recommendations from leaders all over Latin America.

## Opinions

1. It is still premature to make predictions regarding the impact of the GCF.
2. It is clear that the GCF is an effort to generate a new mode of articulation for dialogue among Christians.
3. The good thing is that it does not attempt to become institutionalized but rather builds a meeting space.
4. It has strengthened the vision of a healthy, inclusive ecumenism.
5. We need leaders and congregations tto ake part in these kind of forums.
6. The GCF should propose for itself the goal of overcoming the exclusions and accusations Christians hurl at each other.
7. The existence of the Forum does not seem too defined yet; it appears rather like an event and not an ongoing process.
8. The Forum should be a centre for the analysis of social, political and economic changes that are produced on a global level and their incidence in the life and the mission of Christian churches.
9. From what standpoint do we define "unity"? In some Latin American countries, Catholicism carried out a persecution against Protestants /Evangelicals. In some contexts, Catholics are anti-Evangelical and vice-versa. Therefore, these projects are for us very difficult to carry out.
10. The Forum is welcome to strengthen the forces and strategies in mission.

## Recommendation and Implication for the Future

1. As every effort that comes "from above", it has the task of "weeding out" efforts to find grassroots motivation. Events are the product of effort from above, but processes are the result of efforts from below.
2. It is important to hold seminars aimed at channelling information and generating plural spaces with a view to the diverse kinds of needs Christians face.
3. The GCF should promote sharing pulpits, teaching, engaging in unity projects.

4. What we would like to put forward is that there is little participation of indigenous (Indian peoples) churches in these spaces. The GCF should have a more proactive attitude toward these sectors.
5. We are not interested in taking part in spaces with very rigid organizations or in many institutional aspects. We are rather interested in a network.
6. We must advance in unity of the Spirit and in love, without entering into details in doctrine.
7. The GCF must show that it is an excellent space to extend global relations among Christians.
8. The activities of the GCF should not be circumscribed to one or two events a year; there is a need to find a way to give it more continuity.
9. The GCF must avoid the temptation of creating a very large and scarcely operative structure.
10. The GCF must continue with a global co-ordination team such as the current one to simplify actions avoiding excessive bureaucracy and facilitating more direct contacts.
11. Progress must be made on the inclusion of more churches and organizations.
12. The Forum should affect the national church leadership.
13. We must continue along the road started by the GCF to overcome the lack of understanding that has characterized the Christian churches in their relationship among themselves.
14. There is a need to get past the dialogue and work in church structures, transcending them to move towards the heart of congregations.
15. The GCF must find ways of generating theological reflection in the face of national level issues.
16. It will be vital to maintain continuity in news, reports, communications and activities.
17. It is necessary to progress in micro- and regional level processes attempting to include those churches that are still not participating.
18. It is important to organize meetings by countries.
19. Participant organisms should take on a leading role in spreading the news of the Forum nationally.
20. In order for the churches to reflect the agenda of the Forum there should be a greater personal commitment on the part of the participants.
21. There should be a greater dissemination of the results of the Forum and events.

## Final Observation

As a result of the evaluation made among Forum participants, non-participants and church leaders of Latin America, we can say that:

A. All accept the vision of the Forum.
B. There is no opposition to the Forum.
C. We do not see that the Forum has affected churches yet.
D. Everybody agrees that no superstructure should be created but rather a sufficient structure to enable objectives to be fulfilled.
E. The Forum needs a more decisive attitude to make itself known and become part of the attempts at national and continental unity.

Note: The full FIET report contains another 45 pages with graphics illustrating the statistical findings of the responses to the questionnaires for participants and non-participants, which are not reproduced here for reasons of space and cost.

## STUDIES IN GLOBAL CHRISTIANITY

(Previously GLOBAL THEOLOGICAL VOICES series)

**Series Listing**

Huibert van Beek (ed.)
**Revisioning Christian Unity**
*The Global Christian Forum*
*2009 / 978-1-870345-74-3*

This book contains the records of the Global Christian Forum gathering held in Limuru near Nairobi, Kenya, on 6 – 9 November 2007 as well as the papers presented at that historic event. Also included are a summary of the Global Christian Forum process from its inception until the 2007 gathering and the reports of the evaluation of the process that was carried out in 2008.

David Emmanuuel Singh (ed.)
**Jesus and the Cross**
*Reflections of Christians from Islamic Contexts*
*2008 / 978-1-870345-65-1 / x + 226pp*

The Cross reminds us that the sins of the world are not borne through the exercise of power but through Jesus Christ's submission to the will of the Father. The papers in this volume are organised in three parts: scriptural, contextual and theological. The central question being addressed is: how do Christians living in contexts, where Islam is a majority or minority religion, experience, express or think of the Cross? This is, therefore, an exercise in listening. As the contexts from where these engagements arise are varied, the papers in drawing scriptural, contextual and theological reflections offer a cross-section of Christian thinking about Jesus and the Cross.

Sung-wook Hong
**Naming God in Korea**
*The Case of Protestant Christianity*
*2008 / 978-1-870345-66-8*

Since Christianity was introduced to Korea more than a century ago, one of the most controversial issue has been the Korean term for the Christian 'God'. This issue is not merely about naming the Christian God in Korean language, but it relates to the question of theological contextualization—the relationship between the gospel and culture—and the question of Korean Christian identity. This book examines the theological contextualization of the concept of 'God' in the contemporary Korean context and applies the translatability of Christianity to that context. It also demonstrates the nature of the gospel in relation to cultures, i.e., the universality of the gospel expressed in all human cultures.

June 2009

## REGNUM STUDIES IN MISSION
### Series Listing

In partnership with Paternoster (except titles marked with *)
Web: www.authenticmedia.co.uk/paternoster

Kwame Bediako
**Theology and Identity**
*The Impact of Culture upon Christian Thought in the Second Century and in Modern Africa*
*1992 / 1-870345-10-X / xviii + 508pp*

The author examines the question of Christian identity in the context of the Graeco–Roman culture of the early Roman Empire. He then addresses the modern African predicament of quests for identity and integration.

Everett A Wilson
**Strategy of the Spirit**
*J.Philip Hogan and the Growth of the Assemblies of God Worldwide, 1960 - 1990*
*1997/1870345231/214*

Everett Wilson, a long-time Pentecostal missionary among the Hispanic people, wrote a well-researched contribution on the life and role of J. Philip Hogan, as the primary architect of the missionary work of the U.S. Assemblies of God (AG). The main strength of this work is the vast amount of material and information the author was able to collect, and the enjoyable descriptive way he presents the data as well as an evaluation that readers can easily comprehend.

Christopher Sugden
**Seeking the Asian Face of Jesus**
*The Practice and Theology of Christian Social Witness in Indonesia and India 1974–1996*
*1997 / 1-870345-26-6 / xx + 496pp*

This study focuses on contemporary holistic mission with the poor in India and Indonesia combined with the call to transformation of all life in Christ with micro-credit enterprise schemes. 'The literature on contextual theology now has a new standard to rise to' – Lamin Sanneh (Yale University, USA).

Hwa Yung
**Mangoes or Bananas?**
*The Quest for an Authentic Asian Christian Theology*
*1997 / 1-870345-25-8 / xii + 274pp*

Asian Christian thought remains largely captive to Greek dualism and Enlightenment rationalism because of the overwhelming dominance of Western culture. Authentic contextual Christian theologies will emerge within Asian Christianity with a dual recovery of confidence in culture and the gospel.

Keith E. Eitel

**Paradigm Wars**

*1999 / 1-870345-12-6 / x + 140pp*

*The Southern Baptist International Mission Board Faces the Third Millennium*

The International Mission Board of the Southern Baptist Convention is the largest denominational mission agency in North America. This volume chronicles the historic and contemporary forces that led to the IMB's recent extensive reorganization, providing the most comprehensive case study to date of a historic mission agency restructuring to continue its mission purpose into the twenty-first century more effectively.

Samuel Jayakumar

**Dalit Consciousness and Christian Conversion**

*Historical Resources for a Contemporary Debate*

*1999 / 81-7214-497-0 / xxiv + 434pp*

(Published jointly with ISPCK)

The main focus of this historical study is social change and transformation among the Dalit Christian communities in India. Historiography tests the evidence in the light of the conclusions of the modern Dalit liberation theologians.

Vinay Samuel and Christopher Sugden

**Mission as Transformation**

*A Theology of the Whole Gospel*

*Regnum Books (1999), 522pp, ISBN: 0870345133*

This book brings together in one volume twenty five years of biblical reflection on mission practice with the poor from around the world. The approach of holistic mission, which integrates proclamation, evangelism, church planting and social transformation seamlessly as a whole, has been adopted since 1983 by most evangelical development agencies, most indigenous mission agencies and many Pentecostal churches. This volume helps anyone understand how evangelicals, struggling to unite evangelism and social action, found their way in the last twenty five years to the biblical view of mission in which God calls all human beings to love God and their neighbour; never creating a separation between the two.

Christopher Sugden

**Gospel, Culture and Transformation**

*2000 / 1-870345-32-0 / viii + 152pp*

*A Reprint, with a New Introduction, of Part Two of Seeking the Asian Face of Jesus*

*Gospel, Culture and Transformation* explores the practice of mission especially in relation to transforming cultures and communities. - 'Transformation is to enable God's vision of society to be actualised in all relationships: social, economic and spiritual, so that God's will may be reflected in human society and his love experienced by all communities, especially the poor.'

Bernhard Ott

**Beyond Fragmentation: Integrating Mission and Theological Education**

*A Critical Assessment of some Recent Developments in Evangelical Theological Education*

*2001 / 1-870345-14-2 / xxviii + 382pp*

*Beyond Fragmentation* is an enquiry into the development of Mission Studies in evangelical theological education in Germany and German-speaking Switzerland between 1960 and 1995. This is carried out by a detailed examination of the paradigm shifts which have taken place in recent years in both the theology of mission and the understanding of theological education.

Gideon Githiga

**The Church as the Bulwark against Authoritarianism**

*Development of Church and State Relations in Kenya, with Particular Reference to the Years after Political Independence 1963-1992*

*2002 / 1-870345-38-X / xviii + 218pp*

'All who care for love, peace and unity in Kenyan society will want to read this careful history by Bishop Githiga of how Kenyan Christians, drawing on the Bible, have sought to share the love of God, bring his peace and build up the unity of the nation, often in the face of great difficulties and opposition.' Canon Dr Chris Sugden, Oxford Centre for Mission Studies.

Myung Sung-Hoon, Hong Young-Gi (eds.)

**Charis and Charisma**

*David Yonggi Cho and the Growth of Yoido Full Gospel Church*

*2003 / 1-870345-45-2 / xxii + 218pp*

This book discusses the factors responsible for the growth of the world's largest church. It expounds the role of the Holy Spirit, the leadership, prayer, preaching, cell groups and creativity in promoting church growth. It focuses on God's grace (charis) and inspiring leadership (charisma) as the two essential factors and the book's purpose is to present a model for church growth worldwide.

Samuel Jayakumar

**Mission Reader**

*Historical Models for Wholistic Mission in the Indian Context*

*2003 / 1-870345-42-8 / x + 250pp*

(Published jointly with ISPCK)

This book is written from an evangelical point of view revalidating and reaffirming the Christian commitment to wholistic mission. The roots of the 'wholistic mission' combining 'evangelism and social concerns' are to be located in the history and tradition of Christian evangelism in the past; and the civilizing purpose of evangelism is compatible with modernity as an instrument in nation building.

Bob Robinson

**Christians Meeting Hindus**

*An Analysis and Theological Critique of the Hindu-Christian Encounter in India*

*2004 / 1-870345-39-8 / xviii + 392pp*

This book focuses on the Hindu-Christian encounter, especially the intentional meeting called dialogue, mainly during the last four decades of the twentieth century, and mainly in India itself.

Gene Early

**Leadership Expectations**

*How Executive Expectations are Created and Used in a Non-Profit Setting*

*2005 / 1-870345-30-4 / xxiv + 276pp*

The author creates an Expectation Enactment Analysis to study the role of the Chancellor of the University of the Nations-Kona, Hawaii, and is grounded in the field of managerial work, jobs, and behaviour, drawing on symbolic interactionism, role theory, role identity theory and enactment theory. The result is a conceptual framework for further developing an understanding of managerial roles.

Tharcisse Gatwa

**The Churches and Ethnic Ideology in the Rwandan Crises 1900-1994**

*2005 / 1-870345-24-X / approx 300pp*

Since the early years of the twentieth century Christianity has become a new factor in Rwandan society. This book investigates the role Christian churches played in the formulation and development of the racial ideology that culminated in the 1994 genocide.

Julie Ma

**Mission Possible**

*Biblical Strategies for Reaching the Lost*

*2005 / 1-870345-37-1 / xvi + 142pp*

This is a missiology book for the church which liberates missiology from the specialists for every believer. It also serves as a textbook that is simple and friendly, and yet solid in biblical interpretation. This book links the biblical teaching to the actual and contemporary missiological settings with examples, thus making the Bible come alive to the reader.

Allan Anderson, Edmond Tang (eds.)

**Asian and Pentecostal**

*The Charismatic Face of Christianity in Asia*

*2005 / 1-870345-43-6 / approx. 600pp*

(Published jointly with APTS Press)

This book provides a thematic discussion and pioneering case studies on the history and development of Pentecostal and Charismatic churches in the countries of South Asia, South East Asia and East Asia.

June 2009

I. Mark Beaumont

**Christology in Dialogue with Muslims**

*A Critical Analysis of Christian Presentations of Christ for Muslims from the Ninth and Twentieth Centuries*

*2005 / 1-870345-46-0 / xxvi + 228pp*

This book analyses Christian presentations of Christ for Muslims in the most creative periods of Christian-Muslim dialogue, the first half of the ninth century and the second half of the twentieth century. In these two periods, Christians made serious attempts to present their faith in Christ in terms that take into account Muslim perceptions of him, with a view to bridging the gap between Muslim and Christian convictions.

Thomas Czövek,

**Three Seasons of Charismatic Leadership**

*A Literary-Critical and Theological Interpretation of the Narrative of Saul, David and Solomon*

*2006 / 978-1-870345484 / 272pp*

This book investigates the charismatic leadership of Saul, David and Solomon. It suggests that charismatic leaders emerge in crisis situations in order to resolve the crisis by the charisma granted by God. Regarding Saul, the book argues that he proved himself as a charismatic leader as long as he acted resolutely and independently from Samuel his mentor. He failed, however, because in Samuel's shadow he could not establish himself as a charismatic leader.

Jemima Atieno Oluoch

**The Christian Political Theology of Dr. John Henry Okullu**

*2006 / 1-870345-51-7 / xx + 137pp*

This book reconstructs the Christian political theology of Bishop John Henry Okullu, DD, through establishing what motivated him and the biblical basis for his socio-political activities. It also attempts to reconstruct the socio-political environment that nurtured Dr Okullu's prophetic ministry.

Richard Burgess

**Nigeria's Christian Revolution**

*The Civil War Revival and Its Pentecostal Progeny (1967-2006)*

*2008 / 978-1-870345-63-7 / xxii + 347pp*

This book describes the revival that occurred among the Igbo people of Eastern Nigeria and the new Pentecostal churches it generated, and documents the changes that have occurred as the movement has responded to global flows and local demands. As such, it explores the nature of revivalist and Pentecostal experience, but does so against the backdrop of local socio-political and economic developments, such as decolonisation and civil war, as well as broader processes, such as modernisation and globalisation.

David Emmanuel Singh & Bernard C Farr (eds.)
**Christianity and Cultures**
*Shaping Christian Thinking in Context*
*2008 / 978-1-870345-69-9 / x + 260pp*

This volume is a way of marking an important milestone, 25th anniversary, of the Oxford Centre for Mission Studies (OCMS). The papers here have been exclusively sourced from Transformation, a quarterly journal of OCMS, and seek to provide a tripartite view of Christianity's engagement with cultures by focusing on the question: how is Christian thinking being formed or reformed through its interaction with the varied contexts it encounters? The subject matters include different strands of theological-missiological thinking, socio-political engagements and forms of family relationships in interaction with the host cultures.

Tormod Engelsviken, Ernst Harbakk, Rolv Olsen, Thor Strandenæs (eds.)
**Mission to the World**
*Communicating the Gospel in the 21st Century:*
*Essays in Honour of Knud Jørgensen*
*2008 / 978-1-870345-64-4 / 472pp*

Knud Jørgensen is Director of Areopagos and Associate Professor of Missiology at MF Norwegian School of Theology. This book reflects the various main areas of Jørgensen's commitment to mission. At the same time it focuses on the main frontier of mission, the world, the content of mission, the Gospel, the fact that the Gospel has to be communicated, and the context of contemporary mission - the 21st century.

Al Tizon
**Transformation after Lausanne**
*Radical Evangelical Mission in Global-Local Perspective*
*2008 / 978-1-870345-68-2 / xx + 281pp*

After Lausanne '74, a worldwide network of radical evangelical mission theologians and practitioners use the notion of "Mission as Transformation" to integrate evangelism and social concern together, thus lifting theological voices from the Two Thirds World to places of prominence. This book documents the definitive gatherings, theological tensions, and social forces within and without evangelicalism that led up to Mission as Transformation. And it does so through a global-local grid that points the way toward greater holistic mission in the 21st century.

Bambang Budijanto

**Values and Participation**

*Development in Rural Indonesian*

*2009 / 978-1-870345-70-5*

Socio-religious values and socio-economic development are inter-dependant, inter-related and are constantly changing in the context of macro political structures, economic policy, religious organizations and globalization; and micro influences such as local affinities, identity, politics, leadership and beliefs. The three Lopait communities in Central Java, Indonesia provide an excellent model of a rich and complex negotiations and interactions among all the above factors. The book argues that the comprehensive approach in understanding the socio-religious values of each local community is essential to accurately describing their respective identity which will help institutions and agencies, both governmental and non-governmental, to relate to these communities with dignity and respect.

Young-hoon Lee*

**The Holy Spirit Movement in Korea**

*Its Historical and Theological Development*

*2009 / 978-1-870345-67-5*

This book traces the historical and theological development of the Holy Spirit Movement in Korea through six successive periods (from 1900 to the present time). These periods are characterized by repentance and revival (1900-20), persecution and suffering under Japanese occupation (1920-40), confusion and division (1940-60), explosive revival in which the Pentecostal movement played a major role in the rapid growth of Korean churches (1960-80), the movement reaching out to all denominations (1980-2000), and the new context demanding the Holy Spirit movement to open new horizons in its mission engagement (2000-). The volume also discusses the relationship between this movement and other religions such as shamanism, and looks forward to further engagement with issues of concern in the larger society.

David A. Kerr, Kenneth R. Ross (eds.)

**Edinburgh 2010: Mission Then and Now**

*2009 / 978-1-870345-73-6*

No one can hope to fully understand the modern Christian missionary movement without engaging substantially with the World Missionary Conference, held at Edinburgh in 1910. As the centenary of the Conference approaches, the time is ripe to examine its meaning in light of the past century and the questions facing Christian witness today. This book is the first to systematically examine the eight Commissions which reported to Edinburgh 1910 and gave the conference much of its substance and enduring value. It will deepen and extend the reflection being stimulated by the upcoming centenary and will kindle the missionary imagination for 2010 and beyond.

Ande Titre

**Leadership and Authority**

*Bula Matari and Life - Community Ecclesiology in Congo*

*2009 / 978-1-870345-72-9*

This book proposes that Christian theology in Africa can make a significant development if a critical understanding of the socio-political context in contemporary Africa is taken seriously. The Christian leadership in post-colonial Africa has cloned its understanding and use of authority on the Bula Matari model, issued from the brutality of colonialism and political absolutism in post-colonial Africa. This model has caused many problems in churches, including dysfunctions, conflicts, divisions and lack of prophetic ministry. The book proposes a Life-Community ecclesiology for liberating authority, where leadership is a function, not a status, and 'apostolic succession' belongs to all the people of God.

Alan R. Johnson

**Leadership in a Slum**

*A Bangkok Case Study*

*2009 / 978-1-870345-71-2*

This book looks at leadership in the social context of a slum in Bangkok from an angle different from traditional studies which measure well educated Thais on leadership scales derived in the West. Using both systematic data collection and participant observation, it develops a culturally preferred model as well as a set of models based in Thai concepts that reflect on-the-ground realities. This work challenges the dominance of the patron-client rubric for understanding all forms of Thai leadership and offers a view for understanding leadership rooted in local social systems, contrary to approaches that assume the universal applicability of leadership research findings across all cultural settings. It concludes by looking at the implications of the anthropological approach for those who are involved in leadership training in Thai settings and beyond.

## OTHER REGNUM TITLES

Vinay Samuel, Chris Sugden (eds.)
**The Church in Response to Human Need**
*1987 / 1870345045 / xii+268pp*

Philip Sampson, Vinay Samuel, Chris Sugden (eds.)
**Faith and Modernity**
*Essays in modernity and post-modernity*
*1994 / 1870345177 / 352pp*

Klaus Fiedler
**The Story of Faith Missions**
*1994 / 0745926878 / 428pp*

Douglas Peterson
**Not by Might nor by Power**
*A Pentecostal Theology of Social Concern in Latin America*
*1996 / 1870345207 / xvi+260pp*

David Gitari
**In Season and Out of Season**
*Sermons to a Nation*
*1996 / 1870345118 / 155pp*

David. W. Virtue
**A Vision of Hope**
*The Story of Samuel Habib*
*1996 / 1870345169 / xiv+137pp*

Murray Dempster, Byron Klaus, Douglas Petersen (eds.)
**The Globalization of Pentecostalism**
*A Religion Made to Travel*
*1999 / 1870345290 / xvii+406pp*

Peter Johnson, Chris Sugden (eds.)
**Markets, Fair Trade and the Kingdom of God**
*Essays to Celebrate Traidcraft's 21st Birthday*
*2001 / 1870345193 / xii+155pp*

Deryke Belshaw, Robert Calderisi, Chris Sugden (eds.)
**Faith in Development**
*Partnership Between the World Bank and the Churches of Africa*
*2001 / 978-0821348482 / 246pp*

June 2009

Robert Hillman, Coral Chamberlain, Linda Harding
**Healing & Wholeness**
*Reflections on the Healing Ministry*
*2002 / 978-1- 870345-35- 4 / xvii+283pp*

David Bussau, Russell Mask
**Christian Microenterprise Development**
*An Introduction*
*2003 / 1870345282 / xiii+142pp*

David Singh
**Sainthood and Revelatory Discourse**
*An Examination of the Basis for the Authority of Bayan in Mahdawi Islam*
*2003 / 8172147285 / xxiv+485pp*

For the up-to-date listing of the Regnum books, see:
http://www.ocms.ac.uk/docs/Regnum_Studies_In_Mission_Listing.pdf
http://www.ocms.ac.uk/docs/Studies_In_Global_Christianity_Listing.pdf

regnum

**Regnum Books International**

Regnum is an Imprint of The Oxford Centre for Mission Studies
P.O. Box 70, Oxford, OX2 6HB
Web: www.ocms.ac.uk/regnum

June 2009